KU-696-364

RSA LIBRARY

07466

WITHDRAWN

URBAN CLUSTERING

Urban Clustering

The benefits and drawbacks of location

BORIS A. PORTNOV
EVYATAR ERELL
Desert Architecture and Urban Planning Unit
Jacob Blaustein Institute for Desert Research
Ben-Gurion University of the Negev, Israel

Ashgate

Aldershot • Burlington USA • Singapore • Sydney

© Boris A. Portnov and Evyatar Erell 2001

All rights reserved. No part of this publication may be reproduced, stored in a retrieval system, or transmitted in any form or by any means, electronic, mechanical, photocopying, recording or otherwise without the prior permission of the publisher.

Published by
Ashgate Publishing Ltd
Gower House
Croft Road
Aldershot
Hants GU11 3HR
England

Ashgate Publishing Company
131 Main Street
Burlington, VT 05401-5600 USA

Ashgate website: http://www.ashgate.com

British Library Cataloguing in Publication Data
Portnov, Boris A.
     Urban clustering : the benefits and drawbacks of location.
     - (Design and the built environment)
     1.City planning 2.Cities and towns - Growth 3.Urban
     economics 4.Land settlement patterns
     I.Title II.Erell, Evyatar
     307.1'4'16

Library of Congress Control Number: 00-111534

ISBN 0 7546 1449 2

Printed and bound by Athenaeum Press, Ltd.,
Gateshead, Tyne & Wear.

[13 713]

Contents

List of Figures

List of Tables

Preface

This book has evolved from an attempt to construct a measure of urban location that is both simple and comprehensive. We needed such a measure to control other variables in a study of long-term development patterns of small peripheral towns in Israel.

Initially, we employed several traditional measures of urban location, such as aerial distances, densities, and accessibility indicators. However, we found that none of these measures correlated firmly with the towns' development characteristics we studied, such as unemployment, the rate of construction, migration, etc. This could have had two possible explanations. Either there is in fact no obvious relationship between the towns' location and their long-term socio-economic performance; or, some important aspects of location could have been omitted from the analysis, resulting in a model's misspecification.

Convinced that location did in fact have an effect long-term development of towns, we developed an alternative measure of urban location, which we called the Index of Clustering. Every town has a unique value of the proposed index, which is calculated as a function of two variables - the density of the urban field in a region and the town's remoteness from the closest major population centre of a country. The use of this integrated indicator resulted in the detection of a strong non-linear relationship between the location of peripheral towns in Israel and their various development characteristics. Encouraged by the initial success of this index in analysing the development of peripheral towns, we turned to investigate its effect on centrally located towns in Israel. We discovered that in the country's centre, too, the relationship between a town's location and its development indicators was still strong, though it deviated even further from linearity.

Due to our concern that the relationship in question between location and growth might be peculiar to the conditions in Israel at the time of the study, we tested the performance of the proposed index of clustering in two other countries – in Norway and in New South Wales, Australia. The general pattern of the relationship between location and growth, which was observed in Israel, was detected in these countries as well, albeit slightly modified. The more diversified patterns of these countries' regional development led to the occurrence of a wider range of distinctive development situations, such as centres of peripheral regions, transitional zones between central and peripheral areas, inland and coastal towns, etc, creating in turn a different range of values for the index of clustering.

Encouraged by these empirical findings, we decided to take a closer look at the phenomenon of urban clustering as a whole, trying to understand the general nature of this process and its implications for the development of individual towns.

The methodology of the present analysis is primarily that of regional economics and population geography, but its ultimate concern is regional planning. From our point of view, understanding urban clustering is *not* an end in itself. It is our intention to develop planning policies and strategies, which may help decision-makers to enhance the potential of urban growth, wherever this objective is desirable.

Acknowledgements

In preparing this book, we used numerous sources of data provided by various persons and organizations. For the Israeli case study, we used data provided by the Central Bureau of Statistics of Israel in a joint research project titled 'Interregional Inequalities in Israel: 1948-1995 Census Data.' For the Norwegian case study, we had access to the Municipality Database, maintained by the Norwegian Social Science Data Services (NSD) at Bergen, Norway. Access to this rich database was made possible by a research grant obtained in the framework of the Training and Mobility of Researchers (TMR) programme of the European Union. We gratefully acknowledge the kind assistance of Ms. Astrid Nilsen of NSD in assembling the data for the Norwegian case study. Our thanks are also due to Margaret Young and Dianne Rudd of the University of Adelaide, South Australia, for their assistance in assembling and interpreting the data for the Australian case study.

The preliminary results of the present study were presented at various research meetings. Among them were the 2nd International Conference on 'Urban Development: A Challenge for Frontier Regions,' held on April 4-7, 1998 in Be'er-Sheva, Israel; a meeting at the Department of Geography at Norwegian School of Economics and Business Administration, Bergen, and a seminar at the Department of Architecture and Town Planning at Technion, Israel. The authors are grateful to the participants of these discussions for their helpful comments and suggestions.

Prof. A. Paul Hare deserves our warmest thanks for helping us to understand the processes of interaction in social clusters. Wolfgang Haller provided invaluable technical assistance.

Finally, we would like to acknowledge the generous financial support from the Department of Man in the Desert at Jacob Blaustein Institute for Desert Research, Ben-Gurion University of the Negev (Dr. Yair Etzion – head), and from the Deichmann foundation (Germany).

List of Abbreviations

CBD	Central business district
DUS	Daily urban system
F	F-statistic
IC	Index of clustering
IC1	Index of clustering I (IC1=IS1/IR)
IC2	Index of clustering II (IC2=IS2/IR)
IM	In-country migrants
IR	Index of remoteness
IS	Index of isolation
IS1	Index of isolation I (number of towns within commuting range)
IS2	Index of isolation II (population of towns within commuting range)
LA	Local authority
MB	Migration balance
MB/NG	Migration balance/natural growth ratio index
MI	Material index
MRA	Multiple regression analysis
MSA	Metropolitan statistical area
MTCE	Minimal threshold of the cluster efficiency
NG	Natural growth
NI	New immigrants
OG	Overall growth (MB+NG)
P	Probability of error
SD	Sustainable development
SLA	Statistical Local Area (Australia)
SMR	Stepwise multiple regression
SMSA	Standard metropolitan statistical area (U.S.A)
SUG	Sustainable urban growth
t	t-statistic
tanh	Hyperbolic tangent function
UTCE	Upper threshold of the cluster efficiency
VIF	Variance inflation factor

Introduction

This book revolves around the simple idea that the location of a town in relation to other urban places, and the degree of sustainability exhibited by this town in its population growth and economic development, are interrelated.

This concept was originally introduced by the authors of this book in two separately published papers (Portnov and Erell, 1998a; Portnov *et al*, 2000). The first dealt with the effect of urban clustering on long-term growth of small peripheral towns in Israel, the second with a comparative analysis of centrally located and peripheral towns in Israel and Norway. In the present book, this concept is discussed in greater detail. The discussion is supplemented by an analysis of background studies emphasising the effects of location on urban and regional development.

The book begins with a general discussion of a number of fundamental concepts of urban and regional planning, such as remoteness, isolation, distance measurements and the choice of urban centre *(Part I)*. In this part, we devoted considerable attention to the landmark works of Alfred Weber, Alfred Marshall, Walter Christaller, August Lösch, Edward Ravenstein, George Zipf, Samuel Stouffer and others, which deal with industrial and urban location and the effects of distance on population movements. The discussion of these studies provides the necessary theoretical framework for the book, and places the ideas introduced here in a proper historical perspective.

Most previous studies on urban and regional location focused primarily on the effects of transportation costs, the influence of topography and landscape and on service areas. We chose to treat urban location more broadly, as a tripartite paradigm – remoteness, isolation, and choice of urban centre:

- *Remoteness* is a function of the physical distance from a town to the closest major population centre of a country. It has profound effects on various aspects of urban development, most of which are, as we shall argue, clearly adverse. It causes an increase in the cost of transport, thus affecting the location of employment-generating sectors. Furthermore, it affects the attractiveness of urban areas to migrants and commuters, though the effects of remoteness on the choices of migrants and entrepreneurs regarding location is neither linear nor universal;

- *Isolation* of an urban place is determined by its spatial and functional relationships, or a lack thereof, with other urban places in a region. It is not always a simple function of remoteness, since relatively dense and functionally integrated urban clusters can be found even in a remote peripheral region. The link between remoteness and isolation is complex: The unfavourable effects of remoteness can either be reduced or aggravated by the presence (or a lack thereof) of neighbouring urban localities, which may provide additional employment and cultural opportunities for the town's residents. Although urban and regional studies tend to treat spatial isolation as a marginal issue, closely associated with physical remoteness in general, we preferred to treat this phenomenon as a separate issue and subjected it to an in-depth analysis;

- The *choice of urban centre*, in relation to which the effects of remoteness and isolation are estimated, may not be determined by an analysis of certain quantitative characteristics of urban places alone. We shall argue, in particular, that population size alone may not be sufficient to establish an urban locality as a major population centre. This ranking is mostly determined by the functions the settlement may perform, and specifically by the presence of unique regional functions such as large hospitals or institutions of higher education.

In investigating this tripartite paradigm, we felt a strong need to consider, in some length, other important location-related concepts – gravitation models, distance decay functions, socio-economic potential, density, agglomeration functions, etc. Though each of these concepts is important in its own right, and each has unique advantages and drawbacks, all may be seen as alternative measures of urban location.

Previous empirical studies on regional industrial location and on the spatial preferences of migrants, including those employing sophisticated techniques of multivariate analysis, fail to establish a strong link between development and location, if its effect is studied in isolation from other factors such as availability of utilities, investment climate, macroeconomic cycles, etc. (see *inter alia* Bivand, 1986; Foss, 1996; Ma, 1999; Moore and

Rosenberg, 1995; Portnov and Pearlmutter, 1997; Frenkel *et al*, 2000), Why is this so? Two possible explanations are suggested:

- The ability of an urban place to sustain its growth is an extremely complex phenomenon that can be measured by various indicators, such as migration, unemployment, etc. We shall argue, however, that none of these indicators taken alone may be sufficiently informative for the analysis. In *Part II* of this book, we shall argue that the population growth of a city becomes sustainable once it is based mainly on its ability to attract migrants, rather than on natural causes (fertility-mortality rates). Based on this conclusion, we shall propose an integrated measure of sustained population growth in towns, estimated as the ratio between the net migration balance and the natural growth (the MB/NG index). We shall argue that the significance of this index surpasses its direct application as a simple measure of population growth, because a settlement's ability to attract migrants and to retain its existing population implies sound economic development and a favourable physical environment, in addition to other desirable characteristics;

- Traditional measures of urban location, widely used in empirical studies (from simple density measurements to more complex formulas of socio-economic potential, and agglomeration indices), are not always sufficiently accurate and may not produce reliable estimates. For instance, many of these indices do not discriminate between concentrated and dispersed patterns of urban development within a region, and unless the physical size of the geographic unit of analysis is relatively small, may be clearly misleading. We shall, therefore, concentrate our efforts on the development of an integrated indicator of urban location which may be more useful than existing measures of location. Such an index, referred to as the Index of Clustering (IC), will be proposed in *Part III* of the book. It is estimated as the combination of two factors – remoteness from the closest urban centre and density of the urban field in a region. This indicator may outperform many traditional measures of urban location and thus help us to demonstrate that location is indeed an important determinant of urban growth.

Following the preparatory discussion (background studies, indicators of location, and measures of sustainable urban growth), we shall turn to the main thrust of this book – *urban clustering*. (By 'urban cluster' we refer to a group of urban places located in close proximity to one another and connected by socio-economic and functional links). In *Part III* of the book, we shall discuss the concept of clustering in a broad range of scientific disciplines, ranging from physics to sociology and statistics. Our attention will then be focused solely on the nature and implications of urban clustering. We shall explain how urban clusters are formed and how urban clustering may influence the development of individual urban localities in various geographic areas.

We shall propose that there is no universal process by which urban clusters are formed. Rather, there are three distinctive and often interrelated mechanisms. First, urban clusters can be formed through the process of bifurcation of existing urban centres as they grow and diseconomies of concentration increase. Second, simultaneous growth and eventual merger of adjacent quasi-urban localities may result in the formation of urban clusters. Lastly, urban clusters may be formed by deliberate planning actions, such as those that led to the establishment of new towns around major population centres in various countries. We shall also demonstrate that the effect of clustering on the development of individual towns is not uniform: In sparsely populated regions, the concentration of urban development in selected locations may be conducive to more sustainable growth of the individual towns, due to greater opportunities for inter-urban exchanges. However, in centrally located regions, any further increase in the density of the urban field may have adverse effects on the development of individual towns due to intensifying inter-town competition for potential investors and migrants and to increasing diseconomies of concentration.

In *Part IV* of the book, we shall attempt to illustrate the theoretical arguments above using a number of case studies – Israel, Norway, and New South Wales (NSW) in Australia. Although these places differ substantially with respect to their land areas and to patterns of urban development, they share one important characteristic in the context of the present analysis, namely considerable inequalities in the distribution of population and economic activity across the space. All of these case studies exhibit a strong non-linear relationship between the location of towns (as measured by the proposed index of clustering) and their long-term socio-economic performance.

Another important conclusion, drawn from the results of these case studies, is that there are two distinctive thresholds of clustering: The *minimal threshold of cluster efficiency* (MTCE), above which tangible benefits of cluster location may come into play; and the *upper threshold of cluster efficiency* (UTCE), above which any further increase in the density of the urban field may have undesirable consequences for the individual towns forming the cluster.

These findings, concerning the different effects of clustering on the development of centrally-located and peripheral urban places, led us to the development of two mutually complementary regional strategies – *development clusters* and of *redirecting priorities*. These are described in detail in *Part V* of the book. According to these strategies, development resources should be concentrated primarily on a limited number of selected urban clusters in the peripheral areas until they reach the minimum threshold of cluster efficiency and become sufficiently attractive to migrants and private developers. As soon as such a threshold is achieved, development support may be redirected on a step-by-step basis to urban concentrations elsewhere. This process of temporary and hierarchical concentration of resources can thus be moved deeper and deeper into outlying areas where further urban growth is desirable.

We realize that in this book we could not address all aspects of urban clustering. This phenomenon appears to be considerably more complex than we envisioned at the outset, when this book was first discussed. In particular, there are a number of important issues related to urban clustering which we did not consider even in part. These are inter-urban interactions in clusters (commuting, economic exchanges, etc.), the effects of changing macro-economic conditions, the perception of quality of life in urban clusters as opposed to a stand-alone pattern of settlements, and many others. We shall leave these important issues for future study.

PART I
MEASURING URBAN
LOCATION

If you were to say to the grown-ups: 'I saw a beautiful house
made of rosy brick, with geraniums in the windows and doves
on the roof,' they would not be able to get any idea of that
house at all. You would have to say to the: 'I saw a house that
cost $20,000 Then they would exclaim: 'Oh, what a pretty
house that is!'

A. de Saint-Exupery, *The Little Prince*

1 Effects of Remoteness

A town located far away from the major population centres of a country has obvious drawbacks holding back its development. The cost of infrastructure and of the transportation of goods, especially building materials, is almost inevitably higher in a remote area than in a centrally located region. Unless a remote urban community is quite large, it may suffer from a lack of economic diversity, while businesses located there are likely to experience substantial problems in recruiting skilled labour, which is more readily available in large centres of population, near universities and other educational institutions (Golany, 1978; Saini, 1980; Portnov and Erell, 1998b; McCann and Sheppard, 2000). Unless a geographically remote region has unique natural resources, such as mineral deposits or cheap energy sources, or it is supported by various government grants and subsidies, new businesses are more likely to be established in more central locations.

The remoteness of a town from major population centres of a country also has an adverse effect on population growth. Both foreign immigrants and in-country migrants prefer, all else being equal, to settle in less remote areas, in which choice of employment is less restricted, and opportunities for cultural life, entertainment and leisure are more diverse (Fischer, 1976; Beely, 1988; Borjas, 1989; Clark, 1982; De Jong and Fawcett, 1981; Kupiszewski *et al,* 1998; Lipshitz, 1996b; Greenwood and Stock, 1990; Portnov, 1998a,b).

When we describe a town as *remote*, we mean that it is far from any of the major population centres of the country. The actual distances may, of course, vary by country, but in any case these distances are likely to *exceed those considered to be practicable for daily commuting* (under local conditions).

The definition of a major urban centre, from which the extent of remoteness is determined, is, however, not always straightforward. It depends on the overall population size of the country, its geographic extent, historical patterns of urban development, location of services and facilities, and many other factors (see *inter alia* Weber, 1921 (1958 English edition); Hudson, 1976; Oliver, 1997). In particular, services provided by cities of a particular population size may vary from country to country, depending on local economic and social patterns, environmental conditions, quality of transportation and road infrastructure (Christaller, 1933 (1966 English edition); Clark, 1982; Woldenberg, 1979; Kupiszewski *et al*, 1999).

Another problem associated with remoteness is its quantification and measurement. This problem is both theoretical and applied. The effects of remoteness may be related to several measures, including aerial distance, distance by road, time required to travel to the centre, etc. Each of these measures has both advantages and disadvantages. Aerial distance, for instance, is 'objective' and simple to measure. However, as we will see later, this indicator tends to perform poorly if landscape conditions are complex (mountainous or hilly areas, large rivers or fjords), or when road infrastructure and quality of service are not uniform throughout the area. Under such circumstances, aerial distances may tell us little about actual travel conditions, and may even be misleading.

In this and the following chapters we will discuss in some detail the effect of remoteness on economic development and on population change; the notion of relativity of remoteness, and the concept of an urban centre. Particular attention will be given to indicators and measures of remoteness and their applicability in the context of population patterns having different spatial characteristics.

Relativity of Remoteness

The concept of remoteness is relative. In Russia, for instance, such cities as *Khabarovsk* and *Vladivostok* are almost 8,000 km away from Moscow and St.-Petersburg. In Japan, the most remote towns are only 800 km away from the largest metropolitan centres of the country (Tokyo, Osaka and Nagoya). In Sweden and Egypt, the distances are similar to those in Japan. While the comparable distances in Israel are much smaller (only 100-200 km separate the most remote urban localities in the Negev from the main cities of Jerusalem and Tel Aviv), these peripheral towns are nevertheless commonly perceived as remote.

Portnov and Erell (1998a,b) explain why even in Israel the notion of remoteness is not without basis. There are two factors, which affect the importance of this spatial indicator even in such a small country:

- First, even the distances in question exceed those normally considered practicable for daily commuting.
- Second, the perception of remoteness may affect investment decisions or movements of population no less than the real distances involved. Thus, it is the 'relative remoteness' of a country's peripheral areas, which may be the influencing factor, rather than absolute distance.

Lonsdale (1998) describes a case of such 'subjective reality' due to which a region is perceived as marginal and remote despite its relatively close proximity to population centres of the country. In his historical study, he describes the changing attitudes towards the Great Plains in the central-west of the United States. This large region of some 1.3 million square kilometres has a population of only four million people. It borders on Oklahoma City and Colorado Springs and is only some 200 km away from large population centres of the United States such as Minneapolis, Kansas City and Dallas. Currently, the population of the region is scattered and declining, which causes difficulties in maintaining even essential public services. According to Lonsdale,

> The indigenous Plains Indians ... successfully based their culture and survival on the immense herds of buffalo (bison) grazing here. On the other hand, Europeans venturing into the area in the first half of the 19th century – fur traders, explorers, and pioneers heading west – all saw the Plains as a poorly watered land, and severe weather. The region was dubbed the 'Great American Desert,' an unpleasant place to cross as quickly as possible. None stayed here. European settlement on the Great Plains came only after the American Civil War (1861-65).

Schmidt (1998) attempts to generalize on the issue of relativity of regional marginality – a phenomenon that is closely related to remoteness. In this analysis, she singles out five distinctive aspects of marginality – a) geometric or geographic marginality; b) ecological marginality; c) economic marginality; d) social and cultural marginality, and e) political marginality.

- *Geographic (geometric) marginality* describes the peripheral or distant position occupied by an area in the geographic space and does not determine automatically its marginal character. Besides the absolute position of the region in the geographic space (i.e. frontiers areas of a nation), geographic marginality is related to the physical accessibility of the area – the extent quality of physical infrastructure, of transportation and of communication;

- *Ecological marginality.* This concept relates to areas that were exposed to strong human intervention and underwent a complete transformation of their ecological equilibrium. Such areas cannot be considered part of a natural ecosystem, but rather as marginal areas;
- *Economic marginality* describes regions that are not well integrated in the 'circuits of economic production and exchange.' The marginal economic position of such regions is indicated by their poor economic performance, high unemployment, and low levels of human welfare;
- *Social and cultural marginality.* This concept relates to the geographic separation of a group within society, which cannot adapt itself to a generally accepted social pattern. Geographic separation of such a group may occur for a variety of reasons, including race, religion, origin, nationality, socio-economic and cultural levels and result in the formation of marginal 'enclaves' within even a centrally located region;
- *Political marginality.* This aspect of marginality refers to geographic areas that are of low interest to policy-makers, because of their sparse population and limited electoral influence. Another example are border communities which have an uncertain geo-political future in view of ongoing conflicts with neighbouring countries. The political uncertainty of such areas often leads to reduced public investment, deficient infrastructure and a high degree of economic dependency on the national institutions of public welfare. An interesting case of such a political marginality is described in detail by Gradus (1983; 1984) in his studies of the Negev region in Israel.

Measuring Remoteness

Distance Decay Function

In 1687, Newton discovered that 'any particle of matter in the universe attracts any other with a force varying directly as the product of the masses and inversely as the square of the distance between them' (EB, 1999). Mathematically, Newton's law of gravitation is formulated as follows:

$$F_{12} = \frac{GM_1M_2}{(r_{12})^2},$$

where F_{12} is the gravitational force between two particles/objects of matter; M_1 and M_2 are the mass of these objects; r_{12} is the distance between them, and G is a universal constant.

Let us assume that the masses of two objects are held constant. Then, the nominator of Newton's equation is equal to $A = GM_1M_2$, where A is a constant. If we take a common logarithm of this ratio and substitute r with another symbol for distance (D), we obtain:

$$log\ (F) = a - 2\ log\ (D),\ where\ a = log\ (A).$$

In this alternative formulation, the equation is nearly identical to what in geography is known as the distance decay function. Descriptively, Tobler formulated this function in his 'First Law of Geography': 'everything is related to everything else, but near things are more related than distant things' (Tobler, 1970; cited in Johnston *et al*, 1994).

There are a number of commonly used distance decay functions, each of which, despite their slightly different mathematical formulation, attempts to capture the same phenomenon – that the intensity of interaction (I) between any two given geographic places i and j declines as distance between them (D) grows:

1. Pareto model: $log\ (I_{ij}) = a - b\ log\ (D_{ij})$.
2. Lognormal model: $log\ (I_{ij}) = a - b\ (log\ (D_{ij}))^2$.
3. Square-root exponential model: $log\ (I_{ij}) = a - b\ (D_{ij})^{1/2}$.
4. Exponential model: $log\ (I_{ij}) = a - b\ (D_{ij})$.
5. Normal model: $log\ (I_{ij}) = a - b\ D_{ij}$.
6. Density function: $log\ (I_{ij}) = a - b\ D_{ij} + log\ (D_{ij})$.

To illustrate differences among these formulations of the distance decay functions, some of them are plotted using identical values of the constants a and b (Figure 1.1).

Though all these functions show that the intensity of interaction decreases in line with distance, the decrease in interaction predicted by the exponential model is considerably larger than that expected from Pareto and lognormal models. For instance, the characteristic feature of the density model is its initial peaking, followed by a steep decline. Such a break point is often seen in the population density of residential areas, which may increase initially at some distance from functionally mixed city centres and then drops towards less densely populated suburbs (see *inter alia* Clark, 1982; Alonso, 1960; 1964; Barrett, 1998). As we shall see later, a similar inflection point is also found in various studies of inter-area migration.

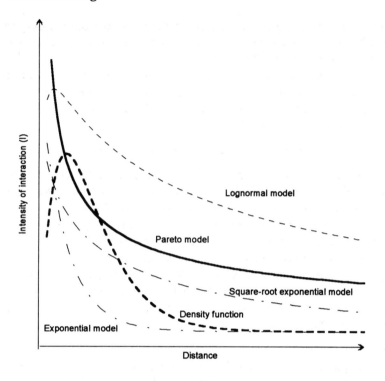

Figure 1.1   Distance decay functions

Calibration Attempts

There have been numerous attempts to calibrate distance decay models for various geographic regions, alternative socio-economic phenomena and different time periods, starting with the early 1930s.

Stouffer (1940; 1962 reprint), for instance, analysed the number of families moving varying distances in the Cleveland area during 1933-35. He used data on residential mobility from the Real Estate Inventory of the Cleveland Metropolitan District and found that the number of families moving was inversely related to the distance moved: the number of families which moved less than 1 km was about 6,000, compared with about 500 families which moved 10 km and only 50 families which moved some 20 km.

In another analysis of the relationship between distance and the intensity of interaction, Zipf (1949; 1972 reprint) compared the overall number of passengers who travelled by railways between 29 cities of the USA in 1933. When the number of passengers was plotted against the derived indicator - $P_1xP_2/D_{12}x10^7$ (where P_1 and P_2 are population sizes of two cities and D_{12} is the aerial distance between them) - an almost perfect correlation between the number of travellers and the index in question was found. Thus, the number of railroad passengers appeared to drop steadily as distance between cities grew and their population size declined. This study predicted, for instance, that two cities of 500,000 residents each, situated 25 km apart, would generate railroad traffic of 100,000 passengers a month, compared with only 100 passengers each month between two similar cities 2,500 km apart.

Krakover and Morrill (1992) studied the spatio-temporal structure of urban growth in the Atlanta area between 1890-1980. They found that in 1890-1920, the rates of growth were highest in the central business district (CBD) of the city and steadily declined in line with increasing distance from it, reaching a minimum at 110-130 km from the city centre. By 1960-1980, however, the peak of urban growth appeared to move from the CBD to a commuting belt 20-40 km from the city centre, and then fell away as the distance from the CBD grew further.

McCann and Sheppard (1999) analysed the distribution of recent graduates of UK universities in 1994-95. They determined that graduates found employment in locations, on average, nearly 100 km away from their place of study. While the maximum distance was almost 1,100 km, nearly 60 per cent of graduates found jobs within a commuting range of 100 km from the university. The proportion of graduates finding jobs further away from their university declined with increasing distance, from 24 per cent in the 100-200 km range to less than 6 per cent in the 200-300 km range.

Stillwell's (1991) analysis of long-distance migration in the U.K. indicated that distance decay is not a function of distance alone but also of the population make up of movers. In particular, he found a relatively strong inverse relationship between the age of migrants and the mean distance they moved (see Figure 1.2). While the mean distance moved by young migrants (15-19 and 30-34 age groups) was, on the average, 165 km, the distance moved by older people averaged only 145-150 km. Notably, the relationship between age and migration distance exhibited little change between the two periods covered by the study (1983-84 and 1985-86). The statistical evidence was fairly robust, and there is little likelihood that the pattern reported occurred by chance.

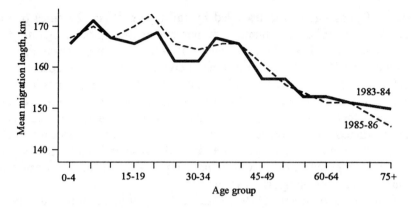

Figure 1.2   **Mean migration distances by age group of migrants in the U.K. in 1983-84 and 1985-86**

Source: Stillwell (1991).

Implications for Industrial Growth

In this section, the effect of remoteness on urban growth will be considered separately in its two distinctive manifestations: implications for industrial development (Weber's and Lösch's theories; location of high-technology industries), and the effect on population change.

Distance-related Factors of Industrial Location - Weber

In his theory of industrial location, Weber (1929, p.17) defined the *location factor* 'an advantage which is gained when an economic activity takes place at a particular point or at several such points rather than elsewhere.' According to Weber's theory, physical distances are determinants of transportation costs, which are considered, in turn, as one of seven major forces affecting the overall cost of industrial production:

1. The cost of land.
2. The cost of buildings, machinery, and other fixed capital.
3. The cost of securing material, power and fuel.
4. The cost of labour.
5. The cost of transportation (assembling the materials and shipping the final product).

6. The cost of financial investment (interest rates).
7. The rate of depreciation of fixed capital (*ibid:* 29-34).

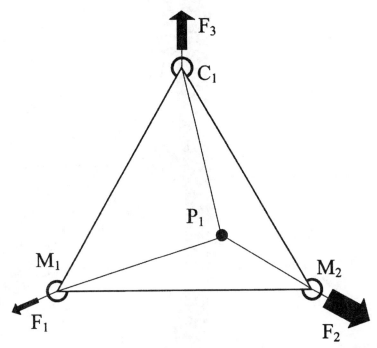

Figure 1.3 **Weber's model of forces determining the industrial location**

M_1 and M_2 are sources of raw materials; P_1 is the place of production; C_1 is the place of consumption; F_1, F_2 and F_3 are forces, which are functions of transportation cost. According to Weber's model, the location of industrial production is determined by the minimal overall transportation cost required to supply the production facility with the raw materials and to deliver the final product to the consumer. In its simplest form, the solution to this problem is determined by the balance of forces 'pulling' the place of production to the source of the heaviest load.

To estimate the effect of transportation on the location of plants, Weber proposed that the transport cost is a function of two variables – distance travelled and the weight of material transported. In this framework, the relative location of the place of production is determined by the material index (MI) of the industry, which is given by the following ratio:

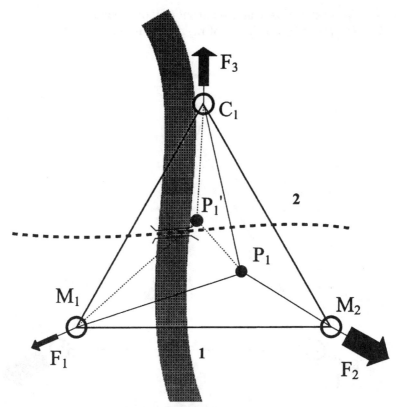

Figure 1.4 Weber's adjusted model of industrial location – actual transportation patterns considered

1 – navigation river; 2 – railroad; P_1' is adjusted position of industrial location (see also notes to Figure 1.3). According to Weber's theory, navigation rivers and railways, which provide relatively cheap means of transportation, may alter, albeit to a relatively small extent, the location of industry determined by plain geometry of weight-mileage minimisation patterns (see Figure 1.3).

$$MI = WM/WP,$$

where WM and WP are the weights of local materials and of the finished product, respectively.

The interplay of these factors may be illustrated by a simplified diagram (Figure 1.3), in which the location of the production plant (P_1) is determined from the location of two sources of raw materials (M_1 and M_2), and a single market, where consumption (C_1) occurs.

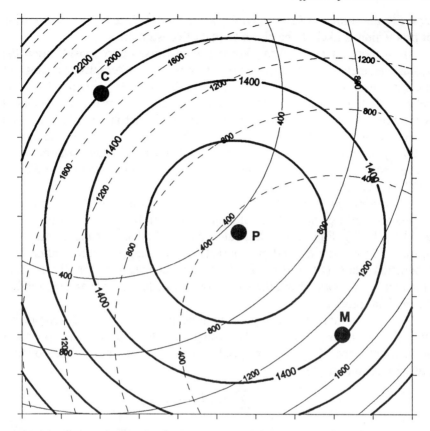

Figure 1.5 Solution to Weber's location problem with isodapanes

The solution for the location of the place of production (P) is diagrammed for one source of raw materials (M) and a single place of consumption (C). The bold lines represent the sum of M and C isodapanes. The distribution of transportation cost in space is assumed to be non-linear.

According to Weber's model, the optimum location of an industrial plant (from considerations of transport alone) will be such that the value of the product 'ton-miles' is at a minimum: Its 'location will be near particular vertices of the transport triangle or far from them according to the relative weight of their location components' (*ibid*, pp. 53-54). If the above material index (MI) of a given industry is substantially higher than 1.0 (i.e. where the finished product weighs much less than the raw materials required to produce it), the location of such industries is expected to be closer to the source of raw materials, while for MI close to 1.0, the location of production is likely to be closer to that of consumption.

In a more advanced form, Weber's model takes into consideration the actual geometry of transportation routes and alternative means of transportation – railroads, waterways, highways, etc. (Figure 1.4). He believes that waterways, highways and railroads may make the distances separating the sources of raw materials, industrial production and consumption 'economically shorter' and thus justify a certain 'deviation' that may 'lengthen the transportation routes' and raise 'transportation costs above those prevailing under the most advantageous conditions' (Weber, 1929, pp.102-103).

A traditional way of solving Weber's location problem involves mapping of *isodapanes* – lines of equal transportation cost (Alonso, 1971; Webber, 1973). Figure 1.5 illustrates this method in a simple case (one source of raw materials and one market). In this diagram, the location of a production plant (P) is determined by the minimal value of the sum of individual *isodapanes* from the source of raw materials (M) and the market for the final product (C).

As an alternative, linear programming can be used as a solution to Weber's location problem. According to this approach, potential production sites (*i*) are analysed so as to minimise the overall transportation cost (Z):

$$Z = \sum_{j=1}^{m} (w_j d_{ij}) + w_c d_{ic} \, ,$$

where Z is the overall cost of transport, m are the raw materials available at site j; w_j is a weight of each material required in production; d_{ij} is the distance between each production site i and the j source of raw material; and w_c and d_{ic} are the weight of the final product and the distance of transporting from the i production site to a c centre of consumption.

Distance-related Factors in the Formation of Economic Regions – Lösch

Like Weber's theory of industrial location, Lösch's concept of the formation of economic regions (1938; 1978 reprint), subsequently developed and quantified in more recent studies (see *inter alia* Wile, 1978; Kanafani, 1978), also emphasises the effect of physical distances and the cost of transportation on the spatial distribution of economic activity.

Lösch first described a simplified case in which raw materials are equally distributed across a totally homogenous plain, and that there are no other inequalities, either political or geographical. It follows that any given

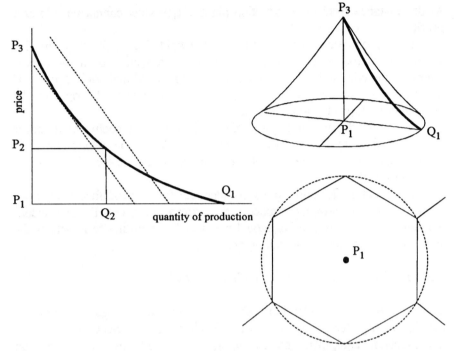

Figure 1.6   Components of Lösch's model illustrating the formation of economic regions in a homogeneous geographic plain

P_1 and Q_1 are respectively the price and demand for a product at the point of production; P_2 and Q_2 are respectively the price and demand a certain distance away; P_3 is the price limit beyond which demand falls to zero, and no goods can be sold.

commodity can be produced anywhere. Figure 1.4 (left diagram) illustrates the effects of transport costs, which are in turn related to distance, on the price of a given product and the demand for it.

Let P_1 be the price of a given product where it is produced (Point #1), while Q_1 is the quantity of this commodity which can be sold at this particular location. Concurrently, P_2 is the price of this product at Point #2, which is a certain distance away, while Q_2 is the demand for this product there. Q_2 is greater than Q_1 due to the cost of transport.

As distance from the production plant to the market grows, higher transport costs are fed into the price of the product. Eventually, the unit price of the product in question is so high (P3) that demand for it is zero.

At this distance from the production plant, the product cannot be sold at a profit.

If the production curve, marked by the bold line on the diagram, lies to the left of the actual demand curve (the dotted line), or if the curves intersect, the commodity in question may be produced and sold at profit. If the production curve (the bold line) exceeds (i.e. lies to the right of the demand curve), production will result in a loss.

In a three-dimensional space, the trade zones for each manufacturer will be limited by a cone that covers the area within which the final product can be sold if the cost of a commodity at the centre of production is equal to P_1 (Figure 1.6).

If production/demand curves are identical for all manufactures and all locations of geographic space, the areas covered by individual manufactures will form a hexagonal net, which, according to Lösch, is the 'most economical shape for trading areas.'

Distance Factors in the Location of Hi-tech Industries

In recent years, a considerable body of research has been generated on the location of high-technology industries. Such industries (electronics, optical and precision equipment, bio-technologies, and software engineering) do not require, as a rule, a considerable input of raw materials and are thus less dependent on transportation than 'traditional' low-tech firms (Shachar and Felsenstein, 1992; Shefer and Frenkel, 1998; Frenkel *et al*, 2000; Shefer and Bar-El, 1993).

These studies indicated a clear tendency for the location of high technology enterprises, particularly small and privately owned firms, in or near major population centres. It is at such cities that they may have access to university facilities, where they may cooperate with established research institutions and where they may find a pool of highly skilled labour (Shefer and Bar-El, 1993).

The particular importance of the proximity of hi-tech industries to a pool of skilled labour is emphasised by the results of Shachar and Felsenstein's (1992) survey of the spatial distribution of labour markets of selected high-technology firms in Jerusalem and Rehovot (see Table 1.1).

As this survey shows, high technology firms in Jerusalem, included in the sample, employ more than 88 per cent of their most qualified personnel (scientists, engineers and administration) from the city itself and its environs, while only 12 per cent of highly qualified workers come from elsewhere. In less centrally located and smaller Rehovot, high technology firms employ only 65 per cent of their most qualified personnel from the city itself and its environs, while 35 per cent of scientist and engineers commute from elsewhere, presumably from Tel Aviv and Jerusalem.

Table 1.1 Labour markets for different skill levels of high technology firms in Jerusalem (after Shachar and Felsenstein, 1992)

Location of firms/ Residence of employees	Skill level				
	Scientists and engineers*	Techni-cians	Production and non-skilled workers	Clerical workers	Total
A. Jerusalem					
Jerusalem	367	196	383	175	1121
Jerusalem's suburbs	59	92	185	22	358
Elsewhere	57	31	22	13	123
Total	483	319	590	210	1602
B. Rehovot					
Rehovot	229	172	324	155	880
Rehovot's environs	185	149	366	110	810
Elsewhere	225	170	241	87	723
Total	639	491	931	352	2413

* Including administration.

This tendency for concentration of high technology industries in close proximity to major population centres is apparently reinforced by the fact that graduates of centrally located universities are often reluctant to leave big cities after graduation and clearly prefer to work and settle nearby (McCann and Sheppard, 2000).

The Effect of Distances on Population Change

In 1885, Ravenstein proposed his 'laws of migration' in a landmark study that shaped the development of migration studies for years. In short, these laws can be formulated as follows (Figure 1.7):

- The intensity of a migration 'current' is inversely proportional to the distance between the migrants' origin and destination. Therefore, the number of migrants in a given population centre declines proportionally to the distance between the city in question and the region of origin of the migrants;

- A great number of migrants proceed over a short distance, but this initial displacement of population triggers subsequent chains of migration ultimately directed towards the major centres of commerce and industry. (According to Ravenstein's theory, the sequence of events is as follows: residents of the countryside surrounding a growing urban centre move into this centre, and the gap left in the rural population is then filled with migrants from more remote districts. Through this 'chain reaction,' the influence of the centres of growth is subsequently felt in the most remote areas of the country);

- Each current of migration produces a counter-current, which moves in the opposite direction. The dispersion of migrants from the major centres of growth is thus the inverse of the tendency for concentration described above, and exhibits similar features;

- Migrants moving over long distances generally go directly into one of the major centres of commerce or industry;

- The native population of urban areas is less inclined to migrate than that of the rural hinterland, while women have a greater tendency to migrate than men (Ravenstein, 1885).

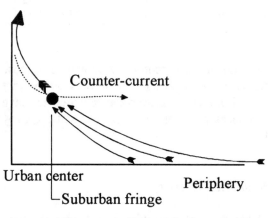

Figure 1.7 An illustration of Ravenstein's model of inter-area migration

The model suggests that the intensity of migration declines as distances between sources of migrants' origin and their destinations grow. Moreover, migration is considered as a multi-step process, in which each current of migration generates its counter-current moving in the opposite direction.

Based on his analysis of the 1871, 1876 and 1881 census counts in Great Britain, Ravenstein found, in particular, that the largest proportion of migrants consists of short-distance movers heading towards adjacent counties in the same kingdom, or border counties in a neighbouring kingdom (Table 1.2). Thus, migrants from Ireland in 1876-1891 settled predominantly in the port towns of Scotland, while nearly 65 per cent of Scottish migrants opted for other counties of Scotland or settled in the border counties of England, rather than in more remote areas.

Stouffer (1940; 1962 reprint, p.70) also emphasises the universal importance of distance in population behaviour:

> Distance is such an important factor that it needs more explicit study than it has received. Where one is seeking to explain 'why' persons go to a particular place to get jobs, 'why' they go to trade at a particular store, 'why' they go to a particular neighbourhood to commit crime, or 'why' they marry the particular spouses they choose, the factor of spatial distance is of obvious significance.

Table 1.2 Proportion of migrants enumerated in 1871-81 in various kingdoms of the U.K.*

Place of birth	Place of residence		
	Border counties	Elsewhere in the same kingdom	Sister kingdom
England and Welsh	52.4	45.1	2.5
Scotland	46.0	29.8	24.2
Ireland	16.2	24.1	59.7

* Source: Compiled from Ravenstein, 1885.

For Stouffer, however, migration does not necessary reflect the relationship between mobility and distance. Instead, he introduces the concept of 'intervening opportunities,' according to which 'the number of persons going a given distance is directly proportional to the number of opportunities at that distance and inversely proportional to the number of intervening opportunities'. In other words, the effect of distance on long-distance migration manifests itself through the commutated (intervening) opportunities that can be found at this distance (see Figure 1.8).

To quantify the relationship between distance, migration and intervening opportunities, Stouffer suggested the following formula:

$$\frac{\partial y}{\partial s} = \frac{a}{x} \frac{\partial x}{\partial s},$$

where ∂y is the number of persons moving from an origin to a circular band of width ∂s; x is the number of intervening opportunities, i.e. the cumulative number of opportunities between the origin and distance s; and ∂x is the number of opportunities within a band of width ∂s.

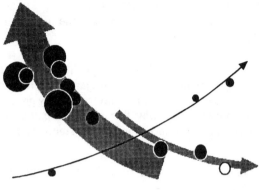

Figure 1.8   A simplified illustration of Stouffer's concept of intervening opportunities

According to Stouffer's concept, the intensity of migration stream is directly proportional to the number of opportunities at this distance and inversely proportional to the number of intervening opportunities between the places of origin and destination.

In contrast, the random utility model of long-distance migration (Maier and Weiss, 1991) does not emphasise any particular effect of distance on migration choices. According to this model, individual migrants select a region which offers the highest utility, as measured by various direct and indirect indicators: prices, individual income opportunities, wage differentials, environmental conditions, local amenities, cultural infrastructure, etc. In its general forms, the random utility function that a region i provides for an individual j is expressed as follows:

$$U_{ij} = U_j \ (R_{ij}, \ p_i, \ y_{ij}, \ \beta_i, \ C_j) + \varepsilon_{ij},$$

where R_{ij} is the utility which region i provides for an individual j in terms of environmental, infrastructure and other primarily physical determinants; p_i is a measure of prevailing prices in the region; y_{ij} are constraints imposed by income; β_i is a vector which contains a set of parameters that determines the shape of the utility function; C_j is a vector of socio-economic characteristics depending on the age, social status and other characteristics of the individual; and ε_{ij} is a stochastic component, which represents all unobserved differences in utility for otherwise comparable individuals.

De Jong and Fawcett (1981) adopt a similar approach to modelling migration behaviour, where distance plays no part. This model, called the value-expectancy model (V-E model), attempts to explain migration as a function of a broad array of economic and non-economic factors, including environmental, cultural and social parameters. Algebraically, this model is formulated as follows:

$$S = \Sigma\ V_i \times E_i,$$

where S is the sum of the value-expectancy products; E_i is the expectancy by an individual i that migration will lead to the desired outcome, and V_i is the value of the migration outcome for the individual i.

This model requires a precise specification of the personally valued goals that 'might be met by moving...and an assessment of the perceived linkage, in terms of expectancy, between migration behaviour and the attainment of goals in alternative locations' (ibid, p. 47). Although this model may provide a perfect explanation of the behaviour of individual migrants, its ability to explain more general migration patterns appears to be limited.

A more general approach to modelling migration behaviour is described in Stillwell and Congdon (1991). In contrast to both the regional utility and the value-expectancy models, this model does incorporate distance as a key determinant of migration:

$$M_{ij} = A \times O_i \times D_j \times f(d_{ij}),$$

where M_{ij} is migration from area i to area j; A = scaling constant or balancing factors; O_i = out-migration; Dj = in-migration; $f(d_{ij})$ = distance function.

Stillwell's attempt to test this model using UK Census data appeared, however, to be inconclusive. For instance, he found that out-migrants from Scotland were relatively unaffected by distance in their migration behaviour. At the same time, migration from Tyne and Wear and the reminder of the North exhibited some effect of distance, as did that from East Anglia and the South West. Concurrently, in the case of the Greater London and the rest of the South East, the distance variable was found to be of relatively low significance.

A more detailed analysis of the UK Census data, performed by Gordon (1991), explained the inconclusiveness of Stillwell's findings concerning the effect of distance on migration as follows: a) The relationship between distance and migration was non-linear; and b) There were heterogeneous migration streams (local, regional and national) existing simultaneously in the country at any given point of time (see Figure 1.9).

As Figure 1.9 shows, the intensity of each of the migration flows initially increases and then, after reaching certain points of inflection (3 miles for the local stream, 12-15 miles for the regional (inter-county) stream, and 50-70 miles for the national stream), declines as distances grow.

An analysis of inter-urban migration in Israel (Portnov, 1998b) provides further evidence concerning the effect of distance on inter-urban population change. Table 1.3 reports the findings of this study concerning the effect of various factors on internal migration and on the initial distribution of foreign immigrants in 1992-95 (the factors are selected using a Stepwise Multiple Regression procedure).

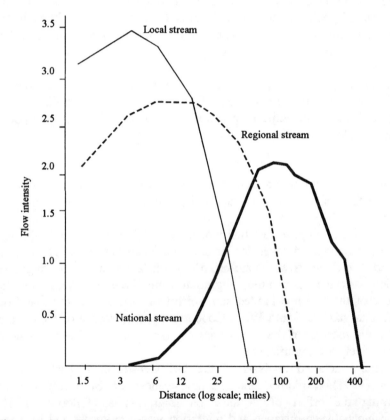

Figure 1.9   Density of migration flows in the U.K. by stream and distance

Source: Gordon (1991).

Table 1.3 Key factors affecting components of population growth of urban settlements in Israel (SMR: linear-log form)

Variable	Foreign immigration, 1,000		Internal migration, 1,000	
	B	t	B	t
Population size of a town, 1,000	1.875	6.2[a]	-2.339	-2.6[a]
Housing construction, 1,000 m^2	-	-	2.973	3.4[a]
Distance to the closest urban centre, km[c]	-0.930	-3.2[a]	1.772	2.9[a]
Indicator of climatic harshness	-	-	0.894	1.7[b]
Share of immigrant population, %	1.041	5.2[a]	-	-
Bank savings, $US per capita	1.121	3.6[a]	-1.474	-2.4[b]
Constant (B$_o$)	-8.026	-7.1[a]	-411	-0.2
F-statistic	56.3		14.80	
R^2	0.839		0.637	

[a] indicates a two-tailed 0.01 significance level; [b] indicates a two-tailed 0.05 significance level; [c] either Jerusalem, Tel Aviv or Haifa; '-' the factor is not included in the SMR model as statistically significant.

Source: Portnov (1998b).

As Table 1.3 shows, the effect of distance to the closest urban centre on the spatial distribution of internal migrants and foreign immigrants appears to be statistically highly significant (P<0.01). The effect of this factor on the behaviour of internal migrants and foreign immigrants is, however, not identical. While the influx of new immigrants to a given locality tends to decline as distance to the closest urban centre increases (B<0), internal migrants in Israel tend to move towards relatively more remote towns, as indicated by the positive sign of the regression coefficient of the distance variable. The following explanation of these opposite trends is suggested: New immigrants, being less informed about the country and local conditions, tend to concentrate in big cities and in neighbouring towns in which they hope to find suitable employment or can count on initial help from friends and relatives. Concurrently, the existing population of these centres (who are potential internal migrants) are more independent economically, are more mobile and better informed about local conditions, and tend to move outwards from overpopulated urban centres to smaller and relatively more remote urban localities in which housing is more available and affordable (ibid.).

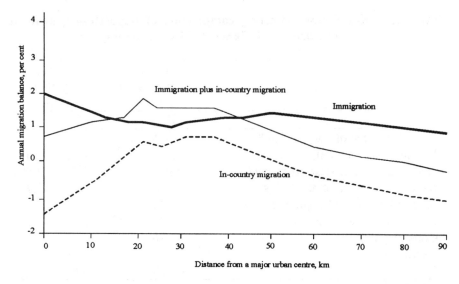

Figure 1.10   Migration streams in Israel as a function of distance from major urban centres

However, the intensity of the outward flow of internal migration increases in line with distance from the major population centres of Israel only up to a certain point. As a more detailed analysis of this phenomenon shows, after reaching a threshold of about 20-40 km, the intensity of internal migration to a town starts to decline (see Figure 1.10; dotted line). A similar break point was observed by Gordon (1991) in the U.K. (see Figure 1.9).

The findings concerning the decline of migration intensity in line with distance from major urban areas are related to the general phenomenon of the distance decay function, discussed in some length in the previous section.

Quantitative Thresholds of Commuting

Table 1.4 attempts to summarise the range of distances considered to be practicable for daily commuting, as indicated by various applied studies. The countries included in the sample have different population size, land area and motorization levels. As the table shows, the distances in question vary from 20-30 km in small and densely populated Israel to some 80-100 km in Australia and the United States.

Table 1.4 **Estimates of distances considered as being practicable for daily commuting in selected countries**

Indicator	Israel	Norway	U.S.A	Australia
Population size, ['000]	5,750	4,440	272,600	18,800
Total area, ['000 km2]	20.1	324.2	9,629.1	7,686.8
Population density [persons per km2]	286	14	28	2
Motorization level, [private cars per 1,000 residents]	290	402	465	460
GDP, [$US per capita]	18,100	24,700	31,500	21,200
Per capita length of highways, [meters]	2.7	20.5	23.6	48.6
Commuting time, [min.]	40-60	45-90	40-45	50-60
Average threshold of commuting, [km]*	20-30	50-60	80-90	90-100

Combined from: CIA, 2000 (population, GDP, highway and land area data); Portnov *et al*, 2000; Shachar and Felsenstein, 1992; U.S. DOT/FHWA, 1990; SN, 1994; SN, 1997-1998; ICBS, 1998. *Authors' estimates.

Conclusions

Remoteness has a profound and complex effect on urban development. It causes an increase in the cost of transportation and thus affects the location of manufacturing facilities. Even in the case of modern high-technology firms, the effect of remoteness from major urban centres on their location may be considerable. Though high technology firms do not generate, as a rule, heavy transport flows, they tend to locate their branches in close proximity to major population centres, in which a pool of skilled labour can be found and where access to existing research infrastructure is immediate.

Remoteness tends to affect a region's attractiveness to migrants adversely, though the relationship between migration currents and distance is neither linear nor universal. The general tendency for inter-area population exchanges to decline with growing distance from major population centres is but one manifestation of the distance decay function.

The distance from major population centres beyond which an area is considered to be remote may differ across different countries, depending on their actual size, population densities, existing infrastructure, motorization levels, and other factors. In any case, this distance is related to that considered practical for daily commuting. Though actual distances may differ, the location of a town or region beyond the commuting range and the perception of remoteness, rather than actual distances, may characterise a town as 'remote.'

2 Defining and Measuring Isolation

The pattern of urban settlement in peripheral areas is normally more scattered than that in densely populated core regions.[1] Because of the lower density of urbanization, distances between urban localities in the periphery exceed greatly those in the core (see Figure 2.1). Thus, for instance, urban and semi-urban settlements located in the Western part of Egypt are typically over 200 km from the nearest neighbouring town, and aerial distances between towns in the Durango region of Mexico are commonly over 100-200 km. These distances are, of course, relatively small compared to those found in the western regions of China, in Russian Siberia or in inland areas of Australia, where neighbouring towns may be some 400-600 km apart (Portnov and Pearlmutter, 1999c).

Physical *isolation* of a peripheral town from other urban places within its geographic region is likely to aggravate the effect of the town's remoteness from major urban centres of the country. Isolation, for instance, almost inevitably causes a shortage of services and cultural infrastructure and limits the choice of job opportunities (Kneese, 1978; Green, 1982). Since small peripheral towns scattered over considerable distances can provide neither diversified employment nor sufficient opportunities for cultural life, economic downturns often result in emigration (Portnov and Erell, 1998b).

In this chapter, the phenomenon of isolation and its implications for the development of peripheral towns will be discussed in some detail. The analysis will start with a brief discussion of the role of climatic conditions and their effect on economic development in the formation of scattered patterns of urban development. This analysis will be followed by a classification of types of isolation of urban communities, and a discussion of the effects of isolation on socio-economic development of urban localities in peripheral areas.

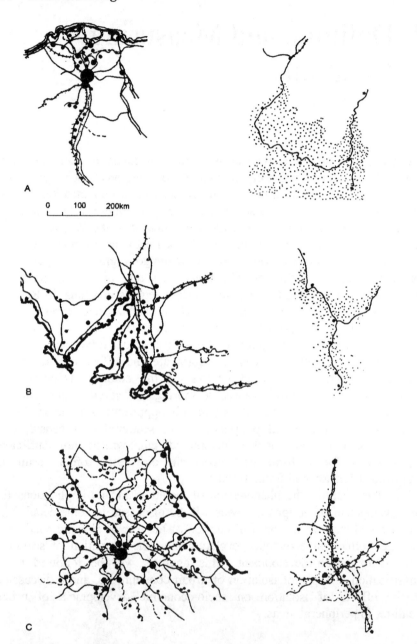

Figure 2.1   Patterns of urban settlement in core (left) and peripheral areas (right) of selected countries (after Portnov, 1999c)

A – Egypt, B – Australia; C – Mexico.

The Role of Climate in Creating Isolated Patterns of Settlements

Scattered patterns of urban settlement, such as those found in most peripheral areas (see Figure 2.1), may have occurred for a number of reasons – historical, economic, etc. It will be argued, however, that spatial isolation of urban localities in peripheral areas is mainly due to the effects of climate, either directly or indirectly. This hypothesis will be discussed separately for agriculture-based settlements and for non-agricultural communities.

Climate and Patterns of Agricultural Settlements

As Figure 2.2 shows, an absolute majority of the urban centres of the contemporary world are located outside of arid and semi-arid regions with harsh climates. The underlying cause is relatively simple: Nearly all of the major population centres of the world were initially established as agricultural communities, whose development relied on a temperate climate and the presence of fresh water. Lacking rain or other sources of potable water, such as rivers, the agricultural potential of arid lands is extremely limited. Without water imports, farming in arid areas provides low yields, compared to those in irrigated areas; and even these low yields tend to decline over time due to soil exhaustion (see Table 2.1).

According to von Thünen's theory of land use,[2] the low productivity of agriculture in arid regions places considerable limitations on the number of people the land can sustain and thus prevents greater concentrations of population, especially in less developed and pre-industrial societies, whose population is dependent primarily on local resources for subsistence.

Weiss (1986) reports the results of an interesting survey of the settlement field of Northern Mesopotamia in 3300-1750 BCE (jointly sponsored by Yale University and the Metropolitan Museum of Art, New York). The region is considered to be agriculturally marginal due to insufficient precipitation (200-300 mm per annum), while substantial inter-annual variability of rain (of about 35-45 per cent) causes frequent crop failure.

Figure 2.3 shows the cluster of settlements established around the town of Tell Leilan between 2500 and 1900 BCE and mapped during the archaeological survey in question.

Figure 2.2 Desert areas and major cities of the world

Source: Portnov, 1999c.

Most of the 15 settlements mapped in the region were small in size: 13 settlements had an area of 1-10 hectares, 2 settlements covered 10-15 hectares and only one settlement (Tell Leilan) occupied nearly 90 hectares.

Not surprisingly, all these settlements were located along the Jarrah River and its tributaries (see Figure 2.3), on which their residents relied for water. Notably, however, the settlements were some 8-15 km from Tell Leilan, and were 5-10 km away from each other.

Table 2.1   Cereal production in dry farming and irrigated areas of Northeast Syria and Iraq in 1909-10 and 1968

District/year	Year	Wheat		Barley	
		Cultivated area, %	Yield, kg/ha	Cultivated area, %	Yield, kg/ha
DRY FARMING:					
Diyarbakir	1909-10	-	1594	-	1214
Mosul	'	-	1235	-	938
Aleppo	'	-	1149	-	965
Kamichli	1968	12.8	1042	24.7	1289
Mosul	'	36.5	852	20.7	1129
Tel Afar	'	35.8	930	13.5	1058
Sinjar	'	27.3	797	13.1	1041
Arbil	'	23.8	961	6.6	1008
Kirkuk	'	9.9	534	3.4	582
IRRIGATION:					
Basra	1909-10	-	2843	-	2927
Massayib	1968	4.5	1524	9.1	1639
Hilla	'	19.0	1694	25.2	1657
Diwaniyah	'	15.2	1600	5.2	1577

Source: Compiled from Weiss (1986). '-' Indicates a lack of data.

Weiss *(ibid.)* attributes this scattered pattern of settlement to the size of the agricultural area required to sustain them, which was estimated to be some 1.5 hectares of cultivable land per person (given the actual productivity of agriculture in the region during the period under consideration).

For the size of Tell Leilan (5,000-6,000 residents), the total area required for agricultural production thus stood somewhere between 13,500 and 15,000 hectares, which corresponds to the radius of some 5.8-7.5 km (excluding the actual size of the town's built-up area). This radius explains why there were no other settlements within 8-15 km from Tell Leilan and why other localities were established at considerable distances from each other. Moreover, the size of this subsistence area was also likely to limit the growth of the central town (Tell Leilan) due to the fact that the range in question (5.8-7.5 km) was effectively the upper limit of village-to-field commuting reported for the region at the historic period in question (Oates and Oates, 1976; cited in Weiss, 1986).

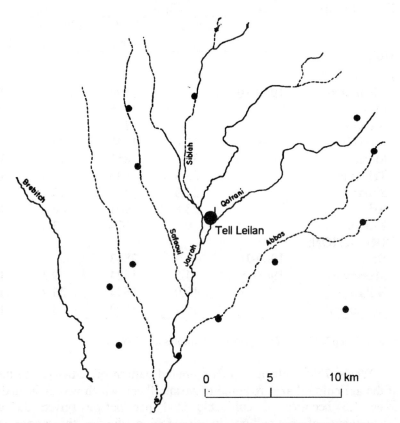

Figure 2.3   Settlements in the Tell Leilan region in 2500-1900 BCE

After Weiss (1986).

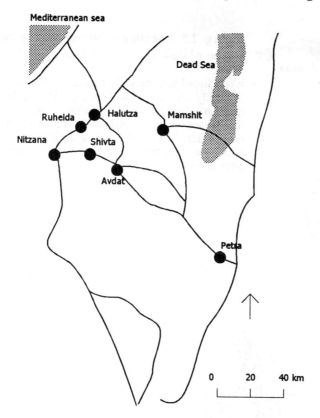

Figure 2.4   Location of Nabataean towns in the Negev desert (200 BCE-700 CE)

The Nabataean towns were established in the Negev as outposts providing patrol services, food and shelter to travellers on the flourishing East-West Spice route. The average distances between towns of some 20-40 km were suited to one-day camel trips across the desert.

Even in present days, climatically harsh areas are, in most cases, sparsely populated, and their settlement pattern remains scattered: subsistence farming requires a relatively large area because the productivity of land in such areas is low. As Middleton and Thomas (1997) point out, current population densities in climatically harsh zones vary mainly according to the productivity of the local environment, but remain generally below 15 persons per km^2 in the extremely arid areas, below 20 persons per km^2 in the arid zones and below 70 persons per km^2 in semi-arid zones. Except for parts of Mexico, dry sectors of northern West

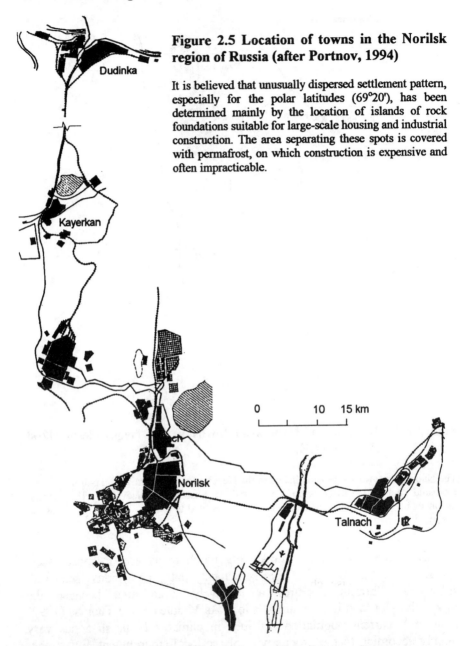

Figure 2.5 Location of towns in the Norilsk region of Russia (after Portnov, 1994)

It is believed that unusually dispersed settlement pattern, especially for the polar latitudes (69°20'), has been determined mainly by the location of islands of rock foundations suitable for large-scale housing and industrial construction. The area separating these spots is covered with permafrost, on which construction is expensive and often impracticable.

Africa, Spain, the Fertile Crescent and much of western Iran, there are few arid lands with population densities of 100-250 persons per km², densities which are common in adjoining humid and sub-humid regions (White,

1966). The reason has been mentioned above: in agricultural economies, larger settlements go hand in hand with greater areas of cultivable land separating individual communities (Oliver, 1997).

In areas with harsh climates, distances between individual towns may be large for another reason – the concentration of essential life-supporting resources. Thus, hyper-aridity is likely to cause the formation of spatially isolated (nucleated) settlements (see Figure 2.1; right diagrams), since their necessary supports, such as water and fertile land, tend to be concentrated around a few oases scattered across the area (Kates *et al*, 1977).

Climate and Non-agricultural Settlements

Restrictions on agricultural production are not, however, the only factor determining the dispersed patterns of settlement in climatically harsh areas. Historically, many settlements in such regions have served as commercial and administrative centres, or have developed around mines, intersections of caravan routes and other local resources (Saini 1980; Golany 1978; Issar, 1999). Thus, the Nabataean towns established in the Negev desert (200 BCE – 700 CE) were located 20-40 km from each other, on the hubs of the then bustling East-West Spice route (see Figure 2.4). The residents of these towns made their living by patrolling the route and providing food and services for the travellers (Negev, 1993).

Some spatially dispersed peripheral towns were established as strategic outposts in response to various geo-political and security considerations. Thus, nearly all of the major population centres of contemporary Russian Siberia (Krasnoyarsk, Irkutsk, Tobolsk, Tomsk, etc.) were established as small military outposts (50-200 residents) scattered across the vast area of the region with, in order to protect Russian settlers from the attacks of indigenous tribes (Portnov, 1992).

In some cases, settlements in climatically harsh areas are located some distance from one another simply because of a lack of land suitable for large-scale construction. Portnov (1994) describes one such case in which the scattered location of towns in the Norilsk region of Russia (Figure 2.5) was determined by the location of spatially dispersed plots of rocky land in an area otherwise characterised by permafrost soil. (Permafrost may provide a strong foundation due to its high ice content. However, if the soil temperature increases, it becomes soft and muddy and may cause severe structural damage or even collapse of buildings. Although numerous technical solutions have been developed to secure the structural stability of buildings on the permafrost soil, these solutions remain extremely expensive, to the point of becoming unfeasible).[3]

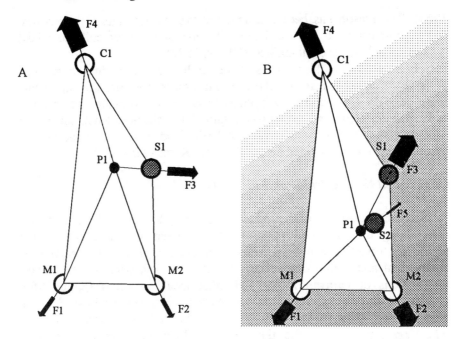

Figure 2.6   Adjustment of a Weberian-type model of industrial location (A) to the variability of climatic conditions (B)

Climatic differences between regions may reinforce the effect of remoteness, and thus cause the establishment of a new town near the location of the production plant but some distance away from the existing settlement.

Theoretically, the effect of climatic harshness on the formation of dispersed patterns of non-agricultural settlements may be illustrated by the adaptation of Weber's model of industrial location. (We may recall that this model, considered in some detail in the previous chapter, does not incorporate climate as one of the factors affecting location).

The adjusted model is plotted in Figure 2.6. Let us assume that the location of production (P1) is determined by four factors: two sources of raw materials (M1 and M2), a market for the final product (C1), and the location of the town (S1) providing labour for the production facility (Figure 2.6A). The geographic plain is homogenous: There are no other differences among alternative locations in the climatic conditions or in the quality of infrastructure and services.

The transport cost of raw materials (F1 and F2) is assumed to be relatively small compared to that of labour (assuming the cost of travel to work is borne by the employer) and of the final product (F3 and F4, respectively). Under such conditions, the location of the factory (P1) is expected to be skewed towards the source of the heavier load – C1 and S1 (see Figure 2.6), as argued in the previous chapter.

Let us now introduce another factor – climatic differences between the areas – and see how the new conditions may alter the established patterns of location. For instance, let us assume that climatic conditions worsen near the sources of raw materials (as indicated by the graduated fill in Figure 2.6B). Under these 'new' conditions, the transport cost of raw materials (F1 and F2) may be expected to increase. For instance, transportation may become less reliable and slower due to frequent snowstorms, poor road conditions, or flooding. Thus, the new bias towards the sources of raw materials (S1 and S3) may 'pull' the optimal place of production (P1) away from the existing settlement (S1; Figure 2.6B). This will increase the overall cost of labour (F3), due to an increase in transportation expenses and to additional compensation paid to commuters. Some existing employees of the production facility may also consider alternative places of employment, commuting to which would be less time consuming or strenuous. As a result, the cost of labour may increase even further due to higher salaries required to retain workers in the facility, especially highly skilled ones. This potential increase of the 'load' in the direction of the sources of raw materials and the residence of the employees is marked by wide arrows 'pulling' the location of the production facility (P1) towards S1, M1 and M2 (see Figure 2.6B).

If additional labour-associated expenses increase even further, the company may consider establishing a 'company' town in close proximity to the production facility (S2 in Figure 2.6B) in order to reduce the overall production cost. This outcome, effectively resulting in the bifurcation of an existing settlement and the formation of a new town, is not, in fact, uncommon: companies in climatically harsh regions, particularly those in primary industries such as mining, have established new communities to house their employees at considerable distances from existing settlements. Examples of such 'company' towns are, for instance, Pilbara in Western Australia (iron mining); Gillette, in Wyoming (coal mining); Bratsk and Divnogorsk, in Russia (power engineering), and Arad in Israel (Dead Sea fertiliser plant). Although the establishment of these towns in close proximity from the place of production cannot be attributed to the effect of the harsh climate alone, the effect of climatic harshness, emphasised in Figure 2.6B was, undoubtedly, one of the decisive factors in these towns' location.

Types of Isolation

Although the concept of *spatial isolation* is not foreign to urban and regional studies, it is not treated as a separate issue, but rather as a marginal problem, closely associated with physical remoteness in general. In sociology, however, the concept of isolation is a core issue that has generated a considerable body of research. Since the research subjects covered by the two fields of science exhibit, as we shall see later, considerable similarities, the wealth of knowledge accumulated in sociology may provide some insights on the effects of isolation on the development of peripheral urban communities. Of particular value in this context is research on 'small groups'.

In his influential book *'Who shall Survive?'*, Moreno (1953; 1978 reprint), defines isolation as an absence of any relationship (neither repulsion nor attraction) between an individual and other persons within a social group. He calls this type of relationship 'social indifference':

> A man is, or at least declares himself indifferent as to whether he works in proximity to A or to B, or to any other individual; ...Or, an individual starts with being attracted to A, B, C, but becomes indifferent towards them in the course of time; he does not care whether they stay with him or leave him, he does not care to replace them. Or, again, an individual A has been indifferent to with whom he works...but the course of time he begins to like these individuals and he does not care to have them replaced (ibid, p. 228).

Moreno identifies eight typical structures of social groups, arranged according to the extent and types of isolation of their members (Figure 2.7):

1. *Total isolation* – the person exhibits neither attraction nor repulsion towards any other individual, either within his own group or within the community, and is not the subject of such emotions by anyone else;
2. *Non-reciprocal outward attraction* – the person is attracted to individuals outside his group who do not reciprocate;
3. *Mutual isolation* - persons, isolated and rejected within their own groups, reject and isolate each other;
4. *Self-inflicted isolation* – a person rejects some individuals in his group and is rejected by others, both within his group and outside it;
5. *Attraction-repulsion* – a person is attracted to some individuals outside his group and rejects others; there are individuals outside his group who are attracted to him, but he does not reciprocate;

6. *Attraction-indifference* – the subject is attracted to individuals within his group; they respond with indifference;
7. *Isolated pair* – there is mutual attraction among individuals, but each of the subjects is otherwise rejected and isolated within his own group; the result is a pair of isolated and rejected persons;
8. *Isolated group* – subjects, each isolated in his group, form a group (cluster) of mutual attraction.

If we substitute urban communities for individuals in this hierarchy, and inter-urban exchanges for inter-personal relationships, we obtain a useful classification of settlement patterns (Table 2.2).

Thus, the type of 'total isolation,' placed by Moreno on the top of his classification, may be used to describe a remote peripheral town isolated both within its geographic region and from population centres elsewhere in the country. Similarly, the term *'isolated group'* can be used to describe a cluster of functionally interacting peripheral towns geographically isolated from the rest of the country's urban places.

The usefulness of Moreno's theory for understanding the phenomenon of urban isolation lies, however, far beyond a simple classification. According to his theory, there are two major causes of isolation – inter-personal differences and physical distances among individuals:

- *Differences.* The farther apart one group develops from another, as evinced by certain distinctions (social, educational, emotional, etc.), the more they tend to become isolated from each other.
- *Distances.* Large distances between individuals normally reduce contacts and enhance the status of isolation.

Moreno proposes 'the law of social gravitation' to describe the effects of distance on interpersonal relationships. Although his law is heavily influenced by Newton's law of gravitation (see Chapter 1 of this book), Moreno's social gravitation law has an important addition, namely the facilities of communication:

People 1 (P1) and People 2 (P2) move towards each other in direct proportion to the amount of attraction given (a1) or received (a2), in inverse proportion to the physical distance (d) between locality X and locality Y, the residences of P1 and P2 respectively, the facilities of communication between X and Y being constant.

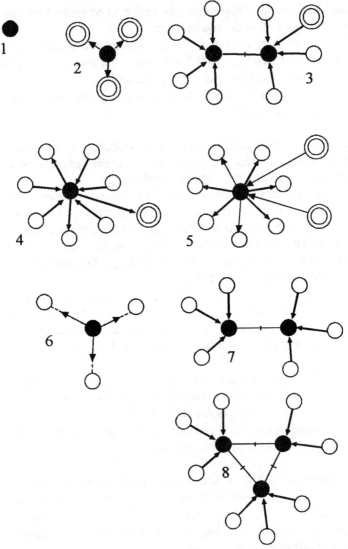

Figure 2.7   Types of isolation in social groups (after Moreno, 1953)

1 – total isolation; 2 – non-reciprocal attraction; 3 – mutual isolation; 4 – self-inflicted isolation; 5 – attraction-repulsion; 6 – attraction-indifference; 7 – isolated pair; 8 – isolated group. Filled circles represents the individuals; empty circles represent other individuals in the group; double circles signify that the individual is a member of a different group from the one charted; solid lines represent attraction; dotted lines indicate indifference; bold lines represent repulsion; crossed lines represent a two-sided relationship (i.e. either mutual attraction, repulsion or indifference); arrows stand for one-sided relationships.

Table 2.2   Classification of urban places according to the extent and type of isolation*

Type of isolation	Description
Total isolation	A town has no functional links with other settlements within its geographic region and only limited links with other population centres of the country. Unless it is quite large, the town's economy is likely to be unsustainable and its population unstable.
One-sided interaction	A town is integrated into the general setting of urban places (as expressed in, for instance, more frequent commuting to major population centres of the country than elsewhere), while its links with other urban communities within a region are either weak or non-existent. Such a situation may occur in remote geographic areas that are well connected by air links to a country's major urban centres.
'Broken link'	Neighbouring peripheral towns provide identical functions and services and do not complement or enhance each other. This may result in more frequent functional exchanges with towns and cities outside the region.
Supra-regional link	A town's economy is unequivocally oriented towards population centres outside its geographic region. Unlike one-sided interaction (see above), this form of functional link may express itself in two-sided (core-periphery) population exchanges, provision of services and industrial cooperation.
Partial integration	A town provides services to surrounding rural and semi-rural communities, but receives no substantial 'back-wash' effect.
'Isolated twins'	Two closely located peripheral towns, isolated from the rest of urban places, provide a joint pool of services, employment and facilities to their residents.
Isolated group	Peripheral towns form a cluster of urban places integrated through a developed system of inter-urban exchanges.

* Partially based on Moreno's (1953) classification of types of isolation in social groups.

In another important study of small group relationships, Hare (1962) also emphasises the importance of proximity in the formation of a social group, arguing that persons who live near each other, work or study together tend to become friends more often than persons who live or work farther apart. He also argues that social cohesion within a group is more likely to continue if the individuals either have common interests or values or can effectively complement ·each other. To illustrate the latter supposition, Hare describes the results of the experiment carried out by Muzafer Sherif and his colleagues in a boys' summer camp in northern Connecticut. For this camp, a group of 11-12 year boys were selected who had not previously met each other. After a few days, it was found that the boys acquired an informal and spontaneous organization based on a division of skills and responsibilities that helped them to form a sustainable 'social atom':

> One boy excelled in cooking. Another led in athletics. Others, though not outstanding in any one skill could be counted on to pitch in and do their level best in anything the group attempted...A few boys consistently had good suggestions and showed ability to coordinate the efforts of others in carrying them through. Within a few days one person had proved himself more resourceful and skilled than the rest. Thus, rather quickly, a leader and lieutenants emerged. Some boys shifted towards the bottom of the heap, while others jockeyed for higher positions (Sherif, 1956, p.55-56; cited in Hare, 1962).

A similar division of functions is inherent to settlement patterns. While some urban communities develop as ports or transportation nodes, others may specialise in food processing or provide service centres to the former, thus supplementing and enhancing the development of each other, despite a lack of immediate spatial proximity (Clark, 1982; Fujita and Mori, 1996; 1997).

Measures of Isolation

In his book on inter-group relationships, Moreno (1953; 1978 reprint) suggests two quantitative indices of social isolation that can, with some essential adjustments, be used for measuring the degree of isolation in settlement patterns. The first index, called the *'interest index for own group'*, is estimated as a ratio between the overall number of personal choices within the group available to an individual and the number of choices actually received:

$$I = (S*C)/R,$$

where I is the interest index; S is the size of the group, indicated by the number of persons; C is the number of personal choices allowed per person (5, 10, etc.), and R is the number of votes received from other members of the group.

For a given size of the group, the values of the index in question are high for one-sided interactions (non-reciprocated choices for which $R \rightarrow 0$) and low for fully reciprocated interactions ($R \rightarrow \infty$).

Moreno's second index is the *'index of attraction for out-groups'* (A) and is estimated as follows:

$$A = (N-N_i)*C/R,$$

where N is the entire population; N_i is population of a group *i;* C is number of choices allowed for an individual (5, 10, etc.), and R is the number of votes received by the individual from outside the group.

In applying these indices to settlement patterns, S can be measured as the total number of towns forming a settlement cluster, N as the total number of urban centres in a given settlement system (which may include several clusters as well as isolated towns), while R may be represented by any appropriate measure of the intensity of inter-urban exchanges – migration, inter-area commuting, number of cross-area phone calls, etc.

Whatever proxy is used, the values of the indices above (I and A) will be in inverse proportion to the intensity of exchanges (R): these indices will return high values for truly isolated communities ($R \rightarrow 0$), and low values for towns which are highly integrated in either intra-regional (I index) or supra-regional (A index) systems of urban settlements ($R \rightarrow \infty$).

Thomas (cited in Clawson and Hall, 1973) suggests another quantitative measure, which may also be used as an indicator of a town's isolation in a settlement system. He called this measure the *'independence index'* (IN). This index is calculated as the ratio between the number of journeys to work occurring within a local area (L) and journeys crossing the boundaries of the local area in question (C):

$$IN = L/C.$$

The resulting index tends to have high value for economically self-contained towns (or local areas) that capture the dominant share of job-related commuting, and low values for towns which exhibit a high degree of integration in the economic activities occurring in other towns, and which thus attract only a small fraction of job-related commuting of their residents.

Though the above indicators of isolation (I, A and IN) may provide accurate estimates, their evaluation requires an extensive and complex input (commuting, inter-area exchanges, etc.), which may not be readily available. A simpler index of isolation is proposed in Portnov *et al.* (2000): the isolation of a town may be measured as either the overall number of neighbouring urban places located within commuting distance from the urban locality in question, or as the total population within this range. This indicator of isolation and its relationship with another measure of urban location – remoteness – will be discussed in more detail in Part III of this book, which deals with urban clustering.

Implications of Isolation

It may be argued that, compared to centrally located towns forming integrated functional clusters, spatially isolated peripheral settlements are more vulnerable to negative changes in the national economy as a whole, such as recession, unemployment, and hyperinflation. A study of peripheral towns in Israel (Portnov and Erell, 1998b) indicated that, although the negative effect of the above economic processes is felt elsewhere, their adverse impact on spatially dispersed peripheral localities is especially profound. This study was based on the 'sample-control' method of analysis and covered two groups of peripheral towns and two groups of controls. The first group of peripheral localities (Set 1) and its core control (Control 1) were formed by cities of 120,000-150,000 residents. Concurrently, the second set of peripheral settlements (Set 2) and their centrally located control (Control 2) consisted of settlements of smaller size (6,000-30,000 residents). The study covered the 30-year period of 1965-95.

The results of a comparative analysis of the sample and control settlements are represented graphically in Figures 2.8 and 2.9. The dynamic of the *overall population growth* of urban localities included in the sample (Figure 2.8) indicates that the population of peripheral settlements (Sets 1 and 2) grew on the average more slowly than that of the respective core control. For example, as Figure 2.8 shows, the overall annual rate of population growth of the small peripheral towns (Set 2) was, on the average, 1-2 percent lower than that of the respective control settlements in the central region (Control 2). While the general course of this trend is not entirely unexpected, one particular phase deserves notice. Since the recent peak of mass immigration to Israel from the former Soviet Union in 1990-91, large urban localities in the core (Control 1) exhibited a substantial decline in their rate of population growth. At the same time, smaller suburban settlements in the core area   (Control 2) continued to grow at a relatively high rate. This trend, which is apparently due to the

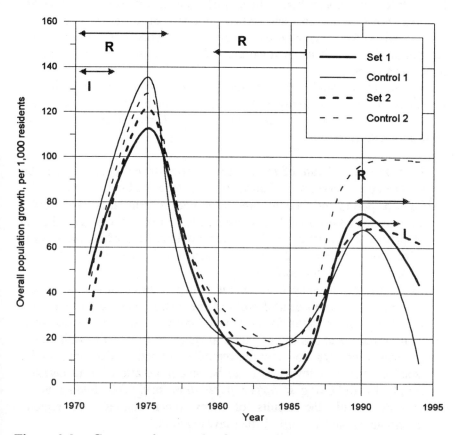

Figure 2.8   Comparative trends of population growth of centrally located and peripheral towns in Israel in 1971-94

Source: Portnov and Erell (1998). The curves represent statistical averages computed separately for the respective sets of peripheral settlements (Sets 1 and 2) and central controls (Controls 1 and 2). The arrows indicate the periods of mass immigration to the country (I), and those of relative economic recession (R).

dispersion of population from major urban centres of the country, was somewhat less evident in peripheral areas. The disparities in growth rates between peripheral localities of different population size (Set 1 and Set 2) are indeed less substantial (Figure 2.8). The prominence of suburbanisation trends in the core and their relative absence in the periphery are an expression of the very different nature of the two types of urban systems. In a densely populated core region, suburban residents may find relief from central city congestion without forfeiting access to employment and services. Since in the sparsely settled periphery distances between towns may render daily commuting impractical, pressures which cause emigration from a particular town may often result in emigration from the region as a whole.

In the above study, the *annual rates of private construction* also appeared to be substantially different in peripheral localities, compared with their 'core' controls (see Figure 2.9). Three general trends are especially noteworthy:

- First, the overall rate of private construction tends to be considerably lower in peripheral towns than in settlements located in the core;
- Second, periods of economic recession and hyperinflation (1973-1977, 1980-1985, 1989-1991) had an especially detrimental effect on the rate of private construction in the peripheral localities, while the positive effect of relatively favourable economic years (1992-94) was somewhat less pronounced there;
- Third, the discrepancy between rates of private construction in large urban settlements in central parts of the country compared with those found in smaller towns in the core (Controls 1 and 2) is substantial, while urban localities in peripheral areas (Sets 1 and 2) exhibit similar patterns of construction activity, regardless of size. It thus appears that isolated peripheral towns *may not* become more attractive to investors simply by *achieving a larger population size*. This finding is not consistent with the results of many other studies of regional development, and is worth further investigation.[4]

Conclusion

Large distances between towns in thinly populated areas, particularly peripheral ones, are likely to aggravate the effects of the remoteness of these localities from major urban centres of a country, effectively preventing the establishment of joint social and economic infrastructures. Different types of spatial isolation may be identified. These range from total isolation (within both a geographic region and from other urban centres of a country) to isolated clusters, in which individual urban localities share essential functions and services. To measure the extent of isolation, different quantitative indices can be employed. For instance, the extent of isolation can be measured as the ratio between intra-regional to inter-regional journeys, as the intensity of inter-urban interaction, or as the number of other urban places located within the area practicable for daily commuting. The choice of a particular index may be determined by the availability of data and by the type of analysis most appropriate for the research objectives.

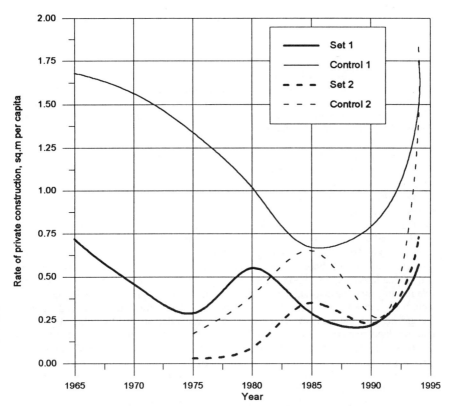

Figure 2.9   Annual rates of private construction in centrally located and peripheral towns of Israel in 1965-94

After Portnov and Erell (1998).

Notes

[1] The core-periphery paradigm is a model of the spatial organisation of human development based on the unequal distribution of power in an economy, society, and polity. According to this theory, whose basics are closely associated with Friedmann (1966), development originates in a relatively small number of centres located at the points of highest potential interaction, defined as the core. The core concentrates major centres of innovative change and dominates over the periphery, which is dependent upon and largely governed by institutions in the core. This dependence manifests itself through the relationships of capital and labour exchanges: Since peripheral regions often lack the resources to sustain their own growth over time, their development potential is largely reliant on processes within the core. This relationship is fundamentally different from the traditional interdependence between a city and its agricultural hinterland. For while in both cases the urban centre provides capital, services and technology, the flow of goods once provided by the hinterland is replaced by a flow of population from the periphery to the core. Core regions thus possess the means of controlling the development of their peripheries and extracting the resources that contribute to their own accelerating growth, which naturally lead to social and political tensions (Friedmann, 1973; Gradus, 1983; Berry, 1973; Johnston *et al*, 1994; Hansen, 1981).

[2] In his book on 'The Isolated State' *(Der Isolierte Staat)* published in 1826, von Thünen (1783-1850) developed his model of concentric land use for an isolated market town. According to von Thünen's model, the location of a settlement is determined in relation to available land resources and transportation cost. This model states that the size of a settlement depends on the area required to provide food for its inhabitants. Farming plots located in close proximity to a settlement or residence are more intensively cultivated, may be used to produce perishable crops (vegetables and dairy products), or crops with high transport costs. More distant plots may be cultivated less intensively, used for production of less perishable crops (grains), or planted with crops requiring less attention and having lower transportation costs. Farming settlements would thus locate in optimal relation to prime agricultural lands, whereas cultivation requiring lower labour inputs would be carried out at greater distances from the settlement. Von Thünen also recognized that the real-world landscape does not offer an undifferentiated plain or uniform land resources, so that land use around a settlement would be adjusted in accordance to variability in land quality and available transportation corridors (such as, for instance, a navigable river). In follow-up cases studies, von Thünen's theory was generally confirmed. In particular, it was found that most intensively cultivated plots tend to be located within one km from the farmer's residence, while plots cultivated less intensively may be as far as 4-5 km away (EB, 1999; Oliver, 1997).

[3] Piles are used to support many, if not most, structures built on ice-rich permafrost. In regions suffering from cold winters, many pile foundations are in ground subject to seasonal freezing. Where this occurs, foundations may suffer from frost heaving, which tends to displace the pile upward and thus to cause great structural damage. The displacement of piling is not limited to the far north, though maximum disturbance is probably encountered most widely in the sub-arctic. Expensive maintenance and sometimes complete destruction of bridges, school buildings, military installations, pipelines, and other structures have resulted from failure to understand the process of frost heaving on foundation piles (EB, 1999).

[4] Numerous studies dealing with the effects of population growth on the economy (see *inter alia* Clark, 1982; Alonso, 1971; Turner, 1993), suggest that reaching a certain population size is an essential precondition for achieving sustained urban growth. This assumption is in line with another popular concept – Perroux's 'growth pole' theory. According to this theory, growth in a propelling region may generate a 'propulsion' effect on surrounding geographic areas. Berry (1973) applied this idea to the hierarchy of urban centres arguing that 'impulses of economic change' are transmitted from growth centres, which are sufficiently large, to their hinterland. He called this phenomenon a 'spread effect.' In the 1960s-1970s, this theory was widely embraced by regional planners in an attempt to accelerate development of underdeveloped peripheral regions. As Hansen (1981) argues, however, optimism relating to the possibility that inducing growth in a few large centres would generate spread effects into their hinterland was soon altered by 'pessimism then the expectations of the earlier phase failed to materialise.' In fact, little evidence has been found to date that the creation of regional growth poles could actually boost the development of their hinterland (Hansen, 1983; Kuklinski, 1978). Instead, in some empirical studies it was argued that 'regional centres' established in underdeveloped peripheral areas actually tend to deplete human and capital resources of surrounding less developed communities (Portnov *et al*, 2000).

3 Choice of Urban Centre

In previous chapters, we discussed the effect of two factors determining the location of a town with respect to a general setting of urban places, namely the distance separating it from the closest major population centre of a country (*remoteness*), and the presence, or lack thereof, of other towns in the region (*isolation*). In the course of this discussion, the choice of urban centres, from which distances are measured, has received no particular attention; it was assumed that this important issue may warrant a separate and in-depth discussion.

Indeed, this issue is not simple and *may not* be resolved by an analysis of certain quantitative characteristics of urban settlements alone. As Table 3.1 shows, the population size of urban settlements described as 'principal cities' appears to vary widely in different countries: from 130,000-700,000 residents in thinly populated Norway to 2,000,000-11,000,000 in China and 2,000,000-13,000,000 residents in India.

Counter to intuition, both the number of principal cities and the number of residents in them do not appear to be a simple function of the overall population size of a country as a whole. For instance, in Denmark and Finland, whose overall population is nearly identical, the population of the largest principal city is 500,000 and 1,300,000 residents, respectively (see Table 3.1). Considerable variation in population size and number of principal cities is also observed elsewhere. Thus, in Morocco and Algeria, the population of principal cities ranges from 670,000 to 3,100,000 and from 350,000 to 1,700,000 residents, respectively, though these countries are nearly identical with respect to their overall population. Two other neighbouring countries - Iran and Iraq - are another example: Although Iran is three time more populated than Iraq, the size of principal cities of the former country exceeds that in the latter by less than twofold. Finally, an equal number of principal cities – four – is found in Sweden, Denmark, Finland, Greece, Morocco, Algeria, Egypt, Syria, Saudi Arabia and Southern Korea, though these countries vary in their overall population and the size of major urban centres.

In the present chapter, factors affecting the choice of urban centre will be discussed in some detail, with particular attention given to the following questions: How are urban centres formed? What are the criteria for defining a locality as a major urban centre? And, finally, what kind of relationships exist between functional characteristics of urban places, their population, their ranking as population centres in countries of different population size, and the level of socio-economic development?

We will argue that in the ranking of an urban locality as a major (principal) population centre, its actual population size is of relatively little importance. This ranking is mostly determined by the functions the settlement may perform, specifically by the *presence of unique regional functions such as hospitals and institutions of higher education.*

Table 3.1   Number and population range of principal cities in selected countries

Country	Population size $[\times 10^6]$	Number of principal cities	Population range of principal cities $[\times 10^3]$
EUROPE:			
Norway	4.4	3	130-700
Sweden	8.9	4	180-1,540
Denmark	5.2	4	150-1,340
Finland	5.1	4	160-500
UK	58.3	6	600-6,400
Ireland	3.6	2	170-1,000
Netherlands	15.5	6	300-1,100
France	58.3	12	400-9,300
Germany	82	15	480-3,500
Switzerland	7.3	5	270-840
Austria	8.0	5	100-1,600
Portugal	10.6	2	1200-2,600
Spain	39.7	10	340-3,000
Italy	58.2	14	230-2,700
Greece	10.5	4	160-3,100
AFRICA:			
Morocco	26.9	4	670-3,100
Algeria	27.9	4	350-1,700
Egypt	61.1	4	840-6,800
Nigeria	88.5	6	430-1,400
Zaire	44.5	3	600-3,800

Country	Population size [x10^6]	Number of principal cities	Population range of principal cities [x10^3]
South Africa	44	3	1,200-1,900
ASIA:			
Israel	5.7	3	250-650
Syria	14.6	4	280-1,500
Saudi Arabia	18.4	4	500-2,000
Iraq	20.2	3	570-3,800
Iran	68.9	4	1,100-6,500
India	943.0	9	2,100-12,600
Sri Lanka	18.4	3	170-1,900
Bangladesh	118.3	3	900-6,100
China	1226.9	13	1,500-9,000
Northern Korea	23.9	3	750-2,600
Southern Korea	45.1	4	1,800-10,600
Japan	125.2	9	1,200-12,000
Burma	46.6	4	150-2,500
Thailand	58.4	3	240-5,900
Vietnam	74.6	4	370-3,900
Malaysia	20.2	5	250-1,200
Indonesia	198.6	5	1,000-8,300

Source: Compiled from Widdows (1996).

Formation of Urban Centres

There is no universal, commonly accepted theory as to how urban centres are formed. An interesting explanation of this process is proposed by Hudson (1976; cited in Oliver, 1997), who suggests that the formation of urban hierarchies undergoes three successive phases:

- *Colonization* – population expands into a region which results in a random settlement distribution;
- *Clustering* – urban growth causes an increase in the number of settlements and in shortening distances among them;
- *Competition* – as urban population grows, successful settlements transform into regional centres. The general settlement pattern becomes more regular as competition for land resources intensifies.

Zipf (1949; 1972 reprint) and Christaller (1933; 1966 English edition) suggested two other explanations for the formation of urban hierarchies and transformation of urban places into major population centres – *the force of industrial innovation* and *concentration of central functions*. Due to exceptionally strong influence of these theories on the subsequent development of urban and regional studies, each of these explanations will be considered in the following subsections in some detail.

Force of Industrial Innovation

According to Zipf *(ibid.)*, the formation of settlement patterns is affected by two interrelated factors – *diversification* and *unification*:

- *Diversification* tends to cause movement of population in the direction of the sources of raw material. The rationale is to minimize the cost of transporting materials to processing plants and to markets. In response to this force, transportation economies tend, ultimately, to split 'the population into a large number of small, widely scattered and largely autarchic communities that have virtually no communication or trade with one another.'
- *Unification* has the opposite effect: it leads to the concentration of all production and consumption in one big city, in which the entire population would live. The effect of this force is stronger if the cost associated with the production and delivery of goods and services to the consumer decreases.

The actual location of population is determined by the balance of these two factors, and depends on the extent to which 'persons are moved to materials and materials to persons in a given system.' Zipf expresses this relationship in terms of two generic equations:

$$N_h = (M+L)_h^2,$$

$$C = P_h(M+L)_h,$$

where N_h is the number of production centres engaged in the production and distribution of an h type of goods; L and M are the costs of producing and of transporting this kind of goods, respectively; P_h is the overall size of the labour force engaged in the production and transportation of the type of goods in question; and C is the overall population of the system consuming this type of goods.

Despite their apparent simplicity and a lack of mathematic rigor, these equations lead to a number of important conclusions. To understand their implications, let us assume that the overall population of the system (C) is held constant and the overall cost of production (M+L) decreases due to, for instance, the introduction of labour-saving devices or more efficient types of transportation. Then, the number of production centres, engaged in the manufacturing of the h type of goods, is expected to decrease ($N_h \to 0$ as M+L$\to$0) and will be located (according to the first formulae) in a smaller number of communities.

Since the overall population size of the system (C) is held constant, each of these production centres will have a larger population than before. This is because the labour force in each of these communities (P_h) will increase in direct proportion to the decrease in the overall cost of production (C=constant; (M+L) $\to$0, than $P_h\to\infty$), as postulated by the latter formulae. In other words, *industrial innovation* (reduction in production and shipping expenses) is expected to lead to the occurrence of a small number of population centres located, according to Zipf, 'in the least-work centre of the terrain,' such that the sum of

> all least-work distances to every person on the terrain will be the minimum...This least-work centre, if viewed dynamically, represents the ideal location towards which the production centres of all kinds of goods migrate as their $(M=L)_h$ cost decrease (*ibid*, p. 355).

Assuming that the overall production cost of different types of goods is not identical, the places of production may thus be concentrated in localities of different population size, ranging from a small number of large population centres (production facilities with relatively low overall production and distribution costs) to a large number of small localities specialising in production of 'low-technology' or bulky goods.

This idea of the relationship between the overall number of urban communities and their population size is captured in the concept of the generalized harmonic 'city-size' distribution, known as the Pareto double-log distribution.[1]

The general formula of the Pareto distribution is as follows:

$$P(x) = \left(\frac{x}{b}\right)^{\alpha+2},$$

where α and b are positive constants.

After the common logarithm is applied, this equation reads as follows:

$$\log (P) = (\alpha+2)*(\log(x)-\log(b)).$$

However, in applied studies of city-size distributions, simplified forms of this equation are commonly used:

$$G_p = AP^{-\alpha} \text{ and } \log (G_p) = A - \alpha \log(P),$$

where G_p is the number of cities with population P or more, A is a positive constant, and α is the Pareto exponent (Alperovich, 1993).

Since the early twentieth century, numerous attempts have been made to test the applicability of this distribution to empirical data on city-size in different countries and geographic regions (see among others Clark, 1982; Carroll, 1982; Alperovich, 1993; Krakover, 1998a,b). It has been shown that city-size distributions differ not only by country but also are subject to change with the passage of time (see Figures 3.1 and 3.2). Nevertheless, all these studies highlight the fact that the number of population centres tends to decrease in an inverse proportion to their population size, so that, in line with Zipf's supposition, a small number of large urban centres 'coexist' in a given spatial system with a greater number of smaller urban localities.

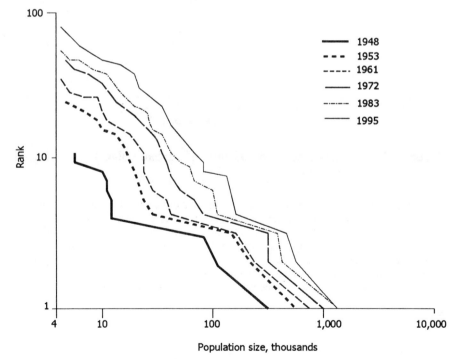

Figure 3.1   Changes in city-size distributions in Israel in 1948-95

After Krakover, 1998b.

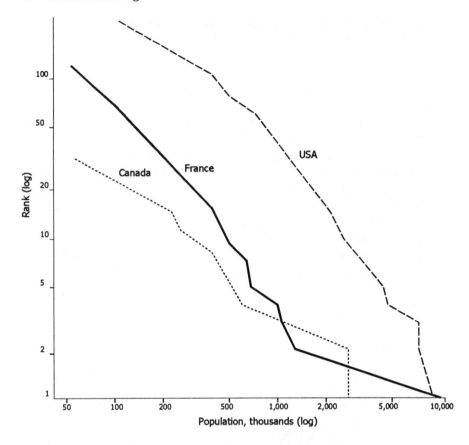

Figure 3.2   **Rank-size distribution of urban places in selected countries**

Though somewhat distorted by the accumulation of the number of urban places above a given population size, the diagram nevertheless indicates that, in line with Zipf's assumption, the number of urban places of a given rank, tends, in general, to decline in inverse proportion to their population size, so that the overall number of large centres is small while smaller urban places are more numerous. Thus, for instance, according to this diagram, France has one urban centre of more than 9,000,000 residents, three urban centres of more than 1,000,000 residents, nine urban centres of more than 500,000 residents, etc.

Source: Clark, 1982.

Concentration of Central Functions

According to Christaller's (1933; 1966 English edition) theory of central places, the position of a town in the hierarchy of urban places is mainly determined by the physical size of its hinterland:

- *Central places of a high order* have major functions that extend over a large region and offer central goods of a high order;
- *Central places of a low order* are those that serve the area in their immediate vicinity and offer central goods of a lower order;
- *Auxiliary central places* are formed by urban localities that have fewer central functions and serve predominantly their own population.

In this framework, each town is assumed to have its own service area, referred to as a 'complementary region.' This region is the area over which a central place tends to exercise its influence: a central place of a higher order has a complementary region of a higher order; a central place of a lower order has a complementary region of a lower order, etc.

According to Christaller, the physical size of a complementary region is a function of many factors, including population densities and traffic conditions. In response to these factors, a region with better access to the central place and a higher concentration of population is expected to have a larger central place than a region with lower densities and poorer transport. Therefore, the concentration of services in population centres is not accidental: services concentrate in such centres because the concentration of population reduces the 'sum of the distances which the inhabitants travel to and from this central place.'

In Christaller's words,

> the consumption of goods, despite equal demands and equal incomes, varies in different places of the region. It is higher near where the central good is offered, and it becomes less with increasing distance until finally, at the periphery, the consumption might cease entirely...The total consumption of central goods is less in regions with weakly developed centres than in regions with strongly developed centres...Eccentric location of central places ...enables the denser population to establish a greater degree of labour specialization, by which many goods, otherwise produced dispersedly, are now centrally produced (*ibid.*, pp. 29-33).

The focal point of Christaller's theory of central places is, however, the notion of 'the range of central goods.' According to this notion, each centrally produced type of goods has two spatial limits:

- *The inner limit*, which is determined by the minimum sales needed to sustain its production of the central good in question, and
- *The upper (outer) limit, which is* determined by the distance from the central place in question beyond which a particular type of goods cannot be sold without a loss, since it can be obtained more economically from another central place.

The net effect of these two forces is a more or less equidistant distribution of production centres. Ultimately a hierarchy of hexagonal cells of different size is created, which Christaller perceives as the 'most efficient' spatial organisation of service areas. Within such a hexagonal structure (see Chapter 4 on measures of distance for a more detailed discussion), the production of central goods with the largest range of markets is concentrated in the largest urban places, while the production of goods with a lower range of markets takes place in both large population centres and in population centres of a lower rank, which generally cannot sustain the production of goods and services of a higher order (Table 3.2).

Table 3.2   Typical characteristics of central places and their complementary regions

Type of central place	Number of central places	Range of region, km	Number of types of goods offered	Population of places	Population of region
L	1	108.0	2,000	500,000	3,500,000
P	2	62.1	1,000	100,000	1,000,000
G	6	36.0	600	30,000	350,000
B	18	20.7	330	10,000	100,000
K	54	12.0	180	4,000	35,000
A	162	6.9	90	2,000	11,000
M	486	4.0	40	1,000	3,500

Source: Compiled from Christaller (1933; 1966 English edition).

However, this simple relationship between the spatial limit of complementary regions and the degree of integration of production facilities into an urban place of a higher rank, which is a cornerstone of Christaller's theory, is not straightforward.

First, the hinterland of a town may be limited due to inter-town competition, when the town's centrality is adversely affected by its close proximity to another 'competing' urban place that performs similar types of functions (According to Christaller's theory, such a situation should not occur, since urban places of a higher rank are not expected to develop so close to each other. This situation is nevertheless quite common in many densely developed countries).

Second, in reality, higher-rank functions may not necessarily be associated with high level urban centres, or contribute sufficiently to lower level ones so as to allow their transformation into an urban centre of a higher rank.

Thus, a number of supra-national and supra-regional functions (such as, for example, data archives, research institutions, resort and tourist complexes) may not necessarily be located in large centres of population. On the other hand, the presence of a nuclear power plant or a classified military installation might affect adversely the degree of centrality their neighbouring towns may otherwise have had, despite the large areas served by these installations.

In other words, the presence of functions that serve extensive areas is not, by itself, a sufficient precondition for the transformation of a town or city into an urban centre of the highest rank. For this to occur, the functions an urban place performs should not only be unique and serve sufficiently wide areas. They should also be capable of being integrated with other types of centrality functions. Furthermore, the town should be attractive to migrants as well as to local inhabitants. This combination of factors may guarantee its leading role as a major population centre and secure its sustained population growth and economic development over a considerable period of time.

In addition to various administrative functions (such as regional and provincial capitals), the list of high-level functions may include large hospitals and institutions of higher education. These facilities often serve extensive areas, and have a sustained 'clientele'. They are not a part of all urban localities (uniqueness). Most important, these functions have, as a rule, a high potential of integration with other urban functions and tend to exhibit numerous 'trickle-down' effects to the local society.[2]

Factors Affecting the Ranking of Urban Places as Principal Cities

To clarify the factors influencing the number and population range of principal cities in countries of different population size and varying levels of economic development, multiple regression analysis (MRA) was employed. This multivariate statistical technique makes it possible to demonstrate the effect of individual variables when the variation of other variables is controlled. In the present analysis, this technique was used to compare the number of principal cities, minimal size of a principal city and population range of principal cities, reported in Table 3.1, with three explanatory factors considered to be relevant in this context:

- *Population size of a country* as a whole [thousands of residents]. Though the raw data reported in Table 3.1 give no clear indication concerning the relationship between quantitative characteristics of principal cities and the population size of countries where they are located, such a relationship may in fact exist: It is logical, for instance, that the number of principal cities, and their population, would tend to increase with the overall population of a country;
- Average *per capita income* [$US]. This factor is considered to be of great significance in influencing a wide range of urban and regional development processes (the extent of urbanisation, interregional income differentials, motorisation levels, inter-area migration, etc.), and as such is included in the present analysis as an explanatory variable;
- *The region* in which a country is located was represented by a dummy variable with the following range of values: 1 for Western Europe; 2 for Eastern Europe; 3 for Asia, and 4 for Africa. (Even at first glance, both the number and population range of principal cities reported in Table 3.1 appear to exhibit considerable variation across regions. Thus, for instance, in countries of similar population size, the number of principal cities seems to be larger in European countries than in countries of Asia and Africa).

Due to restrictions on availability and comparability of data, the analysis was limited to 46 countries located on three continents – Europe, Asia and Africa. The raw data for the analysis were obtained from Widdows (1996), and the list of the countries, in addition to those reported in Table 3.1, included a number of countries in Eastern Europe (Russia, Ukraine, Poland, Hungary, Bulgaria and Albania) and a more extended list of countries in Asia.

To comply with the homogeneity of variance assumption, the initial values of the explanatory variables (population size, income and region) were transformed logarithmically. Subsequent testing confirmed that the variances of the transformed variables are indeed homogenous. The collinearity of the explanatory variables was checked and found to be within tolerable limits.

The results of the analysis are reported in Table 3.3. As this table shows, the MRA models appear to have a reasonably good fit (R^2=0.532-0.655), indicating that the explanatory variables included in the analysis explain the variation of dependent variables (number of population centres, their minimal size and population range) relatively well.

Somewhat to our surprise, the *level of economic development* (measured by the country's average per capita income) appeared to have a statistically significant correlation only with the population range of principal cities, indicating that this range appears to be wider in more economically developed nations. There is insufficient evidence that this factor is in any way correlated with either the lower threshold of population size of a principal city, or with the number of principal cities in a given country.

The location of a country in a given region was found to have a high inverse correlation with the number of principal cities ($P<0.01$). It thus appears that, all else being equal, one may expect to find more principal cities in a European country than in an Asian or African one. Although this conclusion definitely warrants a more in-depth analysis, we suggest that this finding may be attributed to the less centralised nature of European economies and to more developed public services found in these countries, compared to most Asian and African nations. Both factors would lead to the formation of more principal cities than would develop in centralised economies with poorly developed services.

Finally, a country's overall *population size* was found to correlate highly with all three characteristics of the urban field studied ($T>5.6$; $P<0.001$). This implies that the number of principal cities, the minimal population size of a principal city and the range of principal cities in a given country all appear to increase as the population of a given country grows.

Is Population Size a Legitimate Criterion for Defining Urban Centres?

The population of a city may not necessarily be a sufficient indicator of its functional role in a given country. However, population size is often a good proxy for a wide range of development parameters, which are concomitant with a larger population, such as the availability of services, diversity of employment, etc.

Table 3.3   Factors affecting the number, minimal population size and population range of principal cities in selected countries (MRA – linear-log form)

Variable	B	T	T Sign.	Collinearity diagnostics	
				VIF*	Tolerance
Number of principal cities					
Population size	4.437	6.680	0.000	0.737	1.356
Per capita income	1.140	1.741	0.089	0.499	2.005
Region	-1.949	-2.755	0.009	0.471	2.124
Constant	-3.678	-1.235	0.224		
No of cases	46				
R^2	0.543				
F	16.234				
Minimal size of a principal city [1,000]					
Population size	599.254	5.639	0.000	0.737	1.356
Per capita income	136.427	1.303	0.200	0.499	2.005
Region	145.064	1.281	0.207	0.471	2.124
Constant	-910.653	-1.911	0.063		
No of cases	46				
R^2	0.532				
F	15.507				
Population range of principal cities [1,000]					
Population size	4169.988	7.646	0.000	0.737	1.356
Per capita income	1656.577	3.082	0.004	0.499	2.005
Region	1053.527	1.813	0.077	0.471	2.124
Constant	-9689.832	-3.962	0.000		
No of cases	46				
R^2	0.655				
F	25.948				

* Variance inflation factor.

When the population size of urban places is controlled by introducing into the analysis various functional indicators of local development, such as employment, quality of services, location, climate etc., no particular effect of population size *per se* is found (see *inter alia* Portnov and Erell, 1998a).

The fact that population size on its own may have no decisive influence on urban development may be illustrated by a comparative analysis of migration rates across municipalities in Norway (see Table 3.4). For this analysis, the municipalities of the country were divided into a number of groups, according to the presence or absence of two essential regional functions – colleges and hospitals. To allow comparison, municipalities in each group were selected so as to include only those of comparable size (up to 50,000 residents). The average annual rates of migration were then calculated for each municipality.

Table 3.4   Average rates of migration in municipalities of Norway in 1990-91*

Municipality	No. of cases	Migration balance [%]			
		Minimum	Maximum	Mean	Standard Deviation
With college	48	-1.14	1.29	0.15	0.54
Without college	305	-2.87	3.77	-0.28	0.80
With hospital	56	-1.02	1.44	0.15	0.55
Without hospital	266	-2.21	3.77	-0.24	0.76
With both college and hospital	27	-.56	1.29	0.30	0.45
With neither college nor hospital	255	-2.87	3.77	-0.28	0.80

* The analysis was performed using data from the Municipality Database of Norway, maintained by the Norwegian Social Science Data Services, Bergen. Municipalities included in the samples are of comparable size, ranging from 2,000 to 50,000 residents.

As Table 3.4 shows, the average rates of migration in municipalities with colleges and hospitals are positive (0.15-0.30 per cent), while in municipalities lacking these functions, the average rates of migration are characteristically negative (-0.24--0.28 per cent). Since the municipalities included in the analysis are of comparable population size, the differences in question cannot be attributed to variations in population, but rather to the presence or absence of specific functions the municipalities contain, in this particular case by the presence or absence of colleges and hospital facilities.

Choosing among Urban Centres

In some cases, a town might be equidistant from a number of major population centres in a country. In other cases, the distances in question may be comparable, but the population size of the 'competing' principal cities may vary substantially. To which of these centres, should the location of a town be related in determining its remoteness? In answering this question, simple criteria of population size and distances may be neither accurate nor sufficient: The town's economy and patterns of commuting may be directed unequivocally towards a larger principal city, offering a wider range of services, despite the town's close proximity to another, but smaller, major city.

Curiously, a similar problem is discussed in the Jewish religious law – the *Halacha* – and is described in detail by Felsenstein (1998). The question formulated in the *Halacha* is as follows: If a dead calf is found among three towns, which town should be responsible for its burial?

Four different solutions to this problem are suggested in the *Halacha*:

1) If all the towns have similar (or identical) size, the town closest to where the calf was is responsible for its burial;
2) If all the towns are equally close to the place in question, the larger of the towns covers the burial expenses;
3) If the place in question is equally close to two small towns and is farer apart from the third (largest) town, the larger town between the two small towns bears the cost;
4) If both distances and population sizes of the towns are substantially different, the closest town pays for the burial, though this town might be the smallest.

Taking this 'important' problem seriously, Felsenstein suggests exact mathematical formulations for three of the above location situations:

- $Sj/D^2ij<1$ and $(Sj/D^2ij)-(Sk/D^2ik)>0$ (all towns are of equal size),
- $(Sj/D^2ij)-(Sk/D^2ik)>0$ and max $(D^2ij,D^2ik)<$ min $(D^2il,...,D^2in)$ (the two closest towns are of different population size); and
- $Sj/D^2ij>1$ and $(Sj/D^2ij)-(Sk/D^2ik)<0$ (one town is obviously the closest),

where Sj is the size of town j; Dij is the distance from town j and place i in which the dead calf is found.

Of course, the *Halacha* solutions are hardly applicable to the problem of urban interaction at hand. Therefore, in solving it, preference should be given to more common criteria, measuring actual links between the town and alternative urban centres. Hudson (1976) suggests an expanded list of criteria that may be used to this end:

- *The area of newspaper circulation.* The newspapers published in high-ranking towns may be sold even in relatively remote localities. The sphere of influence of a newspaper may thus be determined by examining the sources of small advertisements, such as those published in the classified advertisements sections;
- *The extent of transportation services.* The extent of a city's urban field may be determined by a study of the timetables of bus services. The areas which have a frequent bus service to the city in question may be considered a part of its zone of influence;
- *Retail and wholesale areas.* While it is nearly impossible to find where people who shop at a particular store come from, the area within which central city stores make weekly deliveries (especially food products) may be an indicator of the extent of the urban field;
- *Educational catchment areas.* While small towns and villages may have only primary or secondary schools, technical colleges are generally found in larger urban settlements. However, local governments often make arbitrary decisions concerning the catchment areas of schools in their area of jurisdiction, so this indicator may give misleading results;
- *Journey to work areas.* Arguably, the journey to work is one of the most meaningful criteria defining the range of a major city's influence. However, it should be kept in mind that commuting patterns might differ for different types of manufacturing and non-manufacturing establishments.
- *Miscellaneous criteria* may include the geographic extent of church parishes, the spatial range of listeners of local ratio stations, and the number of telephone calls made between a city and other places.

Not all of these indicators may be readily available for a concrete analysis at hand. Moreover, the use of alternative criteria may result in incomparable and contradictory estimates. A possible solution to this question may thus be successive representation of a town's location in the analysis based on a choice of possible centres of 'functional gravitation' one by one, in an attempt to locate the best performing link.

Conclusions

There is no universal, commonly accepted explanation as to how urban centres are formed and what the criteria are for defining an urban place as a major population centre. The most popular explanations, however, are linked to the overall reduction of production and transportation expenses resulting in the location of production facilities in close proximity to consumers (the force of industrial innovation), and the formation of a concentration of high-centrality functions.

Whichever theory is adopted, the choice of a major urban centre cannot be determined by an analysis of any given quantitative characteristics alone. The population size of urban settlements referred to as 'principal cities' varies in different countries throughout a wide range. In addition, the indicator of population size often represents a mere proxy for a range of development parameters, which are concomitant with a larger population size, namely the availability of services, diversity of employment, etc.

Ranking an urban locality as a major (principal) population centre has relatively little to do with its population size. It owes much more to the presence of complex high-level functions, especially regional facilities such as large hospitals and institutions of higher education.

Notes

[1] According to Pareto's law of distribution of incomes published in the 1890s, the logarithm of the number of incomes at or above an amount n is a linear function of the logarithm of n. In the following studies of Singer and Auerbach, and subsequently in the works of Zipf and Christaller, it was shown that this relationship is also applicable to the distribution of sizes of urban settlements. In particular, it was also shown that the slope of this size-rank relationship, plotted on a log-log scale, is not constant, but is a subject of continuous change; it may differ across countries, regions and time periods (Clark, 1982; Carroll, 1982; Alperovich, 1993; Krakover, 1998a,b).

[2] Felsenstein (1997) singles out four possible effects a large university may have on the development of the town in which it is located: 1) short-term expenditure - purchases by the university itself, by its staff, faculties and students, and by visitors to the university. These result in an increase of the local household income, income of local businesses, and thus of the local tax base through a 'ripple-like effect' of consecutive rounds of

spending and re-spending; 2) induced migration - attracting highly skilled staff and specialists to the town in question, increasing the number of highly educated personnel in the local labour market; 3) accumulation of knowledge and the formation of human capital, leading to growth in the number of high-tech firms, start-up rate, etc.; and 4) geographic spill-over of technological innovations into adjacent areas.

4 Measuring Distance

A wide range of quantitative measures of distance is used in regional planning and in socio-economic studies. For instance, studies of industrial location (see Chapter 1 of this book for a more detailed discussion) often use transportation costs in lieu of physical distances between regions and localities. Migration and urban studies most often use aerial distances to this end (see *inter alia* Ravenstein, 1885; Stouffer, 1940 (1962 reprint); Maier and Weiss, 1991; Stillwell, 1991; Krakover and Morrill, 1992; Portnov, 1998a; McCann and Sheppard, 2000; Kupiszewski *et al,* 1998).

Christaller (1933; 1966 English edition) also built his theory of central places on transportation costs, which he referred to as 'transportation obstacles.' However, his initial assumption of homogenous distribution of population and resources allowed him to use the actual time of commuting (by commuting rings) for the theory's formulation and measurements of aerial distance for its verification.

Although aerial distances are simple to evaluate and to compare, this type of measurement may not always be relevant or informative, particularly when the geographic terrain is not homogenous. Such a situation may occur when urban places are located in mountainous terrain or if they are separated by wide rivers, fjords and other natural obstacles.

In this chapter, these and other factors affecting distance measurements, such as the configuration of transportation routes, traffic conditions, etc., will be discussed, and alternative indicators of distance, such as road distance, time estimates, and journey-to-work areas will be analysed.

The Problems of Heterogeneous Terrain

In most theoretical studies dealing with regional development and urban economics (Weber, 1909; Marshall, 1890; 1892; Lösch, 1938; 1975 reprint; Alonso, 1975; Clark, 1982; Richardson, 1977), the geographic plain, on which production facilities and population centres are distributed, is considered to be homogeneous, i.e. free of any non-economic 'interferences,' such as landscape, climate, etc.

In many practical cases, this simplification is not justified. For instance, it is clearly inapplicable to situations in which cities and towns have been established on steep slops or in climatically harsh areas.

Pavlides (1997) singles out four groups of factors that led to the establishment of urban centres in elevated areas with restricted access, rather than on geographically homogenous plains:

- *Defense.* During periods of political instability, new settlements were frequently built on high, inaccessible sites, as their population sought refuge from invaders. Thus, in the 10th-14th centuries AD, many new settlements in the Mediterranean basin and in the Himalayas were founded in remote mountain areas in order to protect their residents from the Islamic expansion;
- *Health considerations.* In many flat areas, stagnant water often becomes a breeding ground for mosquitoes, while sloping terrain provides better drainage and thus serves as a protection from diseases that are carried by water-born insects;
- *Flood protection.* Many settlements, such as those along the Nile river, were established on low hills which provide protection from the annual flood;
- *Protection of agricultural land.* In order to preserve scarce agricultural land, some urban settlements were built on steep slops, while flat land was reserved for cultivation.

Portnov and Erell (1998b) list other factors that led to the location of urban settlements in climatically harsh desert areas, which fall outside of the theoretically useful description of 'homogeneous terrain':

- *Relocation of territory-consuming industries.* As undeveloped land in core regions becomes more expensive and scarce, military and research installations, particularly those requiring large parcels of flat land, are relocated from the overpopulated core to underdeveloped desert areas, along with accompanying 'dormitory towns';
- *Expansion of mining and power engineering.* With exhaustion of mineral resources in traditional mining centres, primary industries and new settlements move gradually towards more remote and climatically harsh regions;

- *Development of transport infrastructure.* The expansion of roads and improvements in transportation extend the commuting frontier of existing population centers into a more remote periphery. The development of such previously underdeveloped areas becomes more feasible, both economically and socially;
- *Development of means of pumping fresh water* considerable distances from its natural sources, increasing the potential of previously undeveloped drylands;
- *Socio*-economic, *political and ecological considerations* stemming from overpopulation of the core and underdevelopment of the periphery;
- *Acceleration of desertification processes.* By some estimates, desertification affects at least 50,000 km^2 per year, primarily in the developing world (Kates *et al*, 1977). A growing number of urban communities previously situated in mild or semi-arid climates may find themselves faced with arid or hyper-arid conditions.

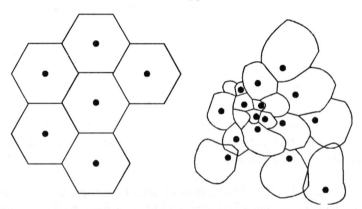

Figure 4.1   Transformation of economic regions under conditions of a non-uniform geographic plain (after Lösch, 1938)

According to Lösch's theory, spatial differences among geographic areas may cause economic regions to deviate from the 'optimal hexagonal shape'. In particular, individual production areas may overlap, and gaps may occur with some areas not being serviced, especially in the periphery.

Implications of Non-homogeneous Terrain: Theoretical Studies

Although Lösch (1938; 1975 reprint) developed his theory of economic regions assuming a spatially uniform plain devoid of any non-economic inequalities, he later introduced the notion of a 'non-homogeneous terrain' on which the 'perfect' hexagonal configuration of economic regions' may be transformed into an overlap of irregular shapes, resembling, in his words, an "irregular layer of slabs of slate," with numerous gaps, especially in the periphery (see Figure 4.1).

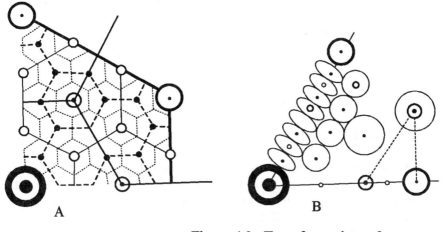

A

B

C

Figure 4.2 Transformations of Christaller's hexagonal model of central places (A) according to traffic (B) and separation (C) principles

According to Christaller's theory, due to the effect of transportation, the majority of central places are expected to concentrate along transportation routes linking central places of higher ranks. Concurrently, away from traffic routes, service areas may be more evenly spread and larger (B). The regular hexagonal structure of central places (A) may also be altered by needs of local governance due to which uninhabited 'border' districts may be excluded from any service area (C).

Christaller (1933; 1966 English edition) also suggests that his spatial system of regularly arranged central places, based on the pure market principle, may be altered if the assumption of perfectly homogenous plain is removed. In particular, he singles out two separate groups of forces (principles) that may cause deviations from 'the most rational hexagonal form' of settlement patterns (see Figure 4.2):

- *Transportation principle* – the distribution of settlements becomes most favourable when most central places lie on a traffic route between towns, assuming that this route is established as straight and as cheaply as possible. The central places of a high order are expected to concentrate along this route with their service zone having 'little depth but greater extension to the side.' Concurrently, away from the main transportation route, service zones of central places are expected to be more evenly spread and larger;
- *Administration (or separation) principle* – according to the needs of the local administration, the number of central places, determined by market forces, may increase considerably to accommodate the needs of local governance. Thus, six of seven places of a lower rank may be established for each central place of a higher rank, rather than three, as predicted by the 'most rational hexagonal model.'

Alonso (1977) refers to actual transportation conditions in a region as 'realistic complications' and suggests that these may have two separate effects on modelling the accessibility of specific geographic areas. First, decreasing marginal cost of transportation over larger distances due to economies of longer hauls may alter evenly spaced concentric circles of *isotims* (lines of equal transportation cost) so that these lines will have wider spacing with increasing distance from the source. Second, if the assumption that transportation is equally possible in all directions does not hold true, *isotims* will take a shape of a 'starfish, with arms extending along the transportation routes.'

Aerial Distance vs. Road Distances

In his book on the principles of human ecology, Zipf (1949; 1972 reprint) suggested that in predicting human behaviour, one should assume that people seek to minimise 'effort' rather than 'work.' Therefore, the path of interaction is

> a strait line when that is the easiest path; otherwise the path will go around swamps and over and around mountains – whatever is the easiest. Naturally, as the traffic between two points increases, it will be economical to straighten the route between them, and to make it more nearly level, as soon as the (probable) amount of work that is saved by the shorter and more level route is sufficient to offset the work of straightening and levelling (*ibid,* p. 348).

The effect of road configuration on distance measurements and opportunities for commuting can be illustrated by a simple example (see Figure 4.3). This figure shows the location of urban settlements along the Oslo Fjord in Norway, and helps to illustrate the possibility of bias introduced by aerial distances.

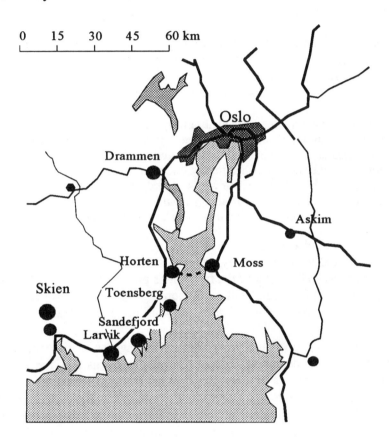

Figure 4.3 Location of towns in the Oslo fjord of Norway

Let us consider, for example, two towns located on different sides of the Oslo fjord – Moss (30.000 residents) and Tønsberg (40.000 residents). As Figure 4.3 shows, these towns are only 24 km apart, as the crow flies. However, in order to reach Moss from Tønsberg by car, one needs to drive nearly 150 km around the fjord. An alternative means is the "Horten-Moss" ferry (marked by dotted line on the diagram), which is both seasonal and infrequent. Thus, daily commuting between them is very limited, although on the basis of aerial distance alone, it would have been possible to reach the opposite conclusion.

Time Estimates

An alternative approach to measuring physical distances between urban communities is to evaluate time spent on travel between them. Characteristically, Howard (1898; 1985 reprint, p.107) based his concept of 'garden cities' on road distances as well as measurement of time:

> There is, first, an inter-municipal railway, connecting the towns of the outer ring – twenty miles in circumference – so that to get from any town to its most distant neighbour requires one to cover a distance of only ten miles, which could be accomplished in, say, twelve minutes...There is also a system of railways by which each town is placed in direct communication with Central City. The distance from any town to the heart of Central City is only three and a quarter miles, and this could be readily covered in five minutes.

The Standard Classification of Municipalities of Norway (SN, 1994) defines an Index of Centrality, which is based on the time spent on commuting, as well as other factors, such as population size and functional characteristics of municipalities. According to this classification, all municipalities of Norway are divided into four levels of centrality:

- *Level 3* is assigned to municipalities forming one of the major urban centres of the country (50,000+ residents or towns that function as a regional centre), or to towns which lie within 75 minutes' traveling time from the centre of a major city (90 minutes, in the case of Oslo);
- *Level 2* is given to municipalities that consist of an urban settlement of 15,000-50,000 residents or lie within 60 minutes' travelling time from the centre of such a settlement;
- *Level 1* includes municipalities that consist of an urban settlement of 10,000-15,000 residents or lie within 45 minutes' travelling time from the centre of such an urban settlement;
- *Centrality Level 0* is assigned to a municipality if it does not fulfill any of the above requirements.

The travel time matrix was also used in the framework of a project funded by the Highlands and Islands European Partnership and aimed at estimating the Index of Economic Potential for various geographic regions of the European Community. In this study, a detailed digital road map of Europe was used, and different average speeds for different classes of road, ferry crossing, check-in times, border crossing delays, and statutory drivers' rest breaks were taken into consideration (Copus, 1999).

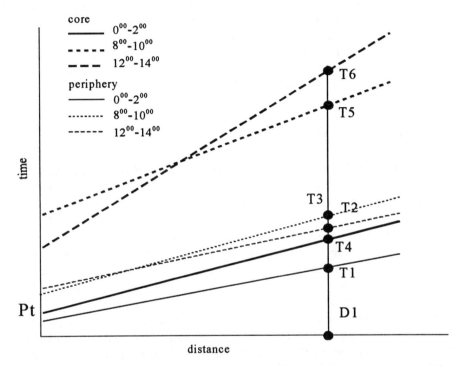

Figure 4.4 **Distance vs. time of commuting in various geographic areas and time of the day, including parking time (Pt) – trend estimates**

The diagrams show that the time required to cover any given distance (D1) may vary during different times of the day, and across various geographic areas. For instance, this time may be longer in densely populated core regions (T6) than in thinly settled peripheral areas (T2), all else being equal. Naturally, the time in question is longer during rush hours (T6) than at night (T4), when roads are less crowded. In winter, when road conditions may worsen, the time required to cover a distance D1 is probably greater in all geographic areas and in all times of the day. This increase may, however, be more substantial in peripheral areas, which are commonly characterised by harsher climatic conditions (see the discussion of the effect of climate on the pattern of human settlement in Chapter 2 of this book). Due to these disparities, the travel time may often be difficult to measure and or to obtain comparable and reliable estimates.

The usefulness of time measurements, even those based on sophisticated GIS technology, may, nevertheless, be questioned on several grounds. First, the actual travelling time may be affected by many exogenous factors, which may not always be allowed for. It may vary for time of the day, day of the week, according to weather conditions, etc. It is, therefore, difficult to measure and obtain comparable and reliable estimates of travel time (see Figure 4.4). Second, the 'importance' of time may change according to people and to circumstances. For instance, business people may attach a very different value to their time compared with tourists on holiday. The concept of so-called 'universal' time is thus of questionable value in this context.

Travel to Work Areas

The concept of 'journey to work' areas is an alternative approach to defining the degree of remoteness of different geographic areas. According to this concept the sphere of influence of a city is determined so as to include counties and communities in which the percentage of resident workers commuting to the central city exceeds a certain limit.

The designation of Metropolitan Statistical Areas (MSAs) in the United States is an example of the implementation of this concept. According to the definition used by the U.S. Department of Census, MSAs are geographic entities, based on the concept of a core area with a large population, plus adjacent communities having a high degree of economic and social integration with the core, as expressed in commuting patterns. In order to qualify as an MSA, a city must have 50,000 or more inhabitants or the Urban Area (UA) should have a total population of at least 100,000 (75,000 in New England). The county or counties containing the largest city, and the surrounding densely settled region, are central counties of the MSA. Additional outlying counties are considered part of the MSA if they meet certain other criteria of metropolitan character, such as a specified minimum population density or percentage of the population that is urban. MSAs in New England are defined in terms of cities and towns, following rules concerning commuting and population density. According to Berry (1973), such rules may be arbitrary. For instance, if less than 15 per cent of the county's working population commute to the central city (urban area), it is not considered a part of the MSA in question.

The concept of Daily Urban Systems (DUSs) developed by Doxiadis (1977) is also based upon the principle of the journey-to-work pattern.

It is clear, however, that these two separate classifications of geographic areas (MSAs and DUSs) are based, albeit indirectly, on estimates of either time or distance.

Thus, according to the 1990 U.S. Census of Population, 85 per cent of journeys to work take place within a 40-45-minute limit of daily commuting (see Figure 4.5), and this travel time does, in fact, determine the spatial boundaries of the country's metropolitan areas.

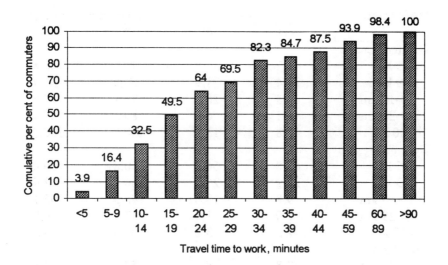

Figure 4.5 Travel time to work for the United States: 1990 Census

Source: Diagrammed using 1990 Census data (U.S. DOT/FHWA, 1990).

The distance covered by daily commuters in the U.K. appears to vary considerably between the country's metropolitan areas. As expected, it is longer in Greater London than in smaller urban areas (see Table 4.1), yet between 85 and 90 per cent of all commuting is limited to some 10-29 km. Characteristically, in recent years, job-related journeys in the U.K. have tended to become longer and more dispersed (Table 4.1). Green *et al* (1999) attribute this trend to the following factors:

• The loss of traditional industrial jobs, which were often staffed locally;
• The continuing dispersal of population away from major urban centres;

- The changing structure of population, in the direction of growth in the number of professional workers, characterized by longer than average journeys; and
- A rise in the use of cars.

Table 4.1   Travel-to-work distances in selected urban areas (UA) of the U.K. in 1981 and 1991 (per cent of employees)

UA/ Distance	Total		Cumulative per cent*	
	1981	1991	1981	1991
Greater London				
< 5 km	41.2	36.8	41.2	36.8
5-9 km	22.4	21.9	63.6	58.7
10-19 km	19.5	20.9	83.1	79.6
20-29 km	6.1	6.7	89.2	86.4
>30 km	10.8	13.6	100.0	100.0
Tyne & Wear				
< 5 km	60.8	56.4	60.8	56.4
5-9 km	25.9	26.0	86.7	82.4
10-19 km	9.8	13.0	96.5	95.4
20-29 km	1.0	1.4	97.5	96.8
>30 km	2.5	3.2	100.0	100.0
Cleveland				
< 5 km	57.8	54.9	57.8	54.9
5-9 km	27.5	25.8	85.3	80.7
10-19 km	11.0	13.4	96.3	94.1
20-29 km	0.9	1.7	97.2	95.8
>30 km	2.8	4.5	100.0	100.0
Merseyside				
< 5 km	54.7	52,0	54.7	52.0
5-9 km	27.7	26.5	82.4	78.5
10-19 km	12.9	14.2	95.3	92.7
20-29 km	2.3	3.5	97.6	96.2
>30 km	2.4	3.8	100.0	100.0

Source: Compiled from Green *et al*, 1999; * Calculated by the authors.

Cost of Commuting

In an attempt to avoid a possible bias that may be introduced by the use of estimates of time, the overall cost of travel is sometime considered as an alternative. Christaller (1933; 1966 English edition), for instance, argues that physical distances, measured in meters or kilometres, are 'quite unimportant,' since actual exchanges among geographic areas are determined by what he calls 'economic distances,' which are determined by

> the cost of freight, insurance and storage; time and loss of weight or space in transit; and, as regards passenger travel, the cost of transportation, the time required, and the discomfort of travel.

Following such an approach, Copus (1999) suggests three alternative formulations of the 'spatial accessibility' problem:

- What is the total cost of travelling from each locality to all the major economic centres?
- How many people can be reached with a daily trip (3-4 hours each way) from each point of the map?, and
- What would be the total cost of accessing a total market of *n* people from each location?

This approach, however, raises a number of questions. First, the cost of travel is not always objective and is given to the influence of a number of variables, each of which is extremely difficult to measure and compare. The actual cost of travel may vary as a function of the overall economic development of a country and of government policies concerning public transport. In countries with low average income, for instance, the average cost of travel (particularly over short distances) is likely to be comparatively lower than elsewhere. This may be attributed to generally lower wage costs. In the Czech Republic, for instance, the cost of a one-way railroad ticket for the distance of some 60 km does not exceed $US1.3, while in Israel, the ticket price for a comparable distance is commonly over $US4-5 (as of March 2000). The cost of travel may vary considerably even between countries with similar levels of development. According to the comparative data cited in the Austrian Federal Railway's (ÖBB) Internet Site, the average cost of railroad travel in Germany exceeds that in Austria by some 85 per cent, while in Switzerland, this cost is almost 105 per cent higher.

Public policies on transport and fuel subsidies may also affect the actual cost of transportation, both directly and indirectly. In Norway, for instance, the government subsidizes many domestic air-links in an attempt to boost the attractiveness of remote peripheral areas.

A similar practice of subsidies for long-distance transport was maintained for many years in the former Soviet Union and other countries of Eastern Europe. Following the collapse of this system of subsidies in the early 1990s, many remote peripheral communities in these countries have been virtually cut off from major population centres, since the operation of airports and railroad stations in thinly populated peripheral areas (such as Siberia and the Far East) was no longer feasible.

In Israel, military personnel, new immigrants and members of agricultural cooperatives are granted substantial discounts or even exemptions on public transportation (specifically on inter-city buses). As a result, privately operated local bus companies tend to increase fares disproportionately on some peripheral, 'less profitable' routes in order to cover the financial losses accrued.

Conclusion

As the present analysis indicates, there is no single, universal indicator to measure commuting distances. While aerial distances provide biased estimates under non-homogeneous landscape conditions, time measurements may also be unreliable due to their seasonal and daily variations, and dependence on the type of transportation. Transport costs reflect the level of economic development and government policies with respect to fuel taxation and subsidies for public transportation, and may thus be difficult to compare. Most studies have incorporated whichever measure appeared to be most appropriate for the specific conditions encountered, but this has tended to complicate comparisons. It is the view of the authors that if the extent of the infrastructure and quality of service are more or less uniform throughout the area under study, road distances are most likely to be the most reliable measure, especially for a cross-country analysis.

5 Indirect Measures of Urban Location

In previous chapters, we focused our attention mainly on distance-related indicators of urban location – remoteness from major population centres, and spatial isolation within a region. These 'straight-forward' measures do not, however, comprise all of the possibilities of determining the status of an urban place in a general setting of urban localities. The means of accomplishing this task include, among others, a number of indirect measures such as the density of development, an index of accessibility, an index of socio-economic potential, and indices of centrality and agglomeration. In this chapter, we will deal with each of these indicators separately, focusing our attention on their comparative advantages and disadvantages in different situations.

Density of Development

Urban and regional development studies generally measure spatial concentration using indicators of population and urban densities, such as people per hectare, floor area ratio (F.A.R.) volume area ratio (V.A.R), etc. (see *inter alia* Smith, 1975; Clark, 1982; Razin and Rosentraub, 2000).

Portnov (1998b) suggests that density of population is a robust general indicator of urban development in a region, and as such helps to explain the processes of migration and population change. In particular, he demonstrates that population density has a statistically significant effect on the inter-regional flow of internal migrants in Israel.

Razin and Rosentraub (2000) use various measures of residential densities (the percentage of dwellings in single-unit detached houses; population per km^2, and the number of housing units per km^2) as proxies for the extent of suburban sprawl. They demonstrate that housing densities in North American cities are closely related to the extent of municipal fragmentation.

In an early study of industrial location, Weber (1909; 1929 reprint) argued that housing density is inversely related to agglomeration, so that in more densely developed areas the weakening effect of 'deglomeration,' attributed primarily to high land prices, is generally stronger.

However, the performance of density measurements as spatial indicators of urban development may be questioned on several grounds; the most serious problems include the lack of a spatial dimension and of relativity.

Lack of a Spatial Dimension

In his book on the effectiveness of land use in urban areas, Portnov (1992, p.32) cited the following description of the *Irkutsk* stronghold in the East Siberia of Russia made by a visitor at the end of 17th century (comments in brackets are added by the authors):

> The perimeter of the stronghold, excluding fortification towers, is about 200 *sazhen* (*sazhen* is an old Russian unit of length, equal to approx. 2.1 m); the walls are built three *sazhen* and one *archin* (approx. 7 m), and on top of the walls, next to the main entrance and near the *Angara* River, an observation tower is erected; the tower has three residential units, with the storage space underneath; the dining-room is above the storages, and living rooms are on top of it; and on top of the living rooms, a watch tower stands…near the tower, inside the walls, a courtyard is allotted, with peasants and servants living in it; on the same wall, right in the middle, another observation tower – *Spaskaya Bashnia* - is built, with the gate underneath and storage spaces above the gate, and living quarters above the storages.

Keeping in mind that in the 17th century, the population of the *Irkutsk* stronghold amounted to some 700 persons, the density of population within the perimeter of this structure was close to 700 persons per hectare (700/(200*2.1/4)=667), a considerable density even when compared with modern high-rise development.

Doxiadis (1964) argues that population densities in ancient Greek cities were also very high, attributing these high densities primarily to the small physical size of these communities (Table 5.1).

These historical examples illustrate the drawback of population density as an indicator of urban development – its lack of scale: According to what may be an arbitrary definition of a settlement's boundaries, its density may be extremely high, while in neighbouring regions the density may be exceedingly low. (Thus, returning to the example of the *Irkutsk* stronghold, we should note that in the 17th century, the average density of population in the entire region in question was barely 0.1 persons per km^2).

Table 5.1   Population densities and physical dimensions of ancient Greek cities (after Doxiadis, 1964)

City	Built area, ha	Average distance from city centre, m	Population, residents	Population density per ha
Selinus (500 BCE)	63.4	800	20,000	315.4
Athens (400 BCE)	215.0	1000	50,000	200.0
Miletus (400 BCE)	106.0	900	30,000	236.0
Piraeus (400 BCE)	420.3	1,500	50,000	119.0
Olynthos (400 BCE)	60.0	600	15,000	250.0
Priene (350 BCE)	41.4	350	4,000	96.8
Corinth (350 BCE)	520.5	1,500	50,000	86.5
Delos (250 BCE)	100.0	800	30,000	250.0

The insensitivity of density measurements to variations in actual development patterns can also be illustrated by two spatial distributions shown in Figure 5.1 (Though a simple idea conveyed by this diagram may easily be illustrated by a verbal description, this diagram is important for the following analysis: The spatial distributions it compares will be used in the following discussion for testing the performance of various location measures). Though the distributions on the left and on the right of the diagram are quite different, mean density measurements return identical values.

Relativity

Density, even when measured accurately and in a comparable method, may be perceived differently by people in different surroundings. At the urban scale, this may be illustrated by the results of a sociological survey reported in Portnov (1992). For this survey, five types of residential development with different density patterns, ranging from low density development with small open spaces (Type A) to high density development with large open spaces (Type E) were selected. Then, densities in these areas were evaluated by their residents, using a five-point scale: 1- very high; 2- high; 3 – normal; 4 – low, and 5 - very low. The

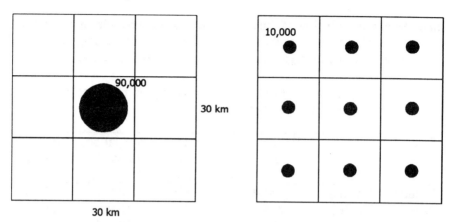

Figure 5.1   Performance of the density indicator in measuring urban location

Although urban distributions shown on two adjacent diagrams are quite different, the indicator of mean density does not discriminate between them: 90,000/(30x30)=10.

results of the survey, after averaging, were compared with actual densities in the respective areas (see Figure 5.2).

As this figure shows, the comparison indicates no clear relationship between actual densities and their evaluations by the residents. The opposite conclusion appears to be true: neighbourhoods consisting of high-rise buildings with large open spaces between them, while having a high *mean* density, were perceived by their residents as underdeveloped; neighbourhoods with a lower mean density consisting of low-rise buildings but with less open space were evaluated by their residents as too extensively developed.

In another study (Williams *et al.*, 1999), twelve residential areas in the U.K. in which different types of urban intensification had taken place, were studied to determine how the neighbourhoods' residents perceived the process of intensification. The changes that occurred included construction on previously undeveloped urban land, an increase in the size of building floor space, etc. The results of the study indicated that the residents' perception appeared to vary considerably, depending, among other factors, upon the age of respondents, length of residence and the type of household tenure (see Table 5.2). The different nature of responses by various population groups to the same types of changes in their neighbourhood is a further indication of the relativity of density indicators.

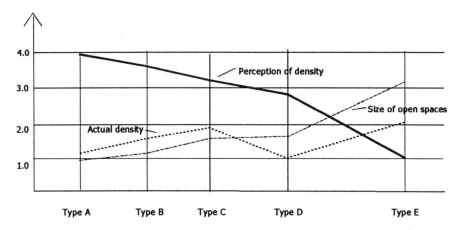

Figure 5.2 **Public perception of development density in different types of development (after Portnov, 1992)**

A survey carried out in residential districts of varying densities found no clear relationship between actual densities and their perception by residents. The same survey indicated that residents appeared to have a much more accurate perception of the size and accessibility of public open space. Areas of high rise development with large open spaces were perceived by their residents as inefficiently developed, while neighbourhoods with less open space, but considerably lower densities, were often characterised as too dense (For the sake of comparison, actual values of each indicator are normalised with the minimal values assumed to be equal 1.0).

Accessibility Index

Some of the drawbacks of simple measures of density may be overcome by more complex methods. One such approach is suggested by the National Centre for Geographic Information and Analysis at the University of California and is reported in Deichmann (2000). This approach combines simple density measurements with those of distance, and with selected parameters describing the transportation network. The resulting *index of accessibility* of a town is calculated as the sum of the square roots of population totals of adjacent towns, weighted by either the travel time to each of them or the distances to them:

$$V_i = \sum_{k=1}^{n} \sqrt{P_k} * e^{-d_{ik}/2\alpha^2},$$

where Vi is the accessibility estimate for a location (an i node of the transportation network); P_k is the population of town k; d_{ik} is the travel time/distance between node i and town k; α is the distance to the point of inflection in the distance decay function (If this parameter is set to one hour, the contribution of a town which is one hour away decreases to about 60 per cent of that of a theoretical town with a similar population requiring no time to travel, while a town which is two hours away contributes only 14 per cent of its total population to the accessibility index); e is the base of the natural logarithm.

Table 5.2   Responses to urban intensifications by different groups of residents (after Williams *et al.*, 1999)

Response	Age group			Length of residence			Tenure	
	16-30	31-60	60+	<2 yrs	2-20 yrs	>20 yrs	Own	Rent
Worse/much worse	27	43	41	23	38	48	45	35
No difference	36	28	33	34	33	27	30	31
Better/much better	37	29	26	43	29	25	25	34

The calculation of population distribution using this index involves five phases:

i)   Construction of the transportation network of the region, including roads, railroads and navigable rivers;
ii) Identification and location of urban centres of different population size, including all existing towns and cities in the area;
iii) Calculation of the accessibility index for each node of the transportation network, based on the location and population size of adjacent urban places and their links to the transportation network;
iv) Interpolation of the accessibility estimates onto a regular raster surface with adjustments for the location of inland water bodies, protected areas, and
v)   Estimation of the population totals for each administrative unit in proportion to the accessibility index measures estimated for each grid cell (It is assumed that the resulting population counts can be converted to densities for further analysis and mapping).

Though the accessibility index has a broader base compared with simple density measurements, it does not appear to be problem-free either. The application of this index to the hypothetical distribution of urban places shown in Figure 5.1 illustrates some of its drawbacks. (In the test, aerial distances between cells were used, while the value of the α parameter was set to 60 km). The results of the calculation of the accessibility index (AI) for each cell *(i)* of these hypothetical distributions are presented in Figure 5.3.

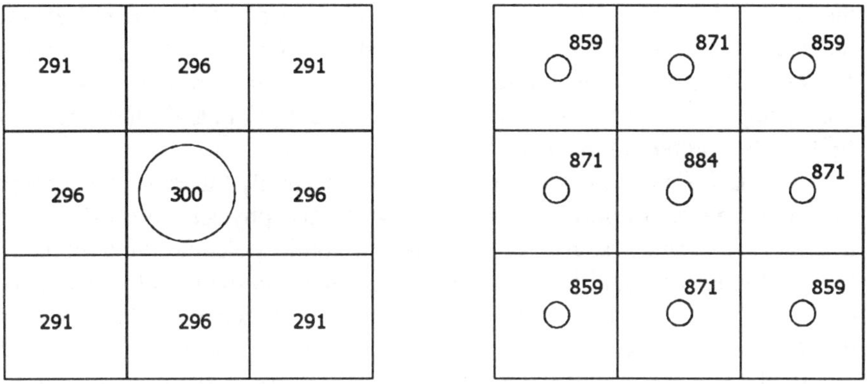

291	296	291		859 ○	871 ○	859 ○	
296	(300)	296		871 ○	884 ○	871 ○	
291	296	291		859 ○	871 ○	859 ○	

Figure 5.3   Accessibility index – test of performance

The values in cells are indices of accessibility calculated using Deichmann's (2000) formulae (see text). As the diagrams show, the accessibility index, unlike densities, returns different values for different types of spatial distribution of population centres; it does not appear, however, to discriminate among adjacent locations and tends to assign relatively high values to unpopulated areas located around a large population centre (left diagram).

Unlike density measurements, the index of accessibility appears to provide different values for the cells in the above example; it also returns different average values for the entire distributions in question (ΣAI_i=2,648; see Figure 5.3, left diagram, and ΣAI =7,804; Figure 5.3, right diagram). However, the differences among adjacent cells are minor (±2-3 per cent). Furthermore, there is little difference between the two contrasting distributions in the example. It is also noteworthy that for the concentrated distribution (Figure 5.3; left diagram), the index of accessibility returns relatively high values for both centrally located and marginal cells, though the latter cells are devoid of any development. Thus, the index in question does not appear to reflect the actual development patterns, but rather produces estimates that better describe spatial influence or potential for development. This leads us to a discussion of a broad array of indicators of socio-economic potential.

Socio-economic Potential

The concept of potential is borrowed from *electrostatics,* which is a field of physics dealing with electro-magnetic fields. According to this concept, the potential of a unit of mass concentrated at a point X is equal at any other point x to the inverse $^1/_{(X-x)}$ of the distance X-x to X. The potential of a general distribution of masses is defined by integration and is harmonic (i.e. changing smoothly with no points of inflection) outside these masses (EB, 1999 – Potential theory).

As Clark (1982) argues, the first attempt to apply this physical concept to population distribution was undertaken by the physicist Stewart in the late 1940s. Stewart suggested that the economic potential of a point in geographic space could be estimated by summing up the populations of the regions accessible to it, each divided by its distance from the point in question. In the following studies, the concept of potential was further modified by using regional incomes, instead of populations, and dividing by 'distance cost.'

Duncan (1959; cited in Clark, 1982) calculated the economic potential of non-metropolitan areas of the U.S. on the basis of population as outlined above, and compared it with the location of manufacturing plants in the same areas. He concluded that an area's economic potential calculated in this manner has a statistically significant effect on the location of heavy manufacturing industries, but not on the location of 'light and footloose' processing industries.

Babarović (1978) argues that simple linear measurements may not be appropriate in estimating the potential of areas and suggests alternative formulae, in which distances between points of geographic space are represented by an exponential function:

$$V_k = \sum_{i=1}^{n} \frac{w_i P_i}{(d_{ik})^\alpha},$$

where V_k is the potential in a given point k; P_i is the population in point i; w_i is a coefficient weighting population P_i according to a selected criterion, such as, for instance, personal income; D_{ik} is the distance between k and each population centre i, and α is an empirical coefficient indicating the degree to which distance adversely affects the potential.[1]

The application of this equation to distributions of urban and rural population in Brazil *(ibid.)* made it possible to define the areas representing the country's 'most dynamic centre' and the actual extent of the periphery, i.e. the area with the highest potential for development and the areas 'with poorer development prospects,' respectively (see Figure 5.4).

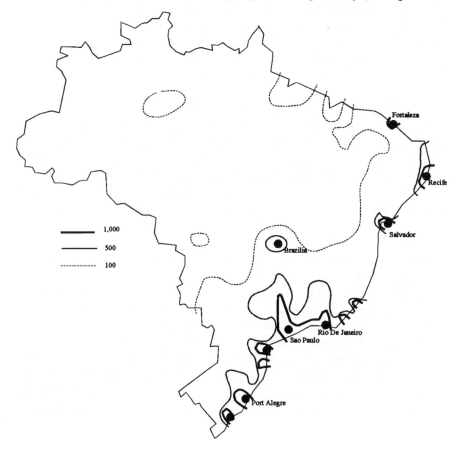

Figure 5.4   Rating of economic potential based on population and income coefficients for urban centres of Brazil (after Babarović, 1978)

Keeble (cited in Copus, 1999) used a similar approach to evaluating changes in the spatial distribution of economic potential in nine European countries between 1965 and 1977. In this study, regional GDP was used in the nominator of the potential equation, while distances were calculated between 'functional centroids' of the regions (largest towns and cities), using a simplified model of the network of major roads and ferries.

The analysis resulted in a clear core-periphery pattern of economic potential, described by Keeble as 'a triangular plateau of high accessibility to Union-wide economic activity with corners on Stuttgart, Hamburg, and Lille. West Berlin, South-East England, and Ile-de-France form outlying peaks of relatively high accessibility around this "golden triangle." This pattern was amended in 1988 into a 'four-sided plateau' of high economic potential, with the addition of the central areas of the UK, including Birmingham.

A repeated analysis, carried out in a GIS framework with a detailed digitised road map of Europe, lead to a similar pattern of potential distribution, in which Keeble's 'golden triangle' was still identifiable, albeit with its southern apex 'separated from its northern base by a 'depression' of lower values in the Reinland Platz eastward into Hessen' *(ibid.)*.

Can the index of socio-economic potential, devised for assessing the prospects for development, also be used as a precise measure of population distribution in general, and urban location, in particular?

Application of this index to the sample distributions proposed in the beginning of this chapter suggests otherwise. Like the index of accessibility (see Figure 5.3), the index of socio-economic potential tends to assign non-zero values to marginal areas, even if they are totally devoid of any development (Figure 5.5; left diagram). Non-zero values, albeit low ones, are obtained even for remote regions having practically no interaction with a given centre of population. Even more significant errors result in regions that are unsuitable for development, such as swamp land or very mountainous areas, if they happen to be in close proximity to large, existing centres of population. Such regions are assigned comparatively high values of this index, in spite of being undeveloped and unpopulated.

Index of Centrality

The status of an urban locality in the general setting of urban places may be determined not only by measures of distance and concentration (indicators of density, accessibility and development potential), some of which were discussed in previous sections, but also functionally, i.e. by a comparison of a town's ranking with that of other urban places. Christaller (1933; 1966 English edition) suggested such a measure for comparing towns – the index of centrality.

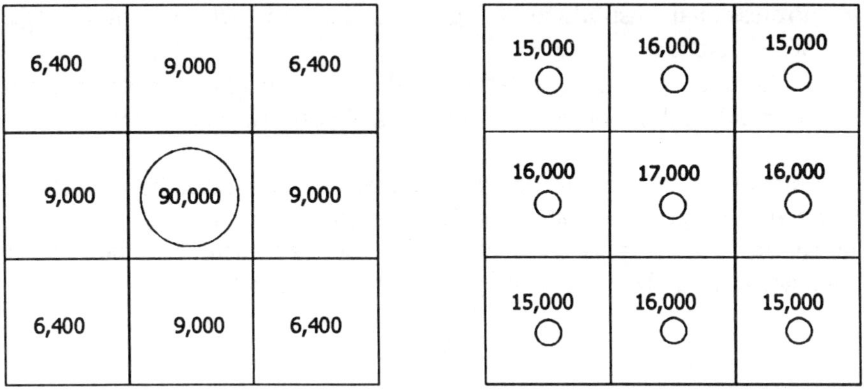

6,400	9,000	6,400
9,000	90,000	9,000
6,400	9,000	6,400

15,000 ○	16,000 ○	15,000 ○
16,000 ○	17,000 ○	16,000 ○
15,000 ○	16,000 ○	15,000 ○

Figure 5.5   Index of socio-economic potential – test of performance

The test is based on the hypothetical distribution of settlements shown in Figure 5.1. Unweighted population figures and aerial distances are used in the calculation, while the value of the distance exponent is set to 1.0.

According to Christaller, it is not possible to determine the centrality of an urban place by means of a simple count of the overall number of high-order functions which take place in it. Such functions may belong to different categories, often rendering their integration and comparison impracticable. In particular, he singles out eight groups of high-centrality functions:

- Institutions of administration (provincial and state governments, high courts and labour offices);
- Institutions of cultural and religious importance (universities, scientific institutes, state libraries, museums, theatres and bishop's seats);
- Institutions of importance in health and sanitation (specialists, scientific institutes, large hospitals and sanatoriums);
- Institutions of social importance (night clubs, stage productions, big newspapers, sport stadiums and radio stations);
- Institutions for the organization of economic and social life (state organisations of artificers, guilds and consumer co-operatives, chambers of commerce and trade);
- Institutions of commerce and finance (large department stores, wholesalers, non-agricultural brokers, foreign trade agents, stock exchanges, branches of the national bank);

- Professional institutions of great complexity (electric plants, gas works, etc.);
- Institutions of transportation and communication (express train terminals, offices of railroad districts and post office districts).

Instead of summing up the number of high-centrality functions, Christaller suggests an indirect index - the centrality of an urban place is represented as a surplus of telephone connections compared to the regional average, and may be calculated by the following formula:

$$Z_z = T_z - E_z \left(\frac{T_g}{E_g} \right)$$

where Z_z is the index of centrality of an urban place; T_z is the number of telephone connections at the urban place in question; T_g is the overall number of telephone connection in the region; E_z is the number of inhabitants in the central place; and E_g is the number of inhabitants in the region.

He thus assumes that a considerable surplus of telephone connections observed in a given urban place, compared with the regional average, indicates a higher importance (centrality) of the town in question, compared with other urban localities.

While the index in question is not spatial by definition and thus cannot be used as a true measure of urban location, it may perform poorly even for the task for which it was originally designed – defining the status of an urban place in a functional hierarchy of urban communities. Indeed, the number of telephone calls may differ substantially for different types of functions, according to their dependence on telephone services. For instance, telemarketing services may have a greater overall number of telephone calls than, for instance, hospitals and express train terminals, despite an apparently higher degree of centrality associated with the latter types of functions. Though truly multi-functional centres should undoubtedly exhibit an excess of telephone communications, the index in question may nevertheless assign a disproportionably higher degree of centrality to some peripheral places than they may actually have.

Partly in response to these deficiencies, Klemmer (1978) proposed an alternative method for determining the degree of centrality of an urban place, which is based on a statistical technique of data reduction known as factor analysis. The use of this technique makes it possible to analyse centrality functions belonging to different functional groups (i.e. hospitals, universities, institutions of culture and administration). This technique leads to a limited number of 'underlying' factors, which explain the variation of individual input variables. Klemmer tested this technique in his analysis of centrality functions in German cities and concluded that factor analysis could indeed result in the selection of a single explanatory variable serving as an integrated measure of urban centrality. However, he had to acknowledge that it was nearly impossible to obtain a single 'predominant factor' with a significance level of about 60-70 per cent.

Agglomeration Indices

As Marshall (1890; 1930 reprint, p. 318) suggests, the *law of increasing returns* is the main force driving industrial agglomeration. This law postulates that 'an increase of labour and capital leads generally to improved organisation, which increases the efficiency of the work of labour and capital'. In a later study of industrial agglomeration, Weber (1909, p. 126) defines the agglomeration factor as

> an 'advantage' or a cheapening of production or marketing which results from the fact that production is carried on to some considerable extent at one place, while a deglomerative factor is a cheapening of production which results from decentralization of production (production in more than one place).

Following this proposition, he suggests the following list of factors affecting agglomeration and deglomeration:

I.   *Agglomerative factors* include economies resulting from enlargement of plants (introduction of labour-saving devices, use of highly specialized machinery; more efficient organisation of management; cheaper credits and discounts on large-scale wholesale purchases);
II. *Deglomeration factors* include primarily the rise of land value resulting from an increase in demand for land that accompanies any agglomeration.[2]

The index Weber proposed to measure the intensity of agglomeration is referred to as the radius of agglomeration, and is calculated from the following formula:

$$R = \sqrt{\frac{M}{\pi\rho}},$$

where R is the radius of agglomeration which determines the distance needed to bring together any given quantity of agglomeration *(M)*, measured in any unit of industrial output; ρ is the density of industrial development in the area; and π is an algebraic constant ($\pi = 3.14159..$).

Since the index in question is inversely proportional to the density of development, it usually has lower values in densely developed core regions and higher values in sparsely developed peripheral regions.

In order to make it applicable to settlement patterns, the following transformation of the index in question may be useful:

$$R_i = \sum_{j=1}^{n} \left(\frac{P_{ij}}{\pi \rho} \right)^{\frac{1}{2}},$$

where R_i is the agglomeration radius for town i, P_{ij} is the total population of town i and an adjacent town j; and ρ is the density of urban development in the region, measured as the number of persons residing in urban localities per unit of land.

The performance of this index is tested in the hypothetical distribution of urban places introduced in Figure 5.1 and reported in Figure 5.6.

Unlike simple density measurements, the index in question appears to differentiate between the distinct distributions of population depicted in the two parts of the diagram. However, like the indices of accessibility and socio-economic potential discussed above, it results in relatively high values being assigned to empty marginal cells in the left diagram.

Richardson (1977) suggests a more sophisticated index of agglomeration, according to which agglomeration economies are assumed to vary in response to a) the number of urban centres (above a certain threshold size); b) the relative size of these centres, with more weight given to the larger centres, and c) the distances between these centres. This agglomeration index is calculated as follows:

$$A = a_1 \left(\sum_{i}^{z} N_i^{a_i} / z \right) + a_2 z + a_3 \left(\sum_{i}^{z} \sum_{j}^{z} d_{ij} / \frac{z!}{2!(z-2)!} \right)$$

where A is the index of agglomeration, a_1, a_2 and a_3 are weighting coefficients (a_1 and a_2 are assumed to be always positive, while a_3 assumed to be negative); z is the number of urban centres in the region, and d_{ij} is the distance between urban centers i and j.

The relationships described by this cumbersome equation are relatively simple - agglomeration economies increase in line with an increase in the number and size of urban centres and decrease as distances between cities grow. However, the presence of weighting coefficients

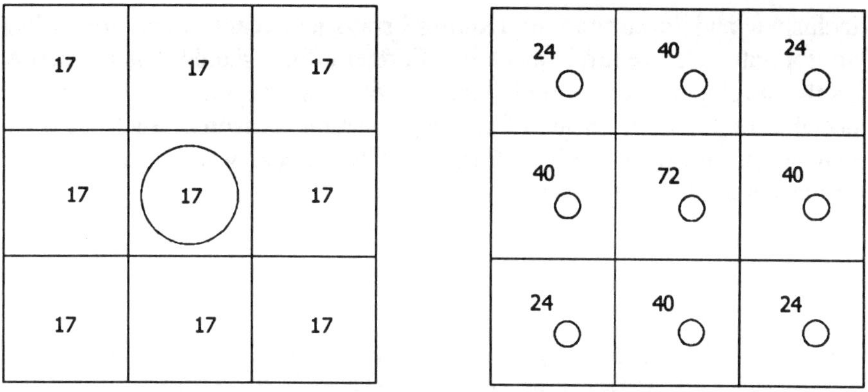

Figure 5.6.   Adjusted index of agglomeration – test of performance

(a₁, a₂ and a₃), whose values are not initially known, makes this formula rather difficult to calibrate and evaluate. The values of these coefficients may be set arbitrary or established by an expert method, but either way, the procedure of their calculation is not clear. The difficulty is that for using a multi-variant statistical technique (such as, for instance, the multiple regression analysis), the values of the dependent variable (A) should be known from the outset. Unfortunately, this is not the case.

Conclusion

Indirect measures of urban location vary from simple density measurements to more complex equations of socio-economic potential and indices of accessibility or agglomeration. In the more complex indices, the effects of density are evaluated in conjunction with the effects of the size of major urban centres and of inter-urban distances. However, none of these indices appears to provide a sufficiently accurate and reliable estimate of urban location. Density measurements, for instance, do not discriminate between concentrated and dispersed patterns of urban development within a region. Unless the physical size of the geographic unit of analysis is relatively small, density estimates may be clearly misleading. On the other hand, indicators of accessibility and socio-economic potential appear to assign relatively high values to locations adjacent to urban concentrations, but otherwise devoid of any development. Although the index of agglomeration seems to be more inclusive and accurate, it requires statistical calibration for which appropriate data are rarely available. Further efforts should thus be focused on the development of a simple indicator of urban location that is as free as possible of the deficiencies of existing location measures. Such an index will be discussed in detail in Part III of this book, which deals with the phenomenon of urban clustering.

Notes

[1] According to Babarović (1978), the value of the α exponent is set to 1 in the classical formulation of the concept of economic potential made by Stewart. However, empirical evidence leads to generalisation of the model in which the value of this coefficient may differ. In particular, a low α exponent ($\alpha < 1$) is more relevant to industrial activities, oriented towards the final consumer market, which require little input of raw materials. For these types of industries, the gradient of economic potential is expected to be smoother than that for manufacturing activities requiring large inputs of heavy raw materials, and which are thus more sensitive to distance. For the latter types of industries, *isopotential* curves are expected to have steeper gradients due to a higher value of the α exponent ($\alpha > 2$). For such values of the gradient, fewer locations have access to external markets. Arguably, the α exponent may also account for variations in a country's economic development, so that more economically developed countries with lower transport costs may have lower values of the exponent in question ($\alpha \approx 1$), while in less developed countries, the values of the exponent are expected to exceed 1.5-2.0.

[2] In more contemporary studies on agglomeration, the list of deglomeration factors is considerably expanded, and include, in addition to high land prices, other 'side-effects' of industrial and population concentration such as air pollution, traffic congestion, etc. (see *inter alia* Barrett, 1998; Turner, 1993).

6 Concluding Remarks

In the first part of the book, we dealt with five major aspects of urban location. Chapter 1 discussed the effects of distance, in general, and remoteness, in particular, on different aspects of urban development, such as location of industries, migration, etc. Chapter 2 focused on defining and measuring the effects of isolation on population growth and economic development of urban localities. The factors affecting the choice of major urban centres, which are 'reference points' for determining the relative location of all other urban places, were considered in some detail in Chapter 3. Chapters 4 and 5 reviewed technical issues associated with urban location, namely the approaches to measuring inter-urban distances (Chapter 4) and possibilities of estimating urban location by various indirect measurements, such as density patterns, location and agglomeration indices (Chapter 5).

Remoteness was demonstrated to have profound effects on various aspects of urban development, most of which are clearly adverse. Thus, remoteness almost inevitably causes an increase in the cost of transport, and therefore affects the location of traditional manufacturing facilities. Though high technology firms are less dependent on transportation and do not generate, as a rule, heavy transport flows, the effect of remoteness on their location is also considerable: these firms tend to locate their branches in close proximity to major population centres, in which a pool of skilled labour can be found and where access to existing research infrastructure is immediate. In addition to purely economic consequences, remoteness tends to reduce a town's attractiveness to migrants and commuters, though the relationship between population flows and distance is neither linear nor universal.

Despite these obvious links between remoteness and development patterns of urban localities, the effects of remoteness cannot be separated from those of other location factors. For instance, the unfavourable effects of remoteness can either be reduced or aggravated by the presence (or a lack thereof) of other urban localities which may form an intra-regional 'safety net' for a given town, supplementing its service functions and providing additional employment and cultural opportunities for the town's residents. Even though two towns may be equally remote from a major population centre of a country, the adverse effects of remoteness upon one of them may be tempered by a developed urban field of urban places linked to one another, resulting in very dissimilar patterns of development. Conversely, the remoteness of a town from a country's population centres might be aggravated by its spatial isolation within the surrounding geographic region. The effects of remoteness on the development of urban places should thus be studied in conjunction with those of isolation: the combination of these location factors may either weaken or aggravate the adverse effects of each of them considered separately. The combined effects of isolation and remoteness will be discussed in more detail in Part III of the book.

Urban and regional studies have traditionally treated spatial isolation as a marginal issue, closely associated with physical remoteness in general. In the present part of the book, this phenomenon was treated as a separate issue and was subjected to an in-depth analysis. This approach allowed us to emphasise the multi-facetted nature of this phenomenon, as well as to identify distinctive types of spatial isolation that may exist in reality. These appear to range from total isolation - both within a geographic region and in relation to other urban centres of a country, to clusters, in which individual urban localities share essential functions and services.

The analysis carried out in the present part of the book seems to indicate that, like remoteness, isolation generally has a negative effect on the development of towns. Indeed, large distances between towns in sparsely populated areas, particularly peripheral ones, are likely to aggravate the effects of their remoteness from major urban centres of a country, effectively preventing the establishment of a joint social and economic infrastructure. However, in densely populated areas, such as in core regions, the effect of distance between towns may not always be negative.

Because extremely dense patterns of urban development result in a lack of land resources for development, and in intense competition for potential investors and migrants, towns in core regions may benefit from being located a certain distance from each other. The effects of distance on urban growth in various geographic areas would therefore benefit from further study. The theoretical aspects of this important issue will be discussed, in some detail, in Part III of the book, while an attempt to verify these theoretical concepts will be undertaken in Part IV, which deals with case studies.

The concept of a major urban centre is central to our understanding of the phenomena of remoteness and isolation. In determining remoteness, urban centres represent 'reference points' from which distances are measured. In measuring isolation, urban centres are 'yardsticks' which help to understand the likely implications of existing patterns of urban settlement for the development of individual towns. There appears to be no universal explanation for the formation of urban centres, nor for the criteria used to define a particular urban place as a major population centre. As our analysis indicates, the choice of a major urban centre cannot be determined solely by an analysis of selected quantitative characteristics of urban settlements. This is partly because the population of urban settlements referred to as 'principal cities' varies in different countries considerably. In addition, the indicator of population size often represents a mere proxy for a range of development parameters, which are concomitant with a larger population size, such as the availability of services, diversity of employment, etc.

Discussion of the phenomenon of the 'major centre' is important in its own right, but it also leads to another extremely important concept, namely the sustainability of urban growth. Sustainable population growth is essential for the transformation of a town into a major population centre. Sustainable growth or, at least the absence of an obvious decline, also has important consequences for the development of other urban places that may not eventually be transformed into such a centre. The phenomenon of sustainable urban growth and the choice of criteria for gauging such growth should therefore be studied in depth and understood. We shall discuss this important concept in the following part (II) of the book.

We also reviewed traditional measures of urban location, which vary from simple density measurements to more complex formula of socio-economic potential, accessibility and agglomeration indices, in which the effect of density is combined with those of size of major urban centres and inter-urban distances. We concluded that such measures are often not sufficiently accurate and may not produce reliable estimates of urban location. For instance, density measurements do not discriminate between concentrated and dispersed patterns of urban development within a region, and unless the physical size of the geographic unit of analysis is relatively small, may be clearly misleading. On the other hand, indicators of accessibility and socio-economic potential appear to assign relatively high values to points of geographic space that are adjacent to urban concentrations but not developed themselves. Although the index of agglomeration seems to be more inclusive and accurate, it requires a sophisticated statistical calibration for which sufficient data are rarely available.

Research efforts should thus be concentrated on the development of a simple indicator of urban location that will overcome the drawbacks of using existing location indices. We shall propose such an index in Part III of this book, which deals with the phenomenon of urban clustering. Concurrently, in Part IV, we shall discuss the performance of this index in a series of case studies.

PART II
MEASURING SUSTAINABLE
URBAN GROWTH

Many succumb on the way, and a few only survive;
those few become stronger with every year, they get a
larger share of light and air with every increase of their
height, and at last in their turn they tower above their
neighbours, and seem as though they would grow on for
ever, and for ever become stronger as they grow.

A. Marshall, *Principles of Economics*

7 Sustainable Urban Growth as a Development Issue

Sustainable urban growth (SUG) is, undoubtedly, an extremely complex and multifaceted phenomenon. Our understanding of this phenomenon as the *enduring ability of urban places to attract newcomers and retain current residents* will be discussed in the context of various other interpretations of the concept. This discussion will be followed by an analysis of indicators and criteria for sustainable population growth, which will lay the basis for the study of the relationship between sustained population growth of towns and attributes of their location.

Interpretations of Sustainable Development[1]

In the wake of rising environmental awareness in the 1970's, various aspects of *sustainable development* (SD) have become the focus of academic study. The term SD itself came into prominence in 1980, when it was introduced by the International Union for the Conservation of Nature (IUCN) in the framework of the World Conservation Strategy, with 'the overall aim of achieving sustainable development through the conservation of living resources' (IUCN, 1980).

The concept of sustainable development (SD) evolved in response to widespread perceptions of a growing global environmental crisis, as forecast by the Club of Rome's Limits to Growth, which contended that the world development trajectory was unsustainable (Meadows *et al,* 1972).

This report conjectured that escalating the impact of human settlements on the physical world would run up against intractable problems some time before the year 2100, precipitating a massive drop in living standards or even the elimination of humanity from the biosphere.

The United Nations Environment Program (UNEP) has since articulated and popularised the concept, which was defined by The World

Commission on Environment and Development (known as the *Brundtland Commission*) as 'development which meets the needs of the present without compromising the ability of future generations to meet their own needs' (WCED, 1987).

With time, the initial concept of SD, oriented primarily towards ecology, has become more inclusive. In particular, it combined an ecological element - protection of the natural environment - with a social component. This resulted in the understanding of SD as protection of the basis of the human life in general (Figure 7.1).

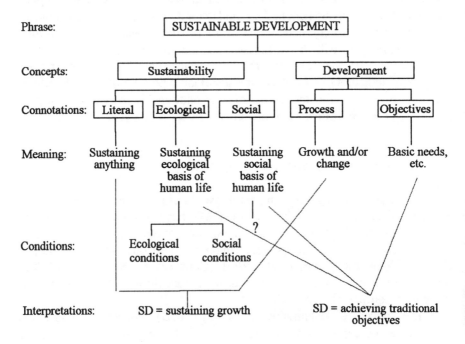

Figure 7.1   Semantics of sustainable development (after Lele, 1991)

The growing consensus that has been built around the issue of SD has been based on the perceived feedback between social and environmental phenomena. In the developing world, for instance, many environmental problems originate from the lack of development, and the struggle to overcome poverty. Environmental degradation impoverishes those dependent directly on the environment for survival, and conversely, that development must be environmentally sound in order to be permanent (WRI, 1996).

As Dampier (1982) assumes, 'environmental quality and economic development are interdependent, and in the long term, mutually reinforcing'. This understanding of SD is thus more complex since it is the basis of causal interrelationships between poverty and environmental degradation which involve not only quality of environment but also technology, consumption patterns and ultimately culture and values in various regions of the world.

In a more recent study, Dodds (1999) attempts to generalise on the alternative approaches to SD and singles out five distinctive interpretations of SD that are currently in use:

- The *economic interpretation* seeks to ensure that economic activity does not undermine the natural (and other) capital on which it is based. Its goal is to achieve 'sustainable income,' primarily through better management of resources and by minimising environmental damage. The key element of this approach is the understanding that environmental information should be incorporated into prices and into the decision-making framework in which decisions concerning resource consumption are made;

- The *ecological interpretation* draws attention to maintaining the integrity and productivity of natural and agricultural systems. Proponents of this interpretation assume that ecological sustainability is an essential precondition for economic sustainability. Therefore, in order to achieve sustainable growth, attention should be given primarily to maintaining ecosystem functions, life support systems and 'representative forms of all other living natural assets;

- The *social equality interpretation* is based on the assumption that encouraging greater equality in society is the key to reducing the negative environmental effects of development. According to this interpretation, poverty and environmental degradation are mutually reinforcing since 'poverty reduces people's opinions and shortens their planning horizons, driving them to inflict long-term environmental damage – particularly in times of crisis;'

- *Socio-economic (demand-side) interpretation:* Unlike the 'supply-side' approach to economic sustainability, this interpretation extends the traditional notion of sustainable income to include non-economic considerations, such as changes in water and air quality, crime rates, values of community and culture, and other factors that are considered to be important in determining the overall well-being, rather than a more narrowly defined economic criterion based on the possession of certain material goods;

- The *ethical and cultural interpretation* is based on the argument that unsustainable growth is caused mainly by a loss of cultural and ethical values in human society, leading in turn to the phenomenon of 'environmental vandalism' and the tendency to 'treat the environment as a commodity which exists only for human benefit.'

In contrast to the 'interpretational' classification above, Bossel (1999) suggests a 'vertical' classification of SD, according to which the phenomenon of SD is subdivided into six subsystems in which sustainable growth is to be obtained:

- *Individual development* (civil liberties and human rights, equality, individual autonomy and self-determination, health, right to work, etc.);
- *Social system* (population development, ethnic composition, social security, medical care and old age provision);
- *Government and administration* (public finances and taxes, political participation and democracy, conflict resolution, population and immigration policies, etc.);
- *Infrastructure* (settlements and cities, transportation and supply systems, waste disposal, education, health system, research and development);
- *Economic system* (production and consumption, finances, labour and employment, income and interregional trade);
- *Resources and environment* (atmosphere and hydrosphere, natural resources, waste absorption, etc.).

According to Bossel *(ibid.),* these six sectors can further be aggregated into three interrelated subsystems:

1. Human system (social system, individual development and governance);
2. Support system (infrastructure and economic system), and
3. Natural system (resources and environment).

Sustainability of Urban Growth

At the level of individual urban settlements, the discussion of SD is primarily focused on three major issues – the reduction of environmental impact associated with urban development; the optimal size of urban places, and the provision of satisfactory urban environments for residents. In the following subsections, each of these issues will be discussed in some detail.

Reduction of Environmental Impact Associated with Urban Growth

The environmental impact of cities is closely related to compact urban form. Efficient use of urban land may help to 'spare' rural land and natural landscapes, that otherwise might have been taken for urban development (Portnov, 1992; Fulford, 1999). High-density urban development may also contribute to a reduction in the transport-related energy consumption, which is a major source of environmental pollution (Newman, 1993).

As Newman and Kenworthy (1989; cited in Fulford, 1999) argue in their study of ten cities in the U.S.A., petrol consumption rates in the cities surveyed varied by 40 per cent. While they found no statistically significant correlation between fuel consumption and such 'traditional welfare' factors as per capita income, car ownership and petrol prices, the intensity of urban land use was found to be related to the use of gasoline at a statistically significant level.

Barrett's (1999) analysis of travel behaviour in the U.K. also indicated that higher urban densities appeared to be associated with generally lower levels of total travel, and, specifically, with a considerably reduced use of private cars (Table 7.1).

Various 'pro-urban' strategies have been developed in order to reduce gasoline consumption and carbon dioxide emissions resulting from extensive use of automobiles in sparsely populated areas: concentration of new development primarily in urban areas; maintaining and revitalising existing urban centres; constraining the development or extension of small rural-type settlements, etc. (Barrett, 1999).

As a result of his analysis of transportation in Australian cities, Newman (1993) suggests that the environmental effect of low-density urban development extends far beyond car-related air pollution. In particular, he puts forward a detailed list of reasons why urban development should be compact if more sustainable urban growth is to be achieved:

Table 7.1   **Travel behaviour in the U.K. as a function of population density, persons per hectare**

Density	Type of travel					
	All modes	Car	Local bus	Rail	Walk	Other*
Under 1	206.3	159.3	5.2	8.9	4.0	28.8
1-4.99	190.5	146.7	7.7	9.1	4.9	21.9
5-14.99	176.2	131.7	8.6	12.3	4.3	18.2
15-29.99	152.6	105.4	9.6	10.2	6.6	20.6
30-49.99	143.2	100.4	9.9	10.8	6.4	15.5
50+	129.2	79.9	11.9	15.2	6.7	15.4
All areas	159.6	113.8	9.3	11.3	5.9	19.1

* Refers to two-wheeled motor vehicles, taxis, domestic air travel and other types of bus (school, hire, express and work).

Source: Barrett (1999).

- *Infrastructure cost.* Inefficient suburban development increases considerably the cost of infrastructure compared to that in old city areas;
- *Transport costs.* The total cost of operating private cars, typical of low-density suburban development, exceeds that of public transportation by some 50-70 per cent;
- *Cost of time.* In societies dependent on transportation by private car, total time spent on traveling is considerably longer than that spent in countries less dependent on private cars;
- *Land waste.* The need for parking lots and roads causes a major loss of rural land and natural landscapes;
- *Housing waste.* Low-density housing in car-oriented suburbs is often in mismatch with market needs but its construction continues;
- *Environmental health problems.* In car-dependent cities, noise, air pollution, road accidents, and respiratory diseases become a major problem;
- *Social inequity.* The young, old, poor or disabled have less access to transport, as do residents of outer suburbs, compared with inner city residents. This places a considerable burden on these groups of population, and leads to increasing social inequity as sprawl continues;

- *Loss of community.* Community and neighborhood interactions decline due to loss of the random interaction that occurs in pedestrian and mass transit systems;
- *Loss of urban vitality.* The vitality and culture of the city are reduced as public spaces are dominated by cars rather than by people.

Optimal City Size

The concept of optimal population size of a city has been under investigation for centuries.

In the 4th century BC, Plato discussed how best to found a *polis* in Crete and presented a detailed program for an 'ideal city-state' with some 5,040 landholders which was to be ruled by 37 curators of law and a council of 360 (*The Laws of Plato;* 1979 English translation). According to Plato's concept,

> the only correct way to determine the adequate size of population is by consideration of the land and the neighbouring cities. The land should be large enough to support a certain number of people living moderately, and no more. This number should be large enough to enable them both to defend themselves, if they suffer an injustice from their neighbours, and to be in a position to give at least some aid to their neighbours if someone else does them an injustice (*ibid.,* p. 124).

The origin of the number of landholders in Plato's 'ideal city' (5040) is not accidental, but it appears to result from an abstract mathematical calculation:

> Let there be five thousand forty landholders and defenders of the distribution; and let there be the same division of the land and the households, each man paired with an allotment. First let the whole number be divided by two, and then the same number by three – for its nature is to be divisible also by four, and five, and so on up to ten... The entire number series is divisible by every number for every purpose. Five thousand forty has no more than sixty, minus one divisors, including all the numbers from one to ten, consequently. And these divisions are useful in war and in peace – in all contracts and associations, in revenue gathering, and in disbursements *(ibid.).*

In reality, as Doxiadis (1964, p.9) argues, pedestrian access, rather than mathematic calculations, determined the physical dimensions of nearly all ancient Greek city-states:

In a state of average size the city was at a 4 hours' walking distance from its edges; in the case of the smaller state it was an hour's walking distance and in that of the larger states 7 hours' distance from the borders. This means that within a day, between sunrise and sunset, one could set forth from his city and reach the furthermost point even of the largest state, whilst in the case of an average size state one was able to set forth from the most distant point, to go to the city and return before sunset.

Howard (1898; 1985 reprint) in his book on 'Garden Cities of To-morrow' envisioned 'garden cities' with an ideal population size of some 32,000, on a site of 1,000 acres. This was to allow easy pedestrian access to the cities' public centres from any, even the most remote, residential neighbourhoods.

The main emphasis in determining the 'optimal city size' has since shifted from concern with pedestrian access toward economic considerations. As Haughton and Hunter (1994) note, the early British New Towns plans indeed considered 30,000 as an 'ideal size,' but this threshold was subsequently increased to 100,000-250,000 residents when it was realised that a certain minimal population base was necessary in order to achieve an economic take-off, especially in supporting key service functions.

Clark (1982) and Richardson (1977), among others, advocate the *minimum cost approach* to the 'optimal city size.' In particular, they argue that urban settlements of a particular population size may be more economically viable than others, at least, when per capita costs of infrastructure maintenance and provision of services are concerned. Alonso (1977), however, criticizes this approach, arguing that cities with higher incomes tend to spend more on amenities and services and, therefore, that rising expenditures in large cities are not necessarily due to higher per capita costs.

The results of the analysis of per capita incomes and expenditures in local authorities (LA) of different population size in Israel (Figure 7.2) appear to be in full agreement with Alonso's conclusion.

As Figure 7.2 shows, per capita expenditures are indeed lower in LA of medium population size (50-100,000 residents) than in both larger and smaller municipalities. However, these municipalities also appear to have a lower per capita income than other groups of LA, so it is questionable whether the above population size is in fact optimal.

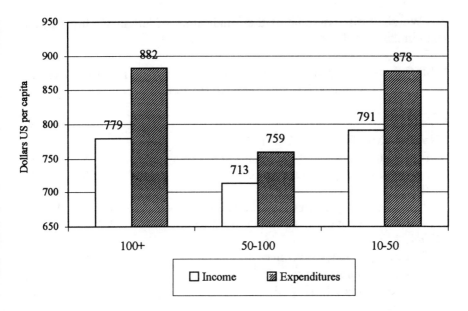

Figure 7.2 **Income and expenditure in urban municipalities of different population size in Israel (as of 1994; unweighted means)**

Social Dimension

Many recent studies attribute sustainable growth of urban places to the degree of satisfaction or security the urban environment may offer to a city's residents.

As Clark (1982) argues, high crime levels are a prominent externality imposed upon large cities, and this may affect public policies concerning an 'optimal city size.' To support this conclusion, he cites above average crime levels in major metropolis of the U.K. and U.S.A., arguing that, according to MRA results, factors aggravating crime rates were all related, to population size (directly or indirectly): unemployment, overcrowding, and the number of males not living with their families.

Alternatively, the 'social vitality' of an urban place may be measured by a range of complementing indicators, commonly known as indicators of the 'quality of urban life.' These indicators range from indices of environmental pollution and crime levels to the availability of employment, cost of living, property values, housing and climatic conditions (Table 7.2).

We shall discuss some of these indicators of 'urban vitality' in more detail in the next chapter.

Table 7.2   Selected indicators of the quality of life in Charlottesville, Virginia (U.S) compared to the national average

Indicator	City stats	Nat'l Avg.
ENVIRONMENTAL POLLUTION:		
EPA watershed rating (100 is best; 0 is worst)	87.3	31.8
Air quality rating (200 is best; 0 is worst)	150	118.9
CRIME:		
Property crime yearly per 100,000 people	3,775.7	4,686.2
Violent crime yearly per 100,000 people	279.8	569.6
ECONOMY:		
Cost of living index (average=100)	95	106.4
Recent unemployment rate, [%]	1.7	5.2
Job growth since 1997, [%]	4.4	1.9
HOUSING:		
Median price for 2-bedroom home, [$]	140,000	110,590
Change in average home value since 1997, [%]	4.7	4.8
Utility costs (Avg. for an 1,800 sq. ft. home), [$]	110	104.9
QUALITY OF LIFE:		
Average commuting time [min]	19.3	19.5
Arts & culture index (100 is best; 0 is worst)	31	46.2
WEATHER:		
Number of sunny days	218	213.1
Average July high [degrees Fahrenheit]	86.1	86.7
Average January low [degrees Fahrenheit]	27.3	27.0
Average annual rainfall [inches]	38.3	36.3
Average annual snowfall [inches]	18.2	23.1

Source: Charlottesville City Hall's Internet Site.

Note

[1] This section is based, in part, on Portnov and Pearlmutter (1999b).

8 Criteria for Sustainable Urban Growth

Considered a multifaceted phenomenon, sustainable development (SD) in general and sustainable urban growth (SUG), in particular, remain open to a variety of interpretations which encompass at least three major dimensions of the issue: environmental, economic and socio-demographic. In this chapter, criteria associated with each of these dimensions of SUG will be discussed. The discussion will be preceded by a brief outline of approaches and criteria commonly used for selecting and testing development indicators.

Criteria for Selecting Development Indicators

Development indicators in urban and regional planning are commonly used in three distinctive ways: 1) measuring the needs or opportunities of each geographic region or settlement as a basis for resource allocation; 2) setting up the contextual 'baseline' of the conditions in an area in order to measure the improvement brought about by public policy intervention, and 3) distinguishing which opportunities or problems are most important for each area as a basis for defining and prioritising policy targets (Wong, 1995).

In the framework of the Global Urban Observatory Programme (GUOP), the United Nations Centre for Human Settlements (Habitat) developed a set of criteria by which urban development indicators may be selected and evaluated. Ten major criteria were suggested:

- *Policy relevance*. Indicators should be relevant to existing or proposed urban policy, and should directly measure its outcomes.
- *Comprehensiveness*. The indicator 'package' should be capable of providing a broad overview of the economic, social and

environmental 'health' of urban areas using primarily existing data sources.

- *Priority.* Indicators should have two levels of priority: The highest priority or 'key' indicators may require only immediately available data, while the secondary priority measurements may contain indicators of a lower policy relevance or which are more difficult to collect or define.

- *Simplicity.* It is assumed that simple indicators are likely to have a far wider circulation and can be used more accurately and readily. In contrast, complex indicators are likely to be misquoted or accused of being unreliable.

- *Measurability.* Urban development indicators should be capable of showing the magnitude of problems. Indicators measured on a dimensionless and time-independent scale are preferable.

- *Reliability.* Indicators should provide a convincing demonstration that objectives are being met; they should be based on sound observation, and not be too subject to statistical 'noise'.

- *Sensitivity.* It is assumed that a measure that stays constant for many years is likely to have little value. On the other hand, indicators that are too volatile are hard to interpret or collect.

- *Unambiguousness.* Indicators should have a clear definition and refer to a specific objective.

- *Independence.* Separate indicators should measure different outcomes.

- *Availability for geographical areas in question.* Indicators that can be disaggregated by urban settlements and geographic areas are likely to be of great interest and thus can be used in a wide variety of circumstances where special needs and equity are policy issues (HABITAT, 1997).

In contrast, Bossel (1999) suggests a shorter list of requirements for development indicators, arguing that these requirements are generally sufficient for gauging the degree of sustainability exhibited by all of the 'systems shaping sustainable development' (descriptive titles for groups of requirements are suggested by the authors):

- *Applicability to different geographic units:* Indicators of sustainable development are needed to guide policies and decisions at all levels of society: village, town, city, county, state, region, nation, continent and world;

- *Conceptual significance:* The indicators must represent only important concerns; an *ad hoc* collection of indicators that just seems relevant is not adequate. A more systematic approach must look at the interaction of systems and their environment;
- *Comprehensiveness:* The number of indicators should be as small as possible, but not smaller than necessary. That is, the indicator set must be comprehensive and compact, covering all relevant aspects;
- *Relevance for the social groups affected:* The process of finding an indicator set must involve the public to ensure that the set encompasses the visions and values of the community or region for which it is developed;
- *Usefulness:* Indicators must be clearly defined, reproducible, unambiguous, comprehensible and practical. They must reflect the interests and views of different stakeholders;
- *Comparability:* Indicators should permit deduction of the viability and sustainability of current developments, and should allow comparison with alternative development paths.

Treatment of Volatility

Whichever indicator (or group of indicators) is used for a concrete task at hand, an important question arises unavoidably and should be addressed: If an indicator provides different values over different periods of time, which of these values describes best the general trend of the process in question?

Let us consider, for instance, a popular indicator of sustainability - the per capita volume of gross domestic product (GDP). The values of this indicator for a given settlement or region may decline or increase intermittently during a period under consideration. Would this indicate that the economy of the place in question is not sustainable?

The answer to this question is rather simple: Though the notion of SD entered the scientific lexicon only in the 1980s, the solution to this problem was, in fact, suggested by the Italian sociologist Vilfredo Pareto at the turn of the 20th century in his book on 'The Mind and Society: A Treatise on General Sociology.' In this book, Pareto (1935 English edition) singles out three different types of fluctuations: a) undulating movement with no trend of change; b) undulating movement with a tendency to decline, and c) undulating movement with a tendency to increase (see Figure 8.1).

In turn, each of these fluctuations may have, according to Pareto, three types of amplitude: a) fluctuations of brief duration; b) fluctuations of medium amplitude; and c) fluctuations of maximum amplitude, which are close to the trend line (*ibid,* pp. 1180-81).

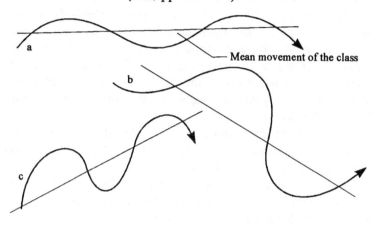

Figure 8.1   **Undulating and mean movements of genera (after Pareto, 1935)**

According to Pareto, the movement of a class in time may be represented by an undulating curve, however, the mean movement of the class, which can be obtained by susceptive measurements over a long period of time, should point at the actual direction of development – no change (a), decline (b), or growth (c).

To find out which of these trends is applicable to the process at hand, Pareto suggests the use of successive measurements extending over a long period of time. Such measurements make it 'fairly easy to eliminate such difficulties' in identifying a general trend, since 'by interpolation one may determine the line...about which the intensity is fluctuating and so discover its mean general direction.'

Applying Pareto's advice to the task of determining the general bias of a development process, it may thus be suggested that the process in question may be characterized as sustainable or non-sustainable by investigating the actual direction of change over the entire time period under consideration. This task can be achieved either by averaging or by ignoring temporary fluctuations within shorter time periods.

Environmental Criteria

The environmental dimension of SD embraces the multiplicative interaction of three nominally independent variables: *population - consumption - technology*. In other words, the concept of sustainability considers the phenomenon in terms of the upward and downward pressure of the population on existing environmental resources, such as food, energy sources, water, etc. (Sage, 1994). Thus defined, the sustainability of a particular geographic area may be quantitatively measured as the ratio between *the percent change in population and that of the use of resources* (Turner, 1993).

Harrison (cited in Sage, 1994) suggests a way of quantifying this concept. Thus, the impact of the population (PI) on the environment is determined by the following ratio:

$$PI = PCP*100/PCR,$$

where PCP is percentage change in population, and PCR is percentage change in the use of resources.

The index in question thus distinguishes between upward and downward pressures of population on the environment scoring them from +100 to –100 per cent, respectively.

As Sage (1994) suggests, the nominator in the above index, which describes the use of resources, may be measured by the annual expansion of farmland, for instance, while population pressure may be estimated in terms of per capita increase in consumption.

Other criteria for measuring environmental sustainability of urban systems include: the amount of wastewater treated, solid waste generated, disposal methods for solid waste, and regular solid-waste collection (HABITAT, 1997).

In contrast to what has been labelled the 'technocentric' version of environmentalism, in which an environmental impact of development is measured by a variety of 'pollution and waste' indicators, the popular notion of 'bio-regionalism' has emerged from the 'ecocentric' wing of the environmental movement. It contends that the environmental crisis cannot be solved by technical and administrative measures alone. The solution, as presented by Atkinson (1992), is not primarily concerned with the physical environment *per se*, but rather with creating a society *that will maintain its environment*.

Bio-regionalism traces its roots to two sources: the conservationist attitudes of Thoreau, Emerson, Muir and Leopold, who revolted against consumerism and insisted that human culture be sensitive to nature and to the specific properties of ecology and place; and to the regionalism of Mumford and others who focused inward, calling for the development of resources and culture *in situ*, as opposed to the expansionist role the west has pursued (Sale, 1985). In this sense, bio-regionalism views the lack of sustainability of Third World cities as a direct result of European colonialism that has eroded indigenous cultural structures of welfare and environmental management without building satisfactory new ones (Atkinson, 1991).

As Portnov and Pearlmutter (1999a) argue, the concept of a bioregion stems from the 'urban hinterland' model developed in the work of von Thünen and other German geographers. This model argues that surplus rural resources are supplied for urban-based processing, to produce a richer variety of products and services for both the city and the rural population in its vicinity. In other words, there is a close connection between the urban and rural components of a discrete region.

It has been suggested that until the 19th century the bulk of the world's population, primarily in Asia, lived in regions of this type in which 'the size of the urban population was closely adjusted to the carrying capacity of its hinterland, and the symbiosis between city and countryside proved to be ecologically sustainable over long periods of time' (Stren *et al,* 1992).

Atkinson (1992) summarizes the general principles of the bioregionalist approach to SD as follows:

1. Bioregions are geophysically and ecologically coherent areas of territory, though not necessarily defined by rigid boundaries. The primary concern is that development strategies should work with the resources of the region, rather than being determined to exploit them.
2. Bioregions are culturally coherent entities, in which development can be better informed by 'local knowledge' than by 'universal' preconceptions.
3. The concept of bioregionalism focuses on changes in lifestyles and consumption patterns, rather than on the dynamics of production. It may be disseminated (marketed) more by the demonstration of alternatives than by analysis and explanation.
4. The measure of wealth of a bioregion is the degree to which it has attained its 'carrying capacity,' a concept that only has relevance if its resources are not overburdened by extra-regional demand.
5. The bioregional economy is self-reliant, which means that practically everything consumed is produced regionally.

The essence of the bioregional model is thus a suggestion that sustainability is intimately connected with some degree of *self-reliance* on the regional level, which may be gauged quantitatively by various indicators of the efficiency of agricultural production (agricultural imports, the size of cultivated area, the volume of production per unit of arable land, etc.).

However, it is worth noting that this regional urban-rural symbiosis, postulated by the 'bio-regional' model of SD, has largely been lost in the modern era, in the sense that cities obtain increasing proportions of their material support from beyond their own natural region (MacNeill *et al*, 1992).

Economic Criteria

The conventional *economic approach* is to treat natural resources as other commodities, assuming their exploitation will be automatically optimised by market forces (Nordhaus and Tobin, 1977). Alternative approaches, however, acknowledge that the environment performs numerous complex functions. First, as emphasized by conventional theories, the environment provides useful material and energy inputs for the economic process. Second, the environment assimilates the waste by-products generated by this process. And, third, the environment provides essential services ranging from recreational, health, cultural, educational, scientific and aesthetic services to the maintenance of essential climatic and ecological cycles (Pearsall, 1984).

These functions emphasise the dependence of the economic process on environmental quality, and the underline the assertion that 'the deterioration of the environment is also an economic problem' (Hueting, 1980). Economic aspects of SD thus consider the phenomenon in terms of economic development that *can endure over time* (Turner, 1993).

Goodland and Ledec (1986) suggested a broad definition of sustainability, which would fit the above prescription. In particular, they defined SD as 'a pattern of development which optimises the economic and other societal benefits in the present without jeopardising the likely potential for similar benefits in the future.' This approach is considered most relevant to industrialised countries, in which growth-oriented development has culminated in the following pattern of resource allocation:

- Decrease in human labour and an increase in capital investment required for a given level of output.
- Increase in the long-term use of energy and raw materials for a given level of production.
- Increase in environmental degradation and ecological stress.

However, the continued substitution of capital and natural resources for labour in the production process is a pattern of economic development that may be unsustainable in the long term, according to Barbier (1989) and Bossel (1999). For instance, Bossel argues that the total money value of the annual flow of goods and services produced in the economy includes both 'social goods' (such as education, food and housing), and 'social ills,' such as the cost of crime prevention, pollution, the treatment of victims of car accidents, disability and poor health.

It is thus suggested that, in order to be useful as an indicator of sustainability, GDP should be corrected by subtracting, rather than adding, the above mentioned 'social ills,' and if policy-makers wish to avoid the high unemployment, resource scarcity, environmental degradation and misallocation of capital which such a pattern of development may engender in the long-run, they should 'abandon the sole emphasis on growth as the primary objective of economic activity.'

Thus, it has been proposed that the definition of economic development in terms of gross national product per capita or real consumption per capita is too narrow. A more comprehensive set of welfare indicators is probably preferable: education, health, and quality of life - a term including, for instance, the number of households below the poverty line, employment rate, number of hospital beds, ownership of durable goods, years of education of best vs. least educated percentiles, lifetime fraction available for leisure, etc.(Turner, 1993; Bossel, 1999).

Population Criteria

Socio-demographic aspects of SD interpret the phenomenon in terms of the *overall stability of population growth* in particular geographic areas, and deal with specific aspects of the issue such as the 'optimal size' of a settlement and the rural-urban balance of a region (Bourne, 1975; Brown and Jacobson, 1987).

Three major indicators are commonly used to measure the extent to which the population growth of urban settlements is sustainable. They are:

a) the overall rate of population growth; b) percentage change of urban population in the area, and c) the average rate of net migration.

Since the present (socio-demographic) definition of SD seems to be most relevant to the main focus of the book, each of these criteria for growth sustainability will be discussed in some detail.

Overall Rate of Population Growth

Though this criterion undoubtedly represents the most obvious and direct datum for gauging the process of urban growth, its reliability and usefulness may be questioned on several grounds.

For example, let us consider two hypothetical towns whose annual overall population growth over recent years has been equal to four percent. Whereas the first settlement steadily exhibited positive natural growth (+5.0 per cent per annum) and a negative migration balance (-1.0 per cent), the respective components of growth in the second locality were both equal to +2.0 per cent annually.

From the standpoint of regional and urban planning, these two settlements clearly represent different cases, while the commonly used criterion of population growth treats them alike.

Let us also consider two communities with identical overall rates of growth (say, +2.0 per cent per annum) but located in countries with very different overall growth rates, say -0.5 and +6.0 per cent, respectively. Clearly, for the first region, a 2.0 per cent rate of growth is much greater than the national average, while for the latter region, the same annual growth rate is rather low.

Percentage Change of Urban Population in the Area

This criterion is commonly used to trace the progress of urban growth in particular geographic areas and regions, and is an important component of national statistics worldwide (Brown and Jacobson, 1987; WRI, 1997). However, we should keep in mind that a region's urban population growth does not necessarily indicate whether this growth occurs evenly across all urban localities, or only in large metropolitan centres, for instance. While this indicator seems to be an essential tool for evaluating the process of urban development in entire countries and large regions, its usefulness for local, urban and regional planning appears to be restricted.

Average Rate of Net Migration

Unlike the previous datum, this indicator is applicable to both single urban settlements and to entire geographic regions. However, it reflects only one component of urban growth – migration - but neglects natural growth, which may offset the effects of migration in terms of the overall population trend of the region in question. Like overall growth, the significance of a given rate of migration can be understood through a comparison with national or regional migration rates. Without reference to these, any analysis of migration may be misleading.

Conclusion

The extent to which the growth of an urban place is sustainable can be gauged by three types of criteria – ecological, economic and socio-demographic criteria, of which population criteria are most relevant to the main thrust of this study. The review of commonly used criteria in this group - overall population growth, percentage change of urban population in the area, and the overall rate of migration - indicates that none of these measures provides a wholly satisfactory tool for analysis on its own. On the other hand, simultaneous use of different indicators creates other problems. For instance, different indicators may highlight different long-term trends, and thus lead to misguided development policies. It is thus suggested that an alternative solution can be found by developing *an integrated indicator* incorporating the comparative advantages of separate direct measurements. Such an indicator will be discussed in the following chapter.

9 Integrated Index

A study of the patterns of population growth of small urban settlements in Israel (Portnov and Pearlmutter, 1997) indicated significant changes in the components of population growth in line with an increase in the settlements' population size (see Figure 9.1). The analysis of these changes led to the development of an integrated index of sustained population growth in urban localities – the *migration balance-natural growth ratio* (the MBNG index), which will be discussed in this chapter in some detail.

Changes in the Components of Population Growth

As Figure 9.1 shows, the relative importance of different sources of population growth (foreign immigration, internal migration, and natural increase) changes as the population size of a town in Israel increases:

- *Foreign immigration.* The attractiveness of an urban settlement to foreign immigrants grows with settlement size. In smaller localities (10-15,000 residents), foreign immigration amounts to 1.0-1.2 per cent per annum, while in larger urban localities (40,000+ residents), its annual rate reaches 1.5-1.6 per cent;
- *In-country migrants.* The attractiveness of urban localities to internal migrants exhibits the opposite trend: the larger a locality, the lower its attractiveness to in-country migrants. While internal migration increases initially in localities of 10-20,000 residents, it drops as soon as the upper threshold of this interval is reached. Finally, after reaching a population size of about 120,000 residents, net internal migration becomes negative;
- *Natural growth.* The annual rates of natural growth decline steadily as the population size of an urban settlement increases. These rates are fairly high in small towns (2.0-3.0 per cent) and drop to 0.3-0.5 per cent in larger urban places.

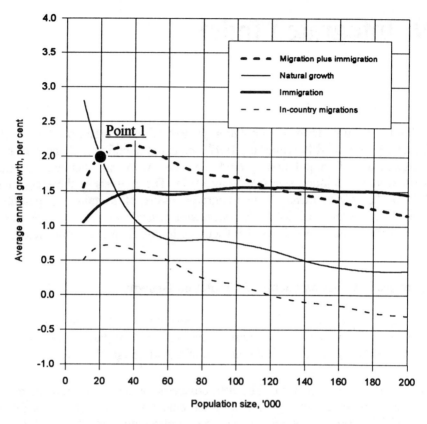

Figure 9.1 Sources of population growth of urban settlements in Israel in 1992-94

The diagram represents 70% Lowess fit lines for 80 urban settlements (10,000+ residents) included in the sample. The filled dot (Point #1) indicates the cross-over point in the settlement's growth after which migration becomes the predominant source of population growth.

Source: Portnov and Pearlmutter, 1997.

One aspect of these trends is of particular importance. It is the drastic change in the components of population growth exhibited by towns whose overall population ranges from approximately 10,000 to 40,000 residents. While the average rates of natural growth in these settlements drop from 2.8 to about 1.2 per cent, their attractiveness to foreign immigrants gradually increases and almost reaches that of larger urban localities, i.e. 1.5 percent per annum (Figure 9.1). In addition, this particular group of towns has a relatively high positive balance of internal migration that varies between 0.5 and 0.6 per cent per annum.

Notably, the structure of growth components within the above group of towns (10,000-40,000 residents) reverses *from the predominance of natural growth to that of the migration and immigration components.* While for settlements of 10,000 residents, natural growth constitutes, on the average, 65 per cent of their overall population increase, for settlements of 40,000 residents it does not exceed 35 per cent. In particular, the 50 per cent crossover point is observed within the group of settlements whose population size reaches the average of 20,000 residents. After reaching this size, the population growth of these urban localities tends to become *less dependent on natural causes (birth and death rates) than on the settlement's ability to attract newcomers and retain current residents.* This is clearly indicative of new growth capabilities, at least in terms of urban and regional planning.

A similar point of inflection is observed in Sweden (see Figure 9.2). Although in this country, both the rates of migration and those of natural growth tend to increase steadily in line with growth of population size of localities, the values of migration and natural growth appear to equalise when population size of localities reaches approximately 40,000 residents. (As mentioned above, in Israel, this point of inflection corresponds to 20,000 residents, and this difference is roughly proportional to that in the overall population size of the two countries in question: 8.9 million vs. 5.4 million residents, respectively).

It is noteworthy that at the inflection point observed in Sweden, both migration balance and natural growth are negative (see Figure 9.2). Characteristically, however, before and after this point, the effect of migration on population growth of Swedish towns is clearly more profound. Thus, in smaller towns (<40-45,000 residents) population decline is mostly due to negative net migration, while in larger localities, positive overall growth (OG) is mainly due to positive net migration supplemented by lower, albeit positive, rates of natural growth.

The MB/NG Index as Integrated Measure of Population Change

The inflection points marked in Figure 9.1 and Figure 9.2 (NG = MB in Figure 9.1 and –NG = –MB in Figure 9.2) are two solutions of the following generic equation:

$$|NG| = |MB|,$$

where |NG| and |MB| are the absolute values of natural growth (NG) and migration balance (MB), respectively.

The full list of solutions to this general equation includes:

1. NG = MG (both NG and MB are positive). This threshold (Point #1 in Figure 9.1) corresponds to the point after which MB becomes the dominant source of a settlement's population growth.
2. |MB| = |NG| (both MB and NG are negative). These conditions result in negative overall growth (OG) and thus correspond to absolute population decline.
3. |NG| = |MB| (one of the growth components is negative). If these conditions are met, the overall population growth of a settlement equals zero. This threshold marks, therefore, the point of inflection that separates the phases of population growth and decline.

Given these thresholds, different values of the MB/NG ratio can be interpreted according to a settlement's ability to sustain its population growth:

- NG > MB, while both NG and MB are positive (0<MB/NG<1): If these conditions are met, the population of a settlement grows mainly due to natural causes (fertility-mortality rates), rather than due to the settlement's attractiveness to newcomers. This phase of growth may be defined as *transitional* (or incipient) growth.
- MB > NG and both NG and MB are positive (MB/NG>1): Under these conditions, the population of a settlement grows primarily because the locality is attractive to newcomers (in-country migrants and foreign immigrants). This phase of growth may be defined as *sustainable*.
- MB > |NG| where MB is positive and NG is negative (MB/NG<-1): The population of the settlement is almost constant, owing to positive MB, which is offset by negative NG. This phase of growth may be defined as *transforming* growth, since the overall growth of the locality can easily become negative if the settlement lacks a 'migration feedback.'
- MB < |NG| when NG is negative (-1<MB/NG<0). These conditions indicate absolute population decline.

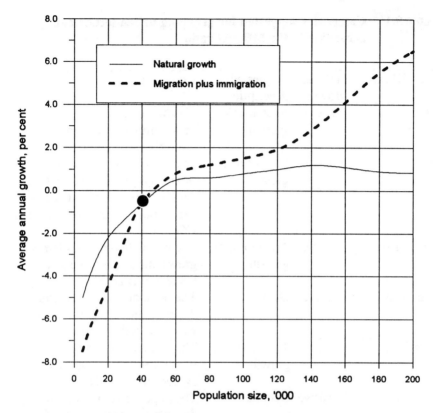

Figure 9.2 Changes in the components of population growth of urban settlements in Sweden as a function of their population size

Source: Plotted from the 1997 population data of Statistics Sweden.

The above list does not encompass the whole range of possible values of the MB/NG ratio. The complete list of these ratios and their interpretations are given in Table 9.1.

Table 9.1   Categories suggested for grouping urban settlements according to the MB/NG ratio

MB/NG ratio	Natural growth	Suggested description	Comment
Above 1.0	Positive	Sustainable growth	The population of a settlement grows primarily due to its attractiveness to migrants
From 0 to 1.0	Positive	Transitional growth	The population of a settlement primarily grows due to natural causes (fertility/mortality rates). MB is positive but is lower than NG.
From -1.0 to 0	Positive	Transforming growth	The population of a settlement grows due to natural causes while MB is negative.
Less than -1.0	Positive	Decline	The population of a settlement declines due to negative MB which exceeds positive NG
Less than -1.0	Negative	Transforming growth	The population of a settlement rises because positive MB exceeds negative NG.
From -1.0 to 0	Negative	Decline	The population of a settlement declines due to negative NG whose absolute value exceeds positive MB
From 0 to1.0	Negative	Decline	The population of a settlement declines due to negative values of both MB and NG
Above 1.0	Negative	Decline	As above

Source: Portnov and Pearlmutter (1999).

MB/NG Index vs. Alternative Indicators of Urban Growth

The importance of the MB/NG index clearly surpasses its direct application as a simple measure of population growth. Indeed, the ongoing attractiveness of a particular urban place implies its 'sound' economic development, favourable physical environment, and other preconditions that are essential for 'sustainable urban growth' in general.

Table 9.2 Natural growth, net migration and per capita GDP in selected countries

Country/region	Natural growth rate, % per annum	Net migration per 1,000 residents	GDP, $ per capita
A. Western Europe			
Austria	0.0	1.3	22,700
Belgium	-0.1	1.0	23,400
Denmark	0.1	3.2	23,300
Finland	0.1	0.4	20,100
France	0.2	0.5	22,600
Germany	-0.2	2.1	22,100
Italy	-0.1	0.2	20,800
Norway	0.2	1.6	24,700
Portugal	0.0	-1.5	14,600
Sweden	0.1	1.7	19,700
UK	0.1	1.1	21,200
B. Eastern Europe			
Armenia	0.5	-8.3	2,700
Belarus	-0.4	3.1	5,200
Russia	-0.6	2.1	4,000
Ukraine	-0.7	0.6	2,200
B. Middle East			
Egypt	1.9	-0.4	2,850
Israel	1.4	4.4	18,100
Jordan	3.1	0.0	3,500
Syria	3.2	0.0	2,500
C. Asia			
China	0.8	-0.4	3,600
India	1.6	-0.1	1,500
Turkmenistan	2.3	-1.4	3,300
D. Africa			
Burkina Faso	2.8	-1.3	1,000
Chad	2.7	0.0	1,000
Congo	3.1	-1.8	710
Ethiopia	2.3	-1.3	560
Ghana	2.4	-0.9	1,400
Guinea	2,3	-15.1	1,180
Mozambique	2.5	0.0	900

Source: Compiled from CIA, 1999.

Specific advantages of the derived index, compared to more direct indicators of attractiveness to migrants (such as overall population growth, in-migration, out-migration and migration balance), are a) simplification of cross-country comparison, b) comprehensiveness and c) ease of interpretation of results.

Simplification of Cross-country Analysis

The MB/NG index may simplify cross-country comparisons, since a comparison of migration rates, without considering the local differences in natural growth, may often be misleading.

Table 9.2 compares absolute rates of natural growth and net migration in countries characterised by different levels of economic development, and thus helps to illustrate this point.

As Table 9.2 shows, even within the group of West European countries, rates of natural growth vary from -0.2% (Germany) to +0.2% per annum (France and Norway). Considering the actual rates of net migration in these countries (on the average, 0.1-0.2% per annum), these variations in natural growth rates may indeed cause a considerable bias in a cross-country comparison. If, for instance, countries with a similar level of economic development such as Israel (GDP = $18,100; NG = 1.4 per cent), Portugal (GDP = $14,600; NG = 0.0 per cent), and Sweden (NG = 0.1 per cent; GDP = $19,700) are included in the sample, such a comparison would be meaningless unless normalised for differences in the rates of natural growth.

Comprehensiveness

Compared to direct measures of population growth (OG, NG and MB), the MB/NG index provides a more comprehensive demographic 'snapshot' of an urban community, and thus brings an additional dimension to the output of the analysis. For instance, it allows us to conclude whether positive net migration is either offset or enhanced by natural growth rates. Table 9.3, which provides a demographic snapshot of various geographic regions in China in 1982-90, illustrates this point.

As Table 9.3 shows, the *Tianjin, Jiangsu,* and *Anhui* regions exhibited in 1982-90 similar rates of overall growth (OG): 2.0, 1.7, and 1.8 per cent, respectively. At the same time, the first region had nearly equal and positive migration balance (MB) and natural growth (NG) of about 1.0 per cent each; the second region had a small positive MG (0.2 per cent), and relatively high NG of almost 1.7 per cent. Concurrently, in the third region

(*Anhui*), a negative MB (-0.2 per cent) was offset during the years in question by positive NG. From the demographic standpoint, these regions clearly represent different cases, while according to the absolute rate of OG, they may be perceived as nearly identical. Notably, the MB/NG index, calculated for each of these regions, produces different results (see Table 9.3). While for the first region (*Tianjin*), this index equals 1.11 (sustainable growth, as defined in Table 9.1), for the second region (*Jiangsu*), it returns 0.17 (transitional growth), and it is equal to -0.08 ('decelerating growth') for *Anhui*.

Likewise, regions with similar rates of MB may be compared. For instance, *Zhejiang* and *Hunan* provinces had in 1982-90 identical annual rates of migration (-0.28 per cent each). In the former region, however, NG was relatively low (0.87 per cent), resulting in an overall growth of 0.59 per cent, compared with the national average of 1.47 per cent per annum. At the same time, the latter region (*Hunan*) had an NG of 1.70 per cent, resulting in an OG of 1.42 per cent. Again, in these two cases, the MB/NG index produces different results (-0.32 and –0.16, correspondingly), which reflects the differences in the demographic situation between the two geographic regions.

Ease of Interpretation

Unlike those of net migration (whose actual rates may vary substantially), the values of the MB/NG index fall within a simple scale (see Table 9.1), and are thus easier to interpret.

For instance, a MB of 0.5‰ may be considered low in Belarus, where the average rate of net migration exceeds 3.0‰ (Table 9.2). Concurrently, the same MB (0.5‰) may be considered very high in Armenia, for instance, where the net migration rate is approximately –8.0‰.

Identical rates of MB, OG, and those of other 'conventional' indicators may thus be of different significance in different countries and regions. Unless local differences in the overall migration rates and natural growth are taken into consideration, the results of the analysis are difficult to compare and to interpret.

The MB/NG ratio allows this task to be performed more efficiently. For instance, if this ratio exceeds 1.0, and both MB and NG are positive, this indicates unambiguously that a community is attractive and its population is sustained by both internal (natural growth) and external sources (migration). Concurrently, values of this index below –1.0 indicate a substantial migration outflow, which is not compensated by natural growth, and thus causes absolute population decline.

Table 9.3   Components of population growth of regions in China in 1982-90, per cent

Region	Migration balance (MB)	Natural growth (NG)	Overall growth	MB/NG index*
Beijing	2.34	0.79	3.13	2.96
Tianjin	1.05	0.95	2.00	1.11
Hebei	0.39	1.39	1.78	0.28
Liaoning	0.21	0.96	1.17	0.22
Shanghai	2.38	0.50	2.88	4.76
Jiangsu	0.24	1.45	1.69	0.17
Zhejiang	-0.28	0.87	0.59	-0.32
Fujian	-0.06	1.78	1.72	-0.03
Shandong	0.27	1.26	1.53	0.21
Guangdong	0.24	1.67	1.91	0.14
Guangxi	-0.39	1.48	1.09	-0.26
Shanxi	-0.06	1.61	1.55	-0.04
Inner Mongolia	-0.18	1.43	1.25	-0.13
Jilin	-0.30	1.23	0.93	-0.24
Heilongjiang	-0.76	1.22	0.46	-0.62
Anhui	-0.16	1.92	1.76	-0.08
Jiangxi	-0.12	1.79	1.67	-0.07
Henan	-0.07	1.79	1.72	-0.04
Hubei	0.01	1.75	1.76	0.01
Hunan	-0.28	1.70	1.42	-0.16
Sichuan	-0.08	1.07	0.99	-0.07
Guizhou	-0.03	1.66	1.63	-0.02
Yunnan	-0.22	1.59	1.37	-0.14
Tibet	-1.68	1.84	0.16	-0.91
Shaanxi	-0.19	1.70	1.51	-0.11
Gansu	-0.46	1.69	1.23	-0.27
Qinghai	-1.71	1.58	-0.13	-1.08
Ningxia	0.96	1.95	2.91	0.49
Xinjiang	-0.26	1.83	1.57	-0.14

Source: Compiled from Zheng (1997).

* Calculated by the authors.

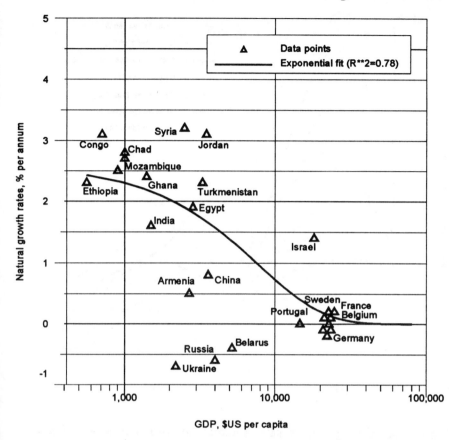

Figure 9.3 Rates of natural growth vs. per capita GDP in selected countries

Source: Plotted using statistical data from Table 9.2.

Emphasis on Migration

The MB/NG index has an obvious emphasis on the migration component of population growth, since it is calculated as the ratio between MG and NG, rather than *vice versa*. In other words, the emphasis is put on migration (nominator), while NG, placed in the denominator, is considered as a control. This is not accidental. The central assumption is that for a settlement's population growth to be sustainable, it must develop on the merit of the settlement's *ability to attract newcomers and retain current residents, rather than on natural causes such fertility and mortality rates.*

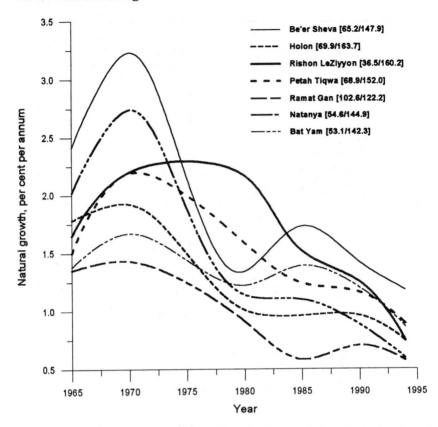

Figure 9.4   Changes in the rate of natural growth in selected cities of Israel in 1965-94

Figures in brackets represent population size of the towns in 1965 and 1995, respectively (thousands of residents)

This approach has a number of justifications. First, as Figure 9.3 shows, the annual rates of NG tend to decline as per capita wealth generated by a nation grows. With the exception of three republics of the former Soviet Union (Belarus, Russia and Ukraine), in which negative NG is attributed to cultural preferences and to economic harshness of a transition period, the trend for the rest of the sample is relatively straightforward: higher per capita GDP is accompanied by lower rates of natural growth. According to this trend line, NG in developed countries is likely to reach zero, and may even become negative.

This relationship between the average level of national wealth and absolute rates of natural growth is not surprising. In fact, Thomas Malthus, an English demographer and economist of the 18th-19th centuries, pointed out this relationship in his influential book 'An Essay on the Principle of Population,' published in 1798 (Malthus, 1798; reprint 1973). In particular, he argued that in virtually all European countries, absolute rates of natural growth had a tendency to decline. He attributed this trend to late marriage, a growing level of education, economic expenses, and 'moral restraint.'

Indications of continuously declining rates of natural growth can also be found in longitudinal studies of time-related changes in population growth. One such study (Portnov and Pearlmutter, 1999a) indicated, in particular, that between 1965 and 1994, the average rate of NG in major population centres of Israel dropped, on the average, more than twofold: from 2.0-2.2 per cent in the beginning of the period to less than 1.0 per cent in the late 1990s (Figure 9.4).

In view of declining rates of NG in line with growth of the national wealth and over time, attractiveness to migrants is the only factor that can ensure sustained population growth across various geographic areas of a developed nation. The role of migration is thus emphasised by the integrated index in question.

MB/NG Index: Problems of Application

Despite its advantages compared to other common indicators of urban growth, the MB/NG index in the originally proposed form (see Table 9.1) has a number of drawbacks. These limitations and methods of overcoming them will be discussed in this section in some detail.

Negative Inputs and Values Close to Zero

The MB/NG index calculated as the simple ratio of two growth components – migration balance (MB) and natural growth (NG) – may have two major problems, related to different inputs:

- First, the sign of the original index reverses when NG is negative and this may complicate the interpretation of results. This is of no concern for countries in which both average national rates of NG and those of individual regions and localities are positive (Africa, Asia, and most of the Middle East). In Europe, however, NG is often negative (see Table 9.2), which may complicate the use of the suggested index;

- Second, the original MB/NG index produces a band of disproportionately high values when the denominator of the ratio (NG) tends to zero.

These two problems are illustrated in Table 9.4, which reports the results of a trial run of calculations for a selected set of MB-NG inputs.

As Table 9.4 shows, the output for the first five cases (both MB and NG are positive) is within the expected range: MB/NG > 1.0 (Table 9.4), since this combination of growth components (MB>0, NG>0 and MB>NG) is defined in Table 9.1 as 'sustainable growth,' for which values of the MB/NG index are expected to exceed 1.0.

Let us, however, consider another set of cases (Cases 7-9) where both MB and NG are negative. Such cases correspond to the conditions referred to in Table 9.1 as 'decline.' However, for all of these cases, the MB/NG ratios are also *positive* (see Table 9.4):

MB=-100, NG=-150, MB/NG index = 0.67;
MB=-200, NG=-250, MB/NG index = 0.80;
MB=-300, NG=-350, MB/NG index = 0.86.

Confusingly, these cases have values of the MB/NG index which are identical to those returned by a very different combination of values for MB and NG, both of which are positive values (cases 12-14):

MB=67, NG=100, MB/NG index = 0.67;
MB=320, NG=400, MB/NG index = 0.80;
MB=602, NG=700, MB/NG index = 0.86.

The MB/NG indices for the cases in which rates of NG are low are even more confusing (cases 17-18 and 23-24):

MB=-50, NG=5, MB/NG index =-10.00;
MB=-100, NG=10, MB/NG index = -10.00;
MB=50, NG=-5, MB/NG index = -10.00.
MB=100, NG=-10, MB/NG index =-10.00.

For all of these cases, the MB/NG indices have high negative values, though the first two cases, in which negative MB exceeds positive NG, are referred to in Table 9.1 as 'decline,' while the second two cases, in which positive MB exceeds negative NG, are defined in Table 9.1 as 'transforming growth.'

Table 9.4   Trial test of the performance of the MB/NG index for different quantitative inputs

Case #	MB	NG	MB/NG Index
1	500	450	1.11
2	400	350	1.14
3	300	250	1.20
4	200	150	1.33
5	100	50	2.00
6	0	-50	0.00
7	-100	-150	0.67
8	-200	-250	0.80
9	-300	-350	0.86
10	-400	-450	0.89
11	-500	-550	0.91
12	67	100	0.67
13	320	400	0.80
14	602	700	0.86
15	890	1000	0.89
16	910	1000	0.91
17	-50	5	-10.00
18	-100	10	-10.00
19	-200	15	-13.33
20	-300	20	-15.00
21	-400	25	-16.00
22	-500	30	-16.67
23	50	-5	-10.00
24	100	-10	-10.00
25	200	-15	-13.33
26	300	-20	-15.00
27	400	-25	-16.00
28	500	-30	-16.67

Solutions

Categorical Scale

A simple solution to improving the performance of the MB/NG index is suggested in Portnov *et al* (2000). According to the suggested approach, the cases included in the research sample are ranked using a 4-point categorical scale: +2.0 (sustainable growth), 0.5 (transitional growth), -0.5 (transforming growth), and –2.0 (decline), based on actual values of the MB/NG index introduced in Table 9.1.

Table 9.5   Repeated calculation of the MB/NG index using a categorical scale and tangential transformations

Case #	MB	NG	Categori-cal scale	Tanh (1)	Tanh (2)
1	500	450	2.00	2.00	2.00
2	400	350	2.00	2.00	2.00
3	300	250	2.00	1.98	1.98
4	200	150	2.00	1.88	1.88
5	100	50	2.00	1.27	1.27
6	0	-50	-2.00	-0.49	-0.49
7	-100	-150	-2.00	-1.70	-1.70
8	-200	-250	-2.00	-1.96	-1.96
9	-300	-350	-2.00	-1.99	-1.99
10	-400	-450	-2.00	-2.00	-2.00
11	-500	-550	-2.00	-2.00	-2.00
12	67	100	0.50	1.37	0.68
13	320	400	0.50	2.00	1.00
14	602	700	0.50	2.00	1.00
15	890	1000	0.50	2.00	1.00
16	910	1000	0.50	2.00	1.00
17	-50	5	-2.00	-0.44	-0.22
18	-100	10	-2.00	-0.84	-0.42
19	-200	15	-2.00	-1.46	-0.73
20	-300	20	-2.00	-1.77	-0.89
21	-400	25	-2.00	-1.91	-0.95
22	-500	30	-2.00	-1.96	-0.98
23	50	-5	-0.50	0.44	0.11
24	100	-10	-0.50	0.84	0.21
25	200	-15	-0.50	1.46	0.36
26	300	-20	-0.50	1.77	0.44
27	400	-25	-0.50	1.91	0.48
28	500	-30	-0.50	1.96	0.49

Table 9.5, where the categorical scale is applied to the example data considered above, illustrates this method. Although the proposed scale does not reflect small differences between individual cases (see, for

instance, Cases 6-11; Table 9.5), it performs well with long-term averages. For instance, if the average value of the (revised) index in question for a given town over a 10-year period equals 1.5, this indicates that its population growth during this period was due mainly to the town's attractiveness to migration (MB/NG>1). As suggested in Table 9.1, this is indicative of sustainable growth. Concurrently, an average of -1.5 on the revised scale indicates an absolute decline in population. In other words, the suggested categorical values, averaged over a period of several years, do not deviate from the original MB/NG scale (see Table 9.1) and are still easy to interpret.

Tangent Transformations

Alternatively, various mathematical transformations can be used in order to increase the sensitivity of the MB/NG index to individual inputs without deviating from the original MB/NG scale (Table 9.1).

Our analysis of various possible transformations suggests that the hyperbolic tangent (*Tanh*) transformation yields reasonably good results (see Figure 9.5). The formulae of this transformation is as follows:

$$MB/NG\ index = a * \tanh((MB + NG)/b) = a * \left(\frac{e^{(MB+NG)/b} - e^{-(MB+NG)/b}}{e^{(MB+NG)/b} + e^{-(MB+NG)/b}} \right),$$

where MB = migration balance; NG = natural growth; e is the base of the natural logarithm (e=2.71828); and a and b are constants.

The proposed transformation has a number of advantages with regard to the calculation of the MB/NG index:

- First, this function has an upper and a lower threshold (see Figure 9.5). Quantitatively, these thresholds are controlled by one of the above mentioned constants: +/-a. Since the resulting values of the transformed MB/NG index cannot exceed these thresholds, it helps to avoid the occurrence of disproportionately high values such as those reported in Table 9.4 (Cases 17-28).
- Second, when absolute values of MB and NG are both positive, this results in high positive values of the MB/NG index, while negative values of these growth components tend to produce negative values of the resulting index. This is the response expected from the index in response to various combinations of its inputs (see Table 9.1).

A test run of this transformation is reported in Table 9.5 (Tanh (1)). A comparison between Table 9.4 (the original MB/NG index) and Table 9.5 shows that the *Tanh* transformation indeed helps to resolve a number of inconsistencies in the original index. In particular, cases where MB and NG are both negative (Cases 6-11, Table 9.4) are assigned negative values of the resulting index (see Table 9.5; Tanh (1)), as would be expected. Another considerable improvement is the treatment of cases where small values of the NG component result in very high values of the index (Cases 17-28, Tables 9.4 and 9.5). In addition to lower values these cases have after the transformation, they are divided into two subsets: negative values of the MB/NG index (Cases 17-22), and positive values of the index (Cases 23-28; Table 9.5). We may recall that such a differentiation was lacking from the original calculation (Table 9.4), even though these subsets represent very different situations: the first subset (Cases 17-22) is characterised by high negative values of MB resulting in absolute population decline, while the second subset has slightly negative NG and large positive values of MB resulting in absolute population growth.

For all these cases, the hyperbolic tangent transformation indeed improves considerably the performance of the integrated (MB/NG) index. However, the transformation in question is still not free of problems. As a close look at its response surface shows the function in question is

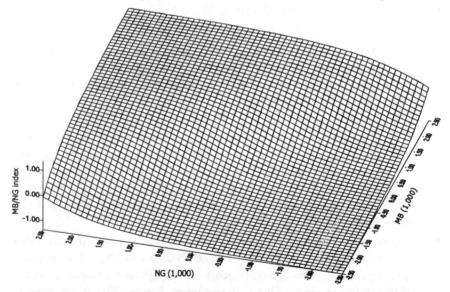

Figure 9.5   Surface response model of the hyperbolic tangent function to different MB and NG inputs

absolutely symmetrical (Figure 9.5). In other words, different combinations of MB and NG may produce identical outputs.

Let us, for instance, consider three different combinations of growth components:

1. MB = 500, NG = -200 (OG = 300);
2. MB = 100, NG = 200 (OG = 300);
3. MB = -200, NG = 500 (OG = 300).

For each of these cases, the resulting MB/NG index is equal, after the *Tanh* transformation, to 1.81. Such identical values are clearly not the response expected from the integrated index (see Table 9.1). Another problem results from the fact that the transformation in question does not discriminate between cases in which both growth components are negative (Cases 7-11; Tanh (1); Table 9.5) and those cases in which only one growth component is negative (Cases 17-22; Tanh(1); Table 9.5). According to the original definition of the MB/NG index (Table 9.1), these two types of cases should be treated differently, rather than uniformly.

Another problem associated with the simple *Tanh* transformation occurs in its treatment of cases in which both MB and NG have high values, and may possibly be equal. This combination returns the highest values of the revised MB/NG index. However, according to the original definition of the MB/NG index (see Table 9.1), its highest values ('sustainable growth') are expected to occur not only when MB and NG are positive, but also when *positive MB exceeds positive NG*, i.e. when a community grows primarily due to its attractiveness to migrants.

These drawbacks of the simple *Tanh* transformation can be dealt with by slight alterations to its formula. In particular, its first constant (*a*) may be treated as a variable, whose values vary in response to different combinations of the inputs – MB and NG (Table 9.6).

As Table 9.6 shows, the proposed adjustments to the constant in question are determined separately for eight sectors, in which MB and NG inputs are distinctively different (MB>0, NG<0, MB>NG, MB<NG, etc.). Since the constant in question controls, as mentioned, the upper and lower thresholds of the *Tanh* function, the values of this constant for each of these sectors are determined according to the maximum values of the MB/NG index which are expected to be found there (see Table 9.1). For instance, for the following combination of the growth components – MB>0, NG>0 and MB<NG (see the second line in Table 9.1), the maximum value of the MB/NG index is 1.0. This value appears in the corresponding row of Table 9.6. For another combination of growth

components (MB>0, NG>0, and MB>NG), referred to in Table 9.1 as 'sustainable growth,' the value of the *Tanh* constant is set to 2.0. As suggested, this value is the absolute maximum that the transformed MB/NG index is allowed to have (Appendix 1).

Table 9.6   Conditional adjustments of the *Tanh* (a) constant

MB	NG	MB vs. NG	Constant (a)
Positive	Positive	MB>NG	2.0
Positive	Positive	MB<NG	1.0
Positive	Negative	MB>|NG|	1.0
Positive	Negative	MB<|NG|	1.0
Negative	Negative	|MB|<|NG|	2.0
Negative	Negative	|MB|>|NG|	2.0
Negative	Positive	|MB|>NG	1.0
Negative	Positive	|MB|<NG	1.0

As both Table 9.5 (Tanh(2)) and Figure 9.6 show, the proposed adjustments to the *Tanh* (a) constant make the transformation more sensitive to individual inputs without altering the *Tanh* response surface as a whole.

The differences between the adjusted and unadjusted model can be illustrated for three characteristic combinations of the growth components marked in Figure 9.6.

- Point #1: MB = 600; NG = 400; MB/NG Index = 2.0 (Adjusted model); MB/NG Index = 2.0 (Unadjusted model);
- Point #2: MB = -400; NG = -400; MB/NG Index = -2.0 (Adjusted model); MB/NG Index = -2.0 (Unadjusted model);
- Point #3: MB = -800; NG = 400; MB/NG Index = -1.0 (Adjusted model); MB/NG Index = -2.0 (Unadjusted model).

While both adjusted and unadjusted models thus provide identical values of the MB/NG index for 'extreme' combinations of growth components (Points # 1 and 2), the adjusted model differentiates between Point #2 and Point # 3, in which negative MG is partially compensated by positive NG.

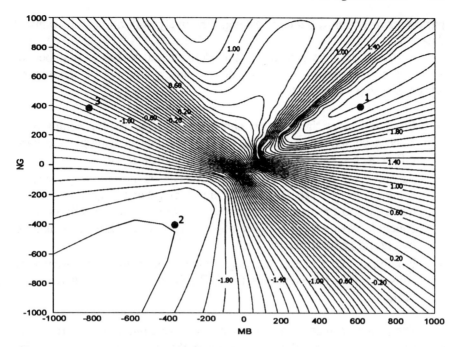

Figure 9.6   Contour plot of the adjusted *Tanh* function

Conclusion

We have shown that sustained population growth of urban settlements in developed countries is *due mainly to migration attractiveness, rather than to natural causes (fertility-mortality rates)*.

Based on this conclusion, an integrated measure of sustained population growth - the migration balance/natural growth ratio (the MB/NG index) - is proposed. The significance of this index clearly surpasses its direct application as a simple measure of population growth, since the ongoing migration attractiveness of a particular settlement implies its 'sound' economic development, favourable physical environment, and other preconditions which are essential for 'sustainable urban growth' in general.

The proposed index was presented in several formats, illustrating potential limitations arising from various combinations of values for its two inputs – NG and MB. The final form of the index, corrected by means of a hyperbolic tangent transformation, uses variable inputs for the parameter a, and is capable of dealing effectively with all combinations of data input.

In this final, revised form, the derived index has a number of advantages compared to more direct measurements of population attractiveness (OG, MB, etc.):

- First, the index in question simplifies a cross-country comparison, since a comparison of migration rates, without considering the local differences in natural growth, may often be misleading;

- Second, the index in question provides a more comprehensive demographic 'snapshot' of a community, and thus brings an additional dimension to the output of the analysis. For instance, it allows us to conclude whether positive net migration is either offset or enhanced by natural growth rates;

- Finally, unlike those of net migration (whose actual rates may vary substantially), the values of the MB/NG index fall within a simple scale.

The proposed index may thus serve as a valuable tool for urban and regional planners, particularly for gauging the impact of public policies aimed at sustaining population growth and economic development in socially and economically lagging regions.

10 Modelling Attractiveness of Urban Places

Attractiveness of urban places refers to their ability to attract resources – human and otherwise, and to retain existing assets. In the first part of this book (Chapters 1-6), we spared no effort to emphasise the importance of location factors such as remoteness, isolation, density patterns, inter-regional climatic differentials, etc. that influence the patterns of industrial location and of population change. It is nevertheless clear that location considerations alone *cannot* be held responsible for unique development trajectories, i.e. either success or failure, of a whole range of urban settlements. Clearly, there is a wealth of other factors, such as availability of housing, employment and services, to name only a few, which affect the development dynamics of towns. In this chapter, some of these additional factors will be discussed in detail, with reference to various empirical studies.

Modelling the Migration Behaviour

The neo-classical *human capital model* (Borjas, 1989; Poot, 1996) represents a common approach to modelling long-distance migration. This model suggests that individuals and families compare the present value of earnings at their current location with that at alternative locations, and the costs of moving. Richardson (1977) argues, however, that this cost-benefit approach appears to be oversimplified. He points out that the model rests upon several critical assumptions which may not always be justified, such as homogenous labour, constant returns to scale, perfectly competitive labour markets, and the absence of other, non-economic migration motives.

De Jong and Fawcett's (1981) *value-expectancy model* represents an attempt to explain inter-regional migration as a function of a broad array of factors, both economic and non-economic (environmental, cultural and social). This model, however, requires a precise specification of the *personally valued goals* that 'might be met by moving...and an assessment of the perceived linkage, in terms of expectancy, between migration behaviour and the attainment of goals in alternative locations.' Although this model may provide a perfect explanation of the behaviour of individual migrants, its ability to explain collective migration patterns appears to be fairly restricted.

Numerous empirical models of inter-urban and cross-district migration can also be found in the recent literature on migration decision-making (see *inter alia* Michel *et al* 1996; Portnov 1998a; Portnov and Pearlmutter 1997; Moore and Rosenberg 1995; Greenwood and Stock 1990). These empirical models cover a wide range of factors affecting migration, such as employment, housing, the level of urbanisation, and climatic differences between geographic areas, and generally employ multiple regression analysis as an analytical tool. While this technique often provides a good fit for specific statistical data at hand, it remains unclear whether such models may be applied outside of their original spatial and temporal framework.

Factors Affecting Migration

Motivations for migration are commonly defined in terms of a 'push-pull' continuum based on George's (1970) classification of international migration. This classification identifies two types of migration: a) migration caused by necessity or obligations, for instance by political and religious persecution or by other hardships at home, and b) migration related to socio-economic and cultural opportunities at the destination. The first type of migration factors are referred to as push factors, while the second group of motives may include both push factors (economic hardship in the area of origin) and pull factors (perceived economic opportunities in the destination).

Based on an extensive survey of the literature on migration, de Jong and Fawcett (1981) singled out six distinctive motives which govern migration patterns: economic motives, social motives, residential satisfaction, maintaining community-based social and economic ties, family ties, and attaining life-style preferences (Table 10.1):

Table 10.1   Main motives for migration (after de Jong and Fawcett, 1981)

Motive	Strength of the motive		Migration groups mostly affected
	Long-distance migrations	Short-distance migrations	
Economic	Strong	Weak	Working age, males
Social mobility/ social status	Moderate to weak	Weak	Young adults, low and middle class families, families with children
Quality of housing	Moderate	Strong	Young families, renters
Maintaining social and economic ties	Moderate	Moderate	Middle and older ages, wealthy migrants
Family ties	Moderate	Moderate to weak	Women, foreigners, young adults
Attaining life-style preferences	Weak but increasing	Moderate to weak	Retired, higher social strata

- *Economic motive.* A common motive for migration is economic: migrants seek better jobs, higher wages, and a materially better life in general. The key role in this process is played by inter-regional variations in the level of technology and socio-economic development that manifest themselves in wage differentials, differences in household income and expenditure, and the average rate of unemployment (Richardson, 1977; Moore and Rosenberg 1995; Portnov and Pearlmutter, 1999a);

- *Social mobility/social status.* Aspirations for higher social status are perceived as an important incentive for migration, especially that directed from rural to urban areas (Ehrlich *et al.* 1972). It is assumed, in particular, that the decision to move may be made either with the goal of enhanced opportunities for social mobility (educational and occupational advancements), or as an attempt to assure the social status of children rather than parents (Findley 1977);

- *Quality of housing.* Availability of housing is traditionally considered a key factor affecting the rates of inward and outward migrations (Lipshitz, 1997; Newman *et al,* 1995; Portnov and Pearlmutter, 1997).

Migration motivated by housing requirements may be attributed to changes in the composition of families which occur as a family goes through its life-circle, as well as from dissatisfaction with residential and environmental conditions of the place of origin;

- *Maintaining community-based social and economic ties.* The presence of relatives and friends in the area of origin is often considered as a constraint on migration; the rate of emigration tends to be greater for those without family connections compared to those with relatives in the area of origin;
- *Family and friends.* Family and friends at potential destinations have a strong influence on 'the decision to move and particularly on the decision where to move.' Family members often settle in the same urban centre or area, so that the newly arrived may obtain aid from relatives already living there;
- *Attaining life-style preferences.* As Rapport (1977, p. 81) notes, 'given an opportunity, people will select the habitat which best matches their needs, preferences, lifestyle and images, whether these be suburbs, old areas, or urban villages; large metropolitan areas or small towns.'

Although family considerations and community links of individual migrants play an important role in decision-making as regards migration in general, the factors determining the attractiveness of particular destinations are not in any way detached from the objective qualities of their environment. Therefore, the classification of migration on the basis of motivation is not the only approach to classification. An alternative one is based on objective socio-economic and physical qualities of the urban environment, such as *climate, location, population size, economy and incentives.* These five groups of factors are assumed to affect the decision-making of individual migrants both directly and indirectly (Portnov and Pearlmutter, 1999a,c):

- *Climate.* The harsh climate of some geographic areas, such as extreme temperatures, blowing dust, or a lack of water resources and vegetation, places considerable limitations on urban amenities and human comfort. Settlements located in unfavourable climatic conditions might therefore be less attractive and desirable to newcomers;
- *Location.* The multifaceted effects of this factor have already been discussed in Chaps. 1-3 of this book. We may recall, for instance, that restricted access to major metropolitan centres, where a great number

of jobs and services are concentrated, and spatial isolation from other urban localities within a geographic region has, in general, a negative effect on a town's attractiveness to potential migrants;

- *Population size.* The role of this factor in influencing the attractiveness of urban places has been widely acknowledged (More and Rosenberg, 1995; Fischer, 1976; Sonis, 1988). Its importance is often attributed to the fact that a certain population size is essential for maintaining a diversity of employment, services and living conditions. A number of studies (Bourne, 1975; Portnov and Pearlmutter, 1997) also suggested that reaching a certain population threshold may trigger a 'built-in mechanism' which ensures population growth of an urban settlement in the future;

- *Economy.* Economic factors influencing population growth of urban communities are extremely complex, and comprise three main components – employment, housing, and services. Each of these factors will be considered in some detail in separate subsections of this chapter;

- *Government incentives.* Many developed countries all over the world (Sweden, Finland, U.K., Japan, Israel, Norway, Republic of Korea, etc.) have regional policies designed to redirect population growth and economic development from overpopulated core regions to underdeveloped peripheral areas. To achieve this strategic goal, various policy mechanisms are employed, such as investment in infrastructure, provision of public housing and financial incentives to domestic and foreign investors in priority development areas. Though these measures are not always ultimately successful in achieving their goals, a number of empirical studies suggest they may have an effect on population movements in such regions (see *inter alia* Balchin, 1990; Diamond and Spence, 1983; Portnov and Etzion, 2000).

Availability of Employment

The predominant role of employment-related factors in interregional migration is emphasised by a neo-classical theory of regional development. According to this theory (Perroux, 1983; Richardson, 1977), inter-area migration is a 'readjustment process' that tends to reduce disequilibrium within local labour markets (Figure 10.1). As Richardson (1977, p. 90) notes, 'migrants tend to move from low-wage to high-wage areas and from areas of labour surplus to those with labour shortages.'

This point of view is also expressed in more recent migration studies (Greenwood and McDowell, 1991; Lipshitz, 1992; Michel et al, 1996).

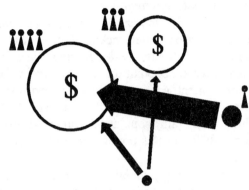

Figure 10.1   A simplified illustration of a neo-classical model of long-distance migration

According to the model, migrants move from low-wage to high-wage areas and from areas of labour surplus to the areas with labour shortages

Armstrong and Taylor (1993, p. 223), on the other hand, argue that labour is not sufficiently mobile. They claim that it does not respond readily to regional differences in either wage rates or unemployment, which are in any case only two of many factors affecting the movement of workers. They also suggest that the migration of labour, rather than decreasing regional disparities, actually increases them, since it causes the outflow of skilled and educated migrants from economically depressed areas.

The validity of this statement appears to be supported by the results of a comparative analysis of long-distance migration in Israel and Japan reported in Portnov (1999a,b). As this study indicates, the effect on migration rates of employment opportunities available in the region indeed appears to be highly significant in Japan (see Table 10.2); However, in Israel, a small country in which inter-regional commuting to jobs does not seem to be an obstacle, there was no statistical evidence of a similar effect.

Moreover, as this study shows, even in Japan, the availability of employment is not the only factor that influences migration patterns: The availability and cost of housing in a region also appear to be statistically significant ($F > 4.2$; $P < 0.05$).

Finally, in Israel, in spite of its small size, the effect of climatic differences between regions is also statistically significant ($F > 3.0$; $P < 0.1$; Table 10.2).

Moore and Rosenberg's (1995) study of migration flows in Canada (Table 10.3) also indicates that in *none* of the ethnic groups of migrants studied were employment considerations the only factors affecting the choice of destination. As Table 10.3 shows, these included - in addition to the unemployment rate, the percentage change in unemployment rate, and percentage change in average household income- the size of the respective immigrant group at the place of destination; the overall population size of the destination city, distance between the areas of origin and destination, differences in the size of housing stock, and the percentage of French-speaking population in the area.

Table 10.2   Factors affecting the attractiveness of geographic regions in Israel and Japan to migrants (analysis of variance)

Factor*	Israel		Japan	
	F	F sign.	F	F sign.
Climate	3.143	0.082	0.008	0.927
Density	0.094	0.761	0.210	0.811
Economy	0.025	0.876	0.577	0.450
Employment	1.033	0.363	10.232	0.002
Employment change	4.364	0.041	1.956	0.127
Housing construction	5.962	0.018	4.258	0.042
Housing prices	3.433	0.069	4.715	0.033
Combined effect	3.357	0.003	5.083	0.000
Mean square (explained)	3.853		1.532	
Mean square (residual)	1.148		0.301	
No of cases	66		100	

Source: Portnov (1999b).

Housing

Availability of housing is often seen as a key factor affecting migration, particularly if it occurs over relatively short distances and if it does not result in a change of the work-place (Kirschenbaum and Comay, 1974; Newman *et al.*, 1995; Portnov and Pearlmutter, 1997; Lipshitz 1997, 1998; Burnley *et al.*, 1997; Portnov, 2000; Stambøl and Sørensen, 1989; Stillwell and Congdon, 1991).

Thus, an extensive survey of in-country migrants in Australia (Burnley *et al.*, 1997) demonstrated that the desire to own an affordable home was the main reason for migration from the centre of Sydney to its periphery.

There is some empirical evidence that the availability of housing may be a driving force behind long-distance migration as well. Thus, in his studies of spatial distribution of foreign immigrants in Israel, Lipshitz (1997; 1998) concluded that some new immigrants chose to settle in the country's peripheral regions despite a shortage of employment there, because government subsidised housing resulted in fairly low housing prices in these districts.

Table 10.3   Modelling the effect of the birthplace of immigrants to Canada in 1981-86 on their choice of destination (regression coefficients)

Variable	Asia	Caribbean	Southern Europe	USA and Western Europe	Canada
Population size	3.72	-	3.67	2.17	1.97
Distance	-0.21	-0.09	-0.16	-0.21	-2.245
Income change	-	-	-	-	0.03
Climatic harshness[a]	-	-	-	-0.001	-
French-speaking population	-	-	-	-0.003	-
Housing change	-	-	-	-0.20	-0.18
Unemployment change	0.37	0.26	0.33		0.78
Unemployment rate	-0.11		-	-0.07	-
Immigrant community[b]	0.08	0.77	-		-
R^2	0.69	0.55	0.56	0.68	0.33
Sample size	140	87	114	194	216

Source: Compiled from Moore and Rosenberg (1995).
Note: Only coefficients significant at a 0.10 significance level are reported.
[a] Number of days with temperatures below 18°F; [b] proportion of the population of the same birth place in the city of destination.

In another study of population migration in Israel (Portnov and Pearlmutter, 1997), it was also argued that in the wake of the mass immigration of 1990-91 and the resulting shortage of housing, some residents of the major metropolitan centres of Israel tended to move to urban localities of smaller size in which housing is more available and affordable.

The effects of housing availability and affordability on migration are also seen in Japan. As Abe (1996) notes, high land and housing prices in the core of the country encourage people to settle in towns outside the major metropolitan areas and to commute daily to work in the central cities.

Moore and Rosenberg (1995) also report that the percentage change in the size of housing stock is one of the most significant factors influencing the choice of destination of immigrants to Canada, specifically those from USA, Western Europe and Canadian-born returnees (see Table 10.3).

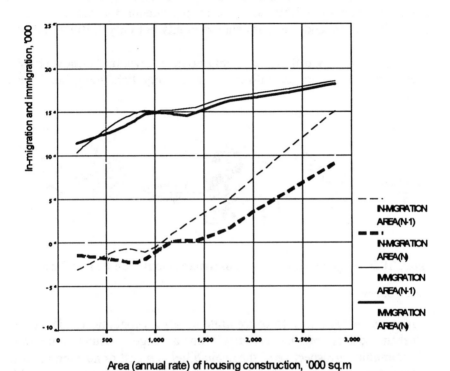

Area (annual rate) of housing construction, '000 sq.m

Figure 10.2   The effect of housing construction on the distribution of internal migrants and foreign immigrants in Israel

Source: Portnov (1998b).

The rates of construction are calculated separately for a given year (N) and the previous one (N-1). Each line is a seven-year (1988-94) average, calculated using data for individual administrative districts. The diagram indicates that availability of housing has a greater effect on the rate of internal migration than on immigration from abroad. While an increase in the rate of housing construction, say from 1,500 to 2,500 m² per annum, is likely to increase considerably the influx of internal migrants to a district, the effect of the same increase in construction rates on foreign immigration is much more moderate. Compared to new immigrants, internal migrants tend to be better informed about housing opportunities available in particular towns and communities.

Portnov's (1998b) study of housing-related migration in Israel helps to gain additional insights on the interrelationship between migration and housing availability in an area. As Figure 10.2 shows, housing construction has a greater effect on the area's attractiveness to in-country migrants (IM) than on its appeal to new immigrants (NI). If housing construction in a district increases from 1,500 to 2,500 m^2 per annum, for instance, it may gain 7,000-12,000 additional internal migrants but only 1,500-2,000 new immigrants.

To explain this difference in migration behaviour, Portnov (1998a) suggests the following generalised model of migration flows (see Figure 10.3):

Figure 10.3   A generalised model of urban population flow in Israel

Source: Portnov (1998a).

- *New immigrants* tend to concentrate in large, economically developed urban centres of the country with a large existing immigrant community, irrespective of the availability and cost of housing in these localities. They are attracted in the hope of obtaining suitable employment in cities which are the most prosperous centres of the country; and they are drawn to friends and relatives, who also provide local information which is generally not available about smaller urban localities with no immigrant communities.

- *Veteran residents* of the country (including former new immigrants) move outward from large urban centres towards localities of smaller size in which housing is more widely available and more affordable. The parallel processes of immigration and internal migration may be correlated indirectly via housing prices: the mass influx of new immigrants to a particular locality boosts housing demand and increases housing prices, which in turn may cause the outflow of current residents, who cannot afford decent housing in the metropolitan centres, to less central locations.

Another interesting trend highlighted in Figure 10.2 is the delayed effect of housing construction on internal migration. Indeed, the line of best fit representing the relationship between the rate of housing construction, lagged by one year (area$_{N-1}$) and the number of internal migrants (IM) is steeper and located relatively higher than the line representing the relationship between internal migration and current housing construction (in-migration/area$_{(N)}$). In other words, there may be a delay of a year or more between the time when housing is completed and the time when internal migration increases, a delay which is apparently caused by the slow spread of information on housing opportunities.

Infrastructure

Although the importance of road and utilities infrastructure as a means of promoting regional growth has been advocated by urban and regional planners since the publication of Marshall (1892) and Weber's (1929) landmark studies, relatively little empirical evidence has been obtained to date to confirm the presence of a causal link between public investment in infrastructure and development processes in a region.

In a recent study, Sasaki *et al.* (1997) investigated the effect of the high-speed rail transit in Japan (*Shinkansen*) on regional development using a supply-oriented econometric model. The results of the study were inconclusive and fell short of confirming that the *Shinkansen* indeed contributed to the dispersion of population and economic activity in Japan.

Rephann and Isserman (1994) investigated the effect of new highways on regional development in the U.S. using a quasi-experimental matching method. This method makes it possible to compare development trends across geographic areas, only some of which underwent certain changes. The results of this analysis showed that the beneficiaries of the interstate links in terms of economic growth were only counties in close proximity to large cities or having some degree of prior urbanization, such as a city with more than 25,000 residents, while rural and more remote counties exhibited fewer, if any, positive effects.

Although Bar-El (2000) found a relatively strong correlation between regional infrastructure investment and various indicators of economic growth across districts in Israel, his study was generally unable to confirm that the relationship in question was causal, i.e. that infrastructure growth indeed caused economic development in a region rather than simply followed it.

Portnov and Pearlmutter (1999b) suggested a dynamic model of the factors determining the location of private construction across urban areas, which incorporates infrastructure as one of its major components (see Figure 10.3).

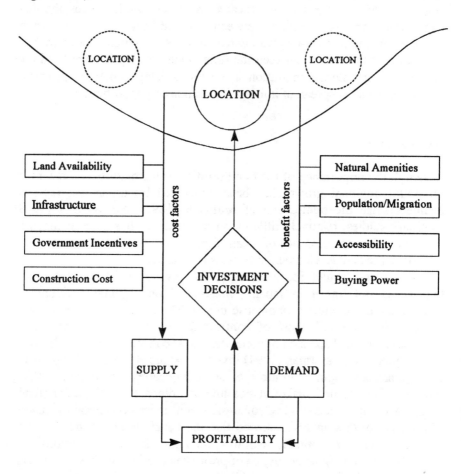

Figure 10.4   A dynamic model of the factors affecting the location of private construction across urban areas

Source: Portnov and Pearlmutter (1999b).

According to this model, cost and benefit factors form a dynamic 'supply-demand' paradigm affecting the potential profitability of investments and, therefore, investment decisions of private developers concerning alternative urban locations. In this framework, the availability of infrastructure is assumed to be an important factor of investment decision-making: Since the availability of roads and engineering utilities in urban areas lowers development costs, areas of developed infrastructure may be more attractive to private investors.

Subsequent testing of this model for towns in Israel confirmed that the effect of infrastructure development on private residential construction in urban localities in Israel indeed appeared to be statistically highly significant (see Table 10.4).

In another study, Portnov and Etzion (2000) analysed the effect of public investment in road infrastructure on population growth in core and peripheral regions of Israel. However, in contrast to the previously mentioned study, no statistically significant effect of infrastructure investment on regional development was revealed.

Services

The quality of social services and facilities, such as schools, shopping facilities and health services, is another factor often mentioned in conjunction with patterns of urban growth (Kirschenbaum and Comay, 1974; Newman *et al*, 1995; Portnov and Pearlmutter, 1999a).

We may recall, for instance, a comparison between municipalities of Norway with and without hospital facilities, reported in Chapter 3 of this book (Table 3.4). This study indicated clearly that municipalities with hospitals appear to have a considerably stronger migration 'pull' compared to municipalities with no hospital services.

Chosen and Kimni (1996) report the results of an in-depth survey of 2,000 migrants to and from Jerusalem, carried out in 1987 and 1989 by the Jerusalem Institute for Israeli Studies. The scarcity of places of entertainment in the city was given as the fourth most frequent reason for leaving the city, cited by 4 per cent of respondents, along with other 'push' factors such as secular-religious friction and Jewish-Arab relations. These factors, however, were greatly outweighed by other motives for out-migration, such as housing, employment and family circumstances. In particular, housing conditions were found to be the main reason for leaving the city; this factor was mentioned by 42 per cent of respondents. Employment-related factors were cited as the third most important motive, and were mentioned by one-fifth of out-migrants. Family reasons were ranked third, with 14 per cent of respondents citing them.

Table   10.4   Factors   affecting   the   rate   of   private   residential   construction   in   towns   of   Israel   in   1994   (MRA   –   linear-log form)

Factor	B	T	Collinearity statistics	
			Tolerance	VIF
Remoteness	-10.689	-0.736	0.620	1.614
Climate	17.010	0.675	0.861	1.161
Population	74.633	4.157[a]	0.522	1.914
Infrastructure	52.882	2.895[a]	0.795	1.257
Savings	39.023	2.488[a]	0.587	1.704
Unemployment	-38.648	-1.411	0.875	1.142
Migration	14.216	1.066	0.858	1.166
Constant	-142.510	-2.139[b]		
No of cases	80			
R^2	.602			
F	15.797[a]			

[a] two-tailed 0.01 significance level; [b] two tailed 0.05 significance level
Source: Portnov and Pearlmutter (1999b).

The motivations for migrating to Jerusalem were unusual, reflecting the city's unique status as a religious centre. While family ties (e.g. relatives in Jerusalem or a marriage to a Jerusalemite) were cited by 18 per cent of in-migrants, the proximity to institutions of higher education were cited by 21 per cent of the respondents, and another 17 per cent mentioned the availability of specific religious services as the main reason for migrating to the city. Somewhat surprisingly, the employment factor came only fifth in the hierarchy of migration reasons (after 'unique atmosphere of the city'), with 12.5 per cent of respondents indicating it as a major cause of in-migration.

In a detailed survey of migration motives in Norway carried out using a similar interview technique (reported in Stambøl and Sørensen, 1989), education-related factors were ranked fourth, 9 per cent of respondents citing this reason for migrating between municipalities, while employment (35 per cent), housing and environment (27 per cent), and family circumstances (12 per cent) ranked higher.

The effects of the quality of social services on the attractiveness of urban communities is also reported in studies utilising more sophisticated statistical techniques and aggregated sources of data. Thus, for instance, Portnov and Erell (1998a) found that educational conditions in urban localities (measured as the average number of pupils enrolled per class) were one of the most statistically significant factors affecting long-term population growth of small towns in Israel (see Table 10.5).

Table 10.5   Factors affecting population growth of small towns in Israel (analysis of variance)

Factor	F-Ratio	F-Probability
Climatic harshness[a]	6.329	0.013
Employment	1.268	0.288
Employment growth	0.106	0.745
Availability of housing	18.411	0.000
Index of clustering[b]	6.552	0.012
Population size	0.180	0.835
Regional centre[c]	0.002	0.967
Services	2.762	0.045
Combined effect	5.640	0.000
Mean Square (explained)	15.478	
Mean Square (residual)	2.744	
No of observations	180	

Source: Portnov and Erell (1998a).
[a] average annual number of days with moderate and severe heat stress; [b] see Chapter 14 of this book for this factor's description; [c] aerial proximity to the closest regional centre, km.

However, the authors of this survey had to acknowledge that the indicator used for the analysis (the average number of pupils per class in elementary and secondary schools) is relatively weak as a general proxy for the average level of services and facilities in a locality, whose use in the analysis was only justified by unavailability of other suitable development data.

Summing up, we may conclude that, despite certain contradictions in the results of existing empirical studies, there is, nevertheless, considerable evidence concerning the effect of non-location factors on inter-area migration. Therefore, these factors cannot be ignored in an attempt to identify and measure the effect of location on the long-term development and population growth of urban communities. With due regard for this, factors mentioned above, such as housing, employment, climatic harshness and services will be introduced as controls in our subsequent case studies (see Chapters 16-18).

PART III
URBAN CLUSTERS

For if they fall, the one will lift up his fellow: but woe to him that
is alone when he falls; for he has not another to help him up.

Ecclesiastes 4:10

11 The Nature of Clustering

Many academic disciplines make use of the concept of clustering, among them astronomy (clusters of galaxies), sociology (clusters of individuals and opportunities), economy (clustering of firms and manufacturing facilities), statistics (clustering of data) and geography and regional planning (clustering of settlements). In all these disciplines, the term cluster describes essentially same phenomenon: *a group of objects or entities located in close proximity to one another and joined by a certain type of link, either functional or gravitational.*

However, interpretations of the causes and consequences of clustering in these disciplines are distinctly different. In the following subsections, the different manifestations of clustering will be considered briefly, in order to gain additional insight into the phenomenon of urban clustering, which is our main concern.

Clustering of Galaxies

Cosmology distinguishes between two distinctive morphological categories of galaxy clusters: regular and irregular. While regular clusters show marked spherical symmetry and have a rich membership, irregular clusters have less well-defined shapes, and usually have fewer members (EB, 1999 – Cosmos).

In 1692, Newton (cited *ibid.*) asserted that the clustered structure of the astronomical universe is due to the effect of gravitation on astronomical masses initially scattered evenly:

> It seems to me, that if the matter of our Sun & Planets & all ye matter in the Universe was eavenly scattered throughout all the heavens, & every particle had an innate gravity towards all the rest & the whole space throughout wch [sic] this matter was scattered was but finite: the matter on ye outside of this space would by its gravity tend towards all ye matter on the inside & by consequence fall down to ye middle of the whole space & there compose one

great spherical mass. But if the matter was eavenly diffused through an infinite space, it would never convene into one mass but some of it convene into one mass & some into another so as to make an infinite number of great masses scattered at great distances from one to another throughout all yt infinite space.

Newton's hypothesis was later formulated mathematically, so that the joint probability (P) for finding two galaxies separated by a distance r is given by the following formulae:

$$P = (r/r_0)^{-1.8},$$

where r_0 is equal to about 2×10^7 light-years (beyond 5×10^7 light-years, the enhancement drops more quickly with distance than $r^{-1.8}$, for reasons as yet unknown).[1]

However, Newton's theory of clustering, based on the effect of gravitation forces, is not the only hypothesis attempting to explain the phenomenon at hand. Other popular theories are:

- *Primordial turbulence.* This explanation emphasizes the role of turbulence during the initial phases of galaxy formation. However, this idea is often criticised on the grounds that turbulence tends to decay over time, so that a magnitude sufficient to cause galaxy formation after decoupling is unlikely;
- *Energetic explosions.* Such explosions may have compressed large shells of intergalactic gas that subsequently became the sites for further galaxy formation and more explosions. This explanation predicts large holes and voids with galaxies at the interfaces, but it fails to provide an explanation for the formation of a 'seed' galaxy at the centre of each shell by some other process, of which there is no evidence;
- *Cosmic strings.* This theory suggests that cluster formation might take place by accretion around 'cosmic strings,' which are long strands or loops of mass-energy, as they are known in elementary particle physics. These strings are envisaged to arise from phase transitions in the very early universe in a fashion analogous to the way faults can occur in a crystal that suffers dislocations because of imperfect growth from, for example, a liquid medium. Though the dynamic properties of cosmic strings are not perfectly understood, it is suggested that they may give a clustering hierarchy similar to that observed for galaxies (EB, 1999 – Unorthodox Theories of Clustering).

Data Clustering

The statistical procedure of data clustering attempts to identify relatively homogeneous groups of cases (or variables) based on their selected characteristics. It sorts objects into groups, or clusters, so that the degree of association is strong between members of the same cluster and weak between members of different clusters. Most often, this technique uses a 'bottom-up' algorithm that starts with each case (or variable) in a separate cluster and combines clusters until only one is left (Nie *et al.*, 1975).

The analysis starts with the formation of a data set in which selected parameters are reported for a number of cases (observations). For instance, geographic locations may be described by characteristics such as population size, economic performance, population makeup, elevation above the sea level, climatic harshness, etc.

At the second stage of the analysis, measures of similarity/ dissimilarity of the cases are calculated, often using a simple method such as the squared Euclidean distance.[2] This distance matrix makes it possible to combine individual cases into clusters with similar properties.

During this procedure, cases are subsequently grouped into bigger and bigger clusters until all are members of a single cluster. When clusters are formed, the first two cases combined are those that have the smallest distance (or greatest similarity) between them. The distance between the new cluster and individual cases is then computed as the minimum distance between the cases outside the cluster and a case contained in it: Initially, all cases are considered separate clusters; there are thus as many clusters as there are cases. Then, two of the cases are combined into a single cluster. At the third step, either another case is added to the existing cluster, or two additional cases are merged into a new one. At every subsequent step, individual cases are added to existing clusters, combined to form new ones, or existing clusters are merged.

There are also 'top-down' techniques of data clustering, which start by dividing a whole set of data into smaller subsets. One such technique is a fast clustering algorithm that uses an initial binary sorting to scale the data to a more manageable size. Given an arbitrary dataset, the algorithm finds a user-specified number of clusters in the data. This technique places the emphasis not on the accuracy of the positions of the clusters, but rather on the time it takes to find them. The fast clustering algorithm first considers the entire data space as one big cluster. After this, the data set is subdivided iteratively until the specified number of clusters is found, or until it makes no sense to subdivide the clusters any further (Ribarsky *et al*, 1998).

Clustering in Social Groups

In the theory of social interaction (see *inter alia* Moreno, 1953; Hare, 1962; Hare, 2000), the successful formation of a social nucleus (cluster) is often attributed to the presence of established channels of communication. As Moreno (1953, 1978 reprint, p. 451) notes,

> the dynamic character of psychological currents which drive individuals and groups towards further and further differentiation produces also its own barriers and controls. One process, the process of differentiation, draws the groups apart; the other, the process of transmission and communication, draws the groups together.

To study interactions among individuals, Moreno suggested an interesting applied tool, called a 'sociogram.' This tool, which was discussed in some detail in Chapter 2 of this book, maps intra and inter-group relationships in a form of a graph, in which vertices represent individuals, while links represent the nature of inter-personal relationships - repulsion, indifference or attraction (see Figure 11.1).

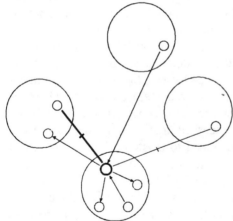

Figure 11.1   'Social atom' of an individual (after Moreno, 1953)

In the sociogram, small circles represent individuals, while big circles stand for spatial locations. Inter-personal attitudes are represented by different lines, which indicate attraction (arrow), mutual attraction (crossed line), and repulsion (bold line). Although sociograms are primarily used to map people's attitudes, they can also be used as a tool for diagramming the intensity of inter-personal interaction.

Though individual sociograms can be extremely complex, nearly all of them appear to share a simple idea, which Moreno calls the 'law of social gravitation. This law states that 'the intensity of inter-personal interaction in a "social atom" declines in inverse proportion to the distance between individuals and in direct proportion to the intensity of inter-personal communication'.

Hare (2000), however, argues that facility of communication among a group's members, emphasized by Moreno, is not a sufficient precondition for the formation of a sustainable social cluster. In contrast to Moreno's concept, Hare places a particular emphasis on distribution of roles among the group's members, as well as on resource provision and the efficiency of leadership. In particular, he suggests that success or failure of a social group is determined by the combination of four factors – meaning, resources, integration and goal attainment:

- Meaning is found in the presence (or lack thereof) of a common task;
- Resources are acquired to accomplish the task at hand;
- Integration is determined by the assignment of distinctive roles for each of the group's members and appointment of the leader;
- Goal attainment means focusing on the work at hand, and avoiding possible detractions.

Each of these components is assumed to be of importance in its own right. For instance, if roles are not appropriately distributed, group members may start to seek additional direction from the leader or engage on a minor 'power struggle,' which is generally destructive for the entire group. Following this conclusion, Hare *(ibid.)* describes a number of possible roles that can be assigned to a group's members in order to strengthen its cohesion:

- The 'leader' (or a 'standard setter'), who evaluates progress toward the goal;
- The 'follower,' who goes passively with the work;
- The 'encourager,' who promotes the general idea of cohesiveness;
- The 'harmoniser,' who resolves disputes interfering with cohesiveness;
- The 'compromiser,' who meets the other by coming half way;
- The 'gatekeeper,' who coordinates the activity in the interest of cohesiveness, and
- The 'group observer,' who keeps records for evaluating the extent to which cohesiveness is maintained.

Clusters of Opportunities

The competing destination model is a popular approach to migration modelling. This model, whose basics are described in some detail by

Fotheringham (1991), assumes that migrants choose their destinations among clusters of opportunities.

This model assumes that an individual migrant cannot analyse every possible destination prior to making a decision about where to move. First of all, it is assumed that migrants do not have all the information necessary to conduct such a sophisticated analysis, particularly when the overall number of possible destinations is large. It is also believed that individuals have a very limited capacity for processing information about multiple opportunities available in different geographic areas.

It is, therefore, suggested that migrants process spatial information on possible destinations hierarchically, first evaluating clusters or groups of alternatives and then evaluating only alternatives within a selected cluster. When the number of alternatives is small, individuals may choose among clusters of opportunities directly. However, when the number of alternatives increases, the number of clusters also grows until it reaches a certain point beyond which there are too many clusters to evaluate and a new tier in the hierarchy needs to be established, i.e. a hyper-cluster of opportunities.

If migrants evaluate all of the alternatives, disregarding their spatial clustering, the attractiveness of a cluster is assumed to be simply the sum of the attractions of the individual destinations within the cluster:

$$V_{is} = n_s V_i$$

where V_{is} is the overall attractiveness of cluster s to migrants from origin i; V_i is a measure of the attractiveness of a destination in the cluster for migrants from origin i, which is measured by summation of all the site attributes essential for migrants such as employment opportunities, housing prices, distance, etc.; and n is the number of alternatives in cluster s.

However, if migrants have a large number of possible destinations, their selection process is assumed to be necessarily hierarchical. To reflect this process, the above formula can be rewritten in the following form:

$$V_{is} = (n_s V_i)^\alpha,$$

where α is an exponent that reflects the relationship between the perceived attractiveness of a cluster and its physical magnitude; this exponent is assumed to be positive; in the presence of agglomeration forces among cluster members, its value will be $\alpha > 1$, whereas if individual clusters are in competition, it will be in the range $0 < \alpha < 1$ *(ibid.)*.

Clusters of Industries

Marshall (1890; 1892) attributes the grouping of production facilities in clusters to the law of *increasing returns*. According to this law, 'an increase of labour and capital leads generally to improved organisation, which increases the efficiency of the work of labour and capital.' He also argues that the law of *diminishing returns*, which means an extra return 'smaller in proportion ...to the last application of capital and labour,' generally leads to dispersion. In the case of a farmer, Marshall (1892, p.92) describes the effect of this law as follows:

> As his sons grow up they will have more capital and labour to apply to land; and in order to avoid obtaining a Diminishing Return, they will want to cultivate more land. But perhaps by this time all the neighbouring land is already taken up, and in order to get more they must buy it or pay a rent for the use of it, or migrate where they can get it for nothing.

In contrast, Weber (1929) considers transport costs the major driving force behind the process of industrial agglomeration in clusters of production facilities. He assumes that the 'agglomeration factor' is an 'advantage or a cheapening of production or marketing which results from the fact that production is carried out on to some considerable extent at one place'. (For further discussion of this concept see Chapter 5 of this book, which deals with indirect measures of urban location).

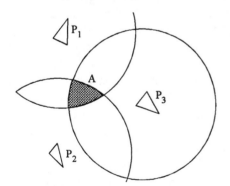

Figure 11.2 Optimal location of the centre of agglomeration for three places of production (after Weber, 1929)

According to Weber's concept, the optimal location of the centre of agglomeration (A) is determined by the minimum point of transportation cost from each of the production facilities (P_1, P_2 and P_3).

In an attempt to address the question as to where agglomeration will take place, Weber suggests that the centre of agglomeration 'must obviously lie within the common segments of the critical *isodapanes* (lines of equal transportation costs – the authors), for within these common segments lie the points at which production may be concentrated without prohibitive deviation costs' so that 'the precise location of the centre of agglomeration will thus be that of the minimum point of transportation cost' (Figure 11.2).

In more recent regional economic studies, clustering is seen as a means of reducing not only the transport costs but also the cost of setting and maintaining support infrastructures such as roads, power, telephone lines, and public services. As Smith (1975) argues, the saving from clustering in terms of land consumption and length of infrastructure may be considerable, though they may neither be attributable directly 'to any of the individuals, nor to pieces of land, whether within or outside the cluster.'

Urban Clusters

In the introduction to his influential book on Central Places in Southern Germany, Christaller (1933; 1966 English edition, p. 1) wrote:

> In the same region we see large and small towns of all categories, one category besides another. Sometime they agglomerate in a certain region in an improbable and apparently senseless manner. Sometimes there are large regions in which not a single place deserves the designation of towns, or even of market…but why are there, then, large and small towns, and why are they distributed so irregularly?

In an attempt to answer this question, Christaller suggested that this 'improbable' pattern of urban settlement is the result of different functions individual urban places may perform: functions with a larger spatial range of service tend to concentrate in a smaller number of evenly distributed larger settlements, guaranteeing a 'safety net' of consumers for high-rank services, while functions of lower rank are found in a larger number of smaller localities which are also more or less evenly distributed (see Chapter 3 of this book for a more detailed discussion). As a result, large cities are surrounded by an 'optimal hexagonal' net of smaller urban localities providing services for more localised populations.

Since these overlapping nets of differently ranked central places are formed, according to Christaller's theory, somewhat independently from each other, the formation of urban clusters is thus perceived essentially as an accidental process. In other words, the presence of adjacent urban places of different rank is attributed to the functional differentiation across urban places according to the principle of market efficiency, and not to a dynamic growth of functionally inter-linked neighbouring urban communities.

Surprisingly, since the publication of Christaller's landmark study, there have been only isolated attempts to examine further the nature of urban clustering, or to investigate the process of cluster formation and the effect of this process on the long-term development of individual towns.

One such study (Golany, 1982), emphasises the role of urban clusters as a means of reducing the perception of spatial isolation in peripheral arid regions. The author of this study argues that, in addition to psychological effects, the clustering of towns in sparsely populated arid zones may result in additional economic benefits, normally associated with agglomeration, such as lowering the costs of infrastructure and transportation. He also argues that, as a result of urban clustering, employment and services provided by the cluster's component towns should be more diversified and better suited to the needs of the local population. He also asserts that with clustering, residential areas can be located advantageously with respect to polluting industries that might be 'placed in another cluster somewhat removed." However, it should be noted that the author of this study provided no empirical evidence of the possible positive effects of urban clustering.

Krakover (1987) went somewhat further, analysing the benefits and drawbacks of urban clustering using a set of statistical data for two metropolitan regions of the U.S. – the North Carolina Piedmont cluster of towns and Philadelphia, which has a more centralised pattern of settlements.

The major hypothesis tested in this study is that towns in clustered and centralised patterns of urban settlements undergo two distinctive phases of growth:

- During the first phase, when towns are relatively small, their prevailing economic, technological, and spatial conditions are conducive to the existence of agglomeration economies. Under such conditions, the rate of economic development may be faster in a single large city than in each of a number of smaller towns forming a cluster of equal overall population size, because firms in a cluster of cities are spread among several centres. Furthermore, a larger city develops earlier a population threshold high enough to justify the entrance of higher order services;

- At the later phase, however, when cities pass a certain population threshold, diseconomies of excessive concentration may become established earlier in the larger city than in a cluster of smaller towns, since an increasing number of entrepreneurs might realise that they may be better off by moving their enterprises to suburban locations. In turn, such an economic spillover may be slower in a cluster of smaller cities, in which the adverse effects of such diseconomies may be less pronounced. Therefore, when economic spillover occurs around towns which are part of a cluster, a wider and more equitable spread of growth may be expected.

To test these assumptions, the dispersed city comprising Greensboro, Winston-Salem and High Point, in the North Carolina Piedmont region was compared with the urban field of Philadelphia, which is characterised by more centralised settlement pattern.[3]

Annual time-series data on employment in retail trade in the two regions between 1962 and 1978 were compared. The results of the analysis for two years covered by the study – 1968 and 1977 – are diagrammed in Figure 11.3.

As Figure 11.3 shows, the differences between the urban fields of Greensboro (the Piedmont cluster) and Philadelphia are clear. In 1968, the rate of economic growth of towns in the Philadelphia region varied with distance from the urban core, with two positive peaks of growth at about 15 and 75-80 miles from the central city. At the same time, towns in the Piedmont appeared to grow at about the same rate, irrespective of distance from the centre of the region.

By 1978, however, the rates of economic growth in both regions varied considerably. While in the Piedmont cluster, the peak of growth shifted towards more remote counties, lying some 75-80 miles from the central city, in the Philadelphia region, the peak of economic growth occurred in closer proximity to the central city, about 25-30 miles from the city centre. In counties located beyond this peak, the index of economic development appeared to be about forty points below the maximum observed in more central counties.

The author of this study concluded that these different spatial patterns of economic growth are evidence that clusters of towns lead to growth having 'a higher likelihood of spreading over space in a wider and more equitable fashion' than in single cities with a comparable overall population.

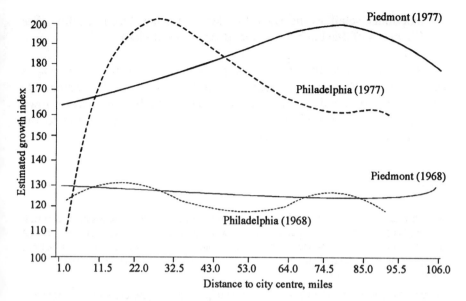

Figure 11.3 **Economic growth in the Piedmont cluster of cities and in Philadelphia's single-centered region as a function of the distance from the central city**

Source: Compiled from Krakover (1987). The lines are polynomial regression fits for the respective groups of counties.

The findings of this survey should nevertheless be treated with some caution, not least because there are considerable differences between the regions studied:

- The regions studied have different overall populations - 1 million residents in the Piedmont region vs. 7 million in the Philadelphia region;
- The two regions differ in the composition of their population (racial and ethnic make-up, etc.), average levels of income, employment base and other essential characteristics.
- Considerable differences between the two regions in the distribution of towns of different sizes (see Endnote 3 below) further limit the accuracy of the comparative analysis;
- Finally, in determining the location of a town in the cluster, aerial distances from the central city were used. This method, while simple, has several drawbacks. In particular, since distances relate only to the main urban centre of the region, the effects of distances among

individual small towns within a cluster are not accounted for. (See Chapter 4 of this book for a more detailed discussion).

Additional in-depth study of the phenomenon of urban clustering is thus required, with particular attention to the provision of fully comparable settlement samples and the development of more reliable estimates of town location both within a cluster of adjacent towns and in relation to the closest major city or group of such cities.

Notes

[1] Recent astronomical surveys indicate the existence of huge regions of space, measuring hundreds of millions of light-years across, in which galaxies are notably deficient or even totally absent. The presence of holes and voids is often considered as a natural complement to the idea of super-clusters, surrounded by thinly 'filled' regions (EB, 1999-Statistics of Clustering).

[2] A major disadvantage of such a matrix is its dependency on the units of measurement. For example, mean humidity for a location may vary from 20 to 100 per cent, while the mean temperature may vary from −5 to 30°C. If variables having different units of measurement are used, they must first be standardised, using z-scores of the initial values.

[3] The area of the Piedmont cluster contains twenty-nine urban places with the following size distribution (as of 1970): two cities of about 150 000; one of about 60 000; five in the range 13 000–17000; six in the range 4000–8000; and fourteen towns with population of fewer than 4 000 inhabitants. The total population of the whole urban field in 1970 was about 1.1 million people. The distance from Greensboro, the major population centre of the cluster, to the population centre of the most remote county is 106 miles. In contrast, the urban field of Philadelphia is characterised by the presence of one large urban unit, the city of Philadelphia. In 1970, the city had close to two million people. The next largest city within the urban field, the city of Allentown, had about 110,000 inhabitants. In general, the urban field of Philadelphia consisted of 233 urban entities in which the population ranged between 2 000 and 110 000. These entities are distributed in twenty-three counties consisting of more than seven million people. The population centre of the most remote county is about 93 miles away from central Philadelphia (Krakover, 1987).

12   Formation of Urban Clusters

There is no universal process through which urban clusters are formed. Instead, there are three distinctive and often interrelated processes. First, urban clusters can be formed through a process of *natural bifurcation* of existing population centres as they grow and diseconomies of concentration increase. Second, *simultaneous growth* and eventual merging of adjacent quasi-urban localities and villages, may result in the formation of urban clusters. Finally, urban clusters may be formed by deliberate *planning actions,* such as those resulting in the establishment of a net of new towns around major population centres in the U.K., the U.S.A., Israel and other countries all over the world. In this chapter, these distinctive mechanisms of the formation of urban clusters will be discussed consecutively.

Urban Bifurcations and Suburban Sprawl

To estimate the extent of suburban sprawl in American cities, Mills (1980) suggested the following simple exponential function:

$$D(x) = D_o e^{-bx},$$

where *D(x)* is population density at distance x from the centre of a metropolitan area, e is the base of the natural logarithm; D_o is the density in the city centre, and b is parameter estimated from the data.

According to this model, if two metropolitan areas have the same total population and radius, the one with a higher value for the parameter b has more inhabitants within any given distance of the centre. Thus, a highly centralised metropolitan area has a large value of b and a decentralised metropolitan area has a smaller one. In the limiting case, where $b=0$, density is constant through the metropolitan area. The parameter b is therefore an indirect measure of suburbanisation, and is called the *density gradient.*

The model in question predicts a continuous drop in residential densities as the distance from the centre increases – a pattern which may not be characteristic of major urban centres. In the central business districts of such cities, residential functions are often replaced by non-residential uses, while high residential densities often occur in suburban rings (see Alonso, 1964; Clark, 1982; Krakover and Morrill, 1992).

The concentration of residential development outside the metropolitan centre may be described by modifying the above density function as follows:

$$D(x) = D_o x e^{-bx}$$

This equation predicts that the maximum population density will occur at a certain distance from the urban centre ($x=1/b$, where $0.0<b<1.0$), rather than at the urban centre itself ($x=0$), and may provide a better description of the patterns of residential concentration around metropolitan areas. However, regardless of which version of the above models provides a better description of the phenomenon at hand, neither attempts to explain its causes and temporal dynamic.

In an attempt to explain this dynamic, Fujita and Mori (1997) developed a 'catastrophic bifurcation' model of an urban system. This model is based on the assumption that as the population of the economy increases gradually, new cities are created periodically as the result of the bifurcation of the existing system, and that as the number of cities increases, the urban system may approach a highly regular central place system. This interesting concept will be discussed below in some detail.

Dynamic Model of Urban Bifurcation

Fujita and Mori's model *(ibid.)*, like most other location studies, starts with the assumption of an unbounded homogeneous plain. (See Part I of this book for a more detailed discussion).

It is also assumed that only one city is situated on this homogeneous plane, and that the population of this city produces all of the manufactured goods in the economy (As assumed, the concentration of the entire production in a single city is due to the endogenous agglomeration force). The city is surrounded by an agricultural hinterland in which all agricultural goods are produced. Because of transport costs, these agricultural goods are cheaper in this city than in more distant places.

It is also assumed that, at some point, the real income of workers in the city starts to rise, attracting more workers from the hinterland. This results in an increase in the number of consumers, leading to a greater demand for manufactured goods, attributed primarily to higher incomes. This, in turn, causes an additional concentration of manufacturing firms in the city, a process that may continue as long as the economy is small and positive effects of agglomeration persist.

As the population of a city grows, and it serves an ever-larger agricultural hinterland, the positive effects of agglomeration are likely to diminish. Locations comparatively far away from the urban centre may become increasingly attractive to new manufacturing firms, while the growing number of firms in the city may make competition there more intense. However, until the population of the city grows sufficiently large, the forces of agglomeration outweigh those of dispersion, preventing the establishment of competing urban centres.

However, increasing population brings the system to a critical point at which a hinterland location is equally attractive to one inside the existing city. The existing mono-centric system may then become unstable, as more and more firms consider relocating to green field sites.

As Fujita and Mori suggest, the existing city may cease to decline when the newer centre reaches equal size. At this point, the mono-centric settlement system has already been transformed into a duo-centric one. If the overall population continues to increase, new frontier cities may be created in the expanding agricultural hinterland, while the older cities survive due to their 'lock-in effects.' Arguably, this may lead in the long run to the creation of a highly regular system of central places.

Compared to the traditional theory of urban location, the concept of 'catastrophic bifurcation' is more dynamic, yet it has a number of drawbacks:

- First, the model has no clear spatial dimension. It neither indicates the physical dimensions of the city at which the 'catastrophic bifurcation' occurs, nor does it reflect the relationship between the direction of urban expansion and the existing patterns of the intra and inter-regional communication network.
- Second, like most neo-classical models of regional development, the Fujita-Mori model in question has no social dimension. According to the basic assumptions of this model, workers follow readily the movements of firms, disregarding other important factors such as commuting thresholds, or the availability and cost of housing, services and facilities, etc;
- Third, the model's assumption that a new city is formed only after an existing urban place has reached the critical point of 'catastrophic bifurcation,' does not seem to be compatible with the simultaneous co-

existence in an urban system of a broad variety of urban places of different sizes, and continuous formation of new settlements, often at considerable distances from the existing urban centres.

Socio-spatial Model of Urban Clustering

The model we suggest may address some of the drawbacks of the 'catastrophic bifurcation' model, particularly those related to its lack of a spatial dimension and overly deterministic approach to migration. Instead of postulating that migrants follow the movements of firms, the suggested model attempts to determine under which circumstances and to which direction the outflow of residents from an 'overloaded' city may occur, in response to a variety of factors – disposable incomes, housing, cost of commuting, etc. The suggested model includes nine major components (Figure 12.1):

1.   *Wages* (W) – the average level of personal income for a given region. This can be measured either as the mean income per employee or as the mean income per family in the region;

2.   *Disposable income* (D) - the proportion of the average income left after deducting mandatory payments, such as taxes, health insurance, education, etc. (not including housing-related payments, which in our model are considered separately);

3.   *Accessibility from the central city* (A) – the proportion of the average income in the region devoted to commuting. This component was introduced because it is assumed that poor access or remoteness of the area may both increase the proportion of income devoted to commuting. (The proportion of income, rather that the actual value, was chosen to allow comparison with other components of the model;

4.   *Housing cost* (H) – the proportion of average income allocated for housing-related payments - either rent or mortgage for a standard housing unit;[1]

5.   *The point of origin* (O) - the geographic location of the city. This point refers to the city's geographic centre or its central business district. We shall mark the origins of all other urban places to be formed in the spatial system by adding subsequent numerals – O_1, O_2 etc.;

6.   *Growth area* (G) - the area in which the most intensive urban growth is expected to occur. Growth may be measured as an increase in the density of population, the overall rate of housing construction, etc.;

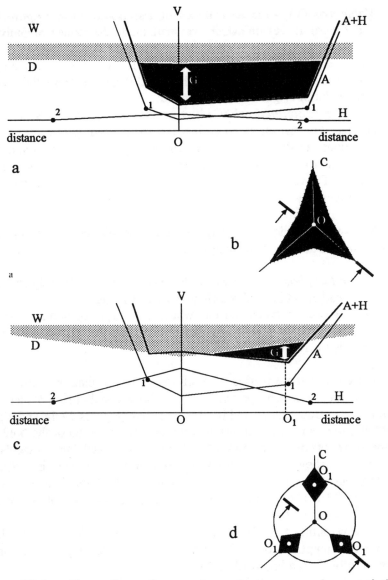

Figure 12.1   **Formation of an urban cluster around an existing urban place – a two-phase dynamic model**

a - initial phase (cross section along the arrow-marked line on the circular diagram below); b – initial phase (two-dimensional pattern of growth); c and d – expansion phase (cross-section and two-dimensional model, respectively); W,D,H,O,C,A and G are model components (see text for definition); 1, and 2 –points of inflection defined in the text.

7.   *Value axis* (V) - the vertical axis of a section diagram (Figure 12.1a and Figure 12.1c) on which we shall mark the values of individual variables;

8.   *Distance axis* (distance) - the horizontal axis of a section diagram (Figures12.1a and 12.1c) on which the distances from the existing city's point of origin (O) are measured;

9.   *Communication network* (C). Let us assume that the city's origin (O) is located on the intersection of major roads, leading to three different directions, as shown in Figure12.1a and Figure 12.1c. This simplified road pattern will help us to illustrate the expected differences in the spread of development in areas adjacent to roads compared with those more remote.

We shall consider separately two different phases of growth which may occur in a given settlement system:

I.   *The initial phase,* during which the existing city is relatively small and its spread effect is localised (Figure 12.1a-b), and

II.   *The expansion phase* during which the city's economic base and territory expand, possibly to the critical point of spatial bifurcation (see Figure 12.1c-d).

For each of these phases, two different types of diagrams are used to represent the settlement pattern: a) two-dimensional 'plan' models (see Figures 12.1b and 12.1d), and b) cross sections (Figures 12.1a and 12.1c). The latter diagrams are sections drawn along the segments of the bold line, in the direction of the arrows on the two-dimensional 'plan' models. As Figure 12.1 shows, the sections are drawn to illustrate the expected development along a major road (drawings right of the V-axis; Figures 12.1a and 12.1c), or in more remote areas (drawings left of the V-axis; Figures 12.1a and 12.1c).

Having outlined the basic components of the model, we may define the main assumptions on which the model rests, starting with the initial phase of growth (see Figure12.1a-b):

1.   *The average wage* (W) that can be earned in the central city (O) is assumed to be constant for all residents of the region (possible differences in the average wages between urban and rural areas are not reflected in the model, which takes into account daily commuters rather than migrants). The horizontal W-line in the diagram reflects this assumption;

2. The share of *disposable income* (D) is assumed to be slightly larger in the hinterland areas than in the central city. For instance, local taxes and expenditure on education may be higher in the city than in hinterland areas. However, as long as the city remains relatively small, these differences are not likely to be substantial (though they may increase considerably as the city grows). This assumption is reflected in a slight slope of the D-line towards the town's location (O) and the widening gap between lines W and D, marked by the grey-hatched area in the diagram;

3. The average *cost of housing* (H) is likely to be somewhat higher in the city than in its hinterland area. However, this difference in the cost of housing should not be considerable while the city is relatively small. This is reflected by the shallow slope of line H in the diagram. As distance from the town grows, no additional decline in housing cost may be expected, because land resources for new development may become virtually unrestricted. The point of inflection, beyond which no further drop in the cost of housing may be expected, is marked by Point #2 in the diagram;

4. *Accessibility* (A) is measured by the cost of transport in proportion to the average salary, and grows as the distance to the town increases. Upon reaching the limits of distance practicable for daily commuting (Point #1; see Figure12.1a), the price of accessibility may increase sharply. This increase is reflected by the changing slope of the line A after Point #1. Away from the main roads, the increase of the accessibility cost is expected to be faster, which is reflected in the steeper slope of the respective line A on the left side of the diagram (see Figure 12.1a).

Let us now introduce the notion of a 'typical employee' – a 'faceless' earner of an average salary, who is distinctive in no way from other employees in the region. (Though similar concepts of an 'economic man' are often criticised by sociologists and anthropologists, this simplified representation is nevertheless quite common in micro-economic and migration modelling and seems to be appropriate for our rather generalised model).

The question we would like to answer is as follows: *Given the above assumptions, where would the 'typical employee' tend to settle?*

The proposed model suggests that the answer to this question is fairly straightforward: he will prefer to settle where the difference between disposable income (D) and expenses on commuting and housing (A+H) is largest, and where money left over for other expenses would be greatest.

In Figure 12.1a, the difference between disposable income (D) and housing/commuting expenses (A+H) is indicated by a black-filled area; the maximum difference is marked by the arrow G. In the plan diagram (Figure 12.1b), the difference between income and housing/commuting expenses area is marked by the black star-like shape, whose arms stretch along the main communication lines (C).

When a town is small and the cost of living in it does not differ considerably from that in the adjacent hinterland area, our 'typical employee' would choose to live in the town itself or in its immediate environs – where there is little commuting cost and where housing is not much more expensive than elsewhere.

Let us assume now that the town's population has grown considerably leading to a greater demand for housing (expansion phase: see Figure12.1c-d). This may in turn result in higher real estate prices in the town and its immediate suburbs, thus increasing the difference between the cost of housing in the town itself and in its hinterland. With a greater population, the cost of obtaining accessibility to the town (A) should also increase, due to increased travel times, traffic jams and other side-effects of accelerating urbanisation.

Though the average wage in the expanded city may increase somewhat, compared to the initial phase of city growth, other expenses in addition to housing and transport may increase as well, thus further reducing the disposable income of our 'typical employee'. This in turn leads to a reduction in the geographic extent of the area where disposable income exceeds the combined costs of transport and housing. (This shrunken area is marked by the small black triangle in Figure12.1a and by three diamond-shaped areas on the plan, located near the threshold of the areas practicable for daily commuting - See Figure 12.1c-d).

As the locations in and around the town become too expensive for our 'typical employee,' he may seek refuge in rural areas, which, in turn, might become the foci for the formation of new urban communities (O_1).

Now, let us leave for a moment our 'typical employee' and consider the behaviour of firms. As migrants and commuters find rural areas increasingly attractive, hinterland locations (O_1) may also become desirable for centrally located firms, particularly those in need of physical expansion and thus most affected by high property prices in the growing city. Like migrants and commuters, such firms may also consider hinterland locations. The combination of these two forces - migration push and centrifugal movements of firms - may become an incentive for the establishment of new settlements (O_1) within the commuting range from the existing town (O).

As these new urban places grow, some of them may eventually undergo a similar process of bifurcation. Eventually, this chain reaction may lead to the formation of clusters of diverse-sized urban places centred around the initial point of origin (O).

An interesting feature of the suggested model is its application as a planning tool. In particular, it may be of help in estimating the effect of changes in infrastructure on the location of areas of potential growth. For instance, we may attempt to investigate the effect of improved means of transportation on the formation of the urban field around the existing town (Figure 12.2).

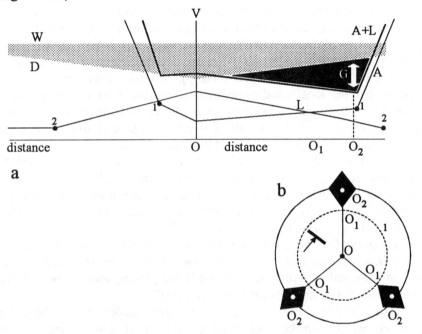

Figure 12.2   Spatial expansion of an urban cluster in response to transportation adjustments

a - cross-section; b – two-dimensional structure of the cluster (see explanations to Figure 12.1).

Due to improved transportation links between the town and its hinterland area, the threshold of the area practicable for daily commuting (Point #1) should also move away from the town's origin (O). This, in turn, may result in centrifugal expansion of the prospective cluster, with the establishment of new towns (O_2) farther outside of the existing centre.

Simultaneous Growth

Often, the formation of new urban clusters starts even before the existing city is 'overloaded', by any means. The changes in the settlement pattern around Tel Aviv, Israel, in 1922-56, illustrate this point (Figure 12.3).[2] As this diagram shows, small clusters of mixed urban-rural localities were already clearly noticeable in 1937 (Marked on the map by thin circles located north, east and south of the city). Though the distances from these clusters to Tel Aviv are not very large by today's standards - some 10-30 km - in the 1930s they were considered substantial, given the inferior state of the road infrastructure and poor public transportation.

Since we may clearly reject a 'catastrophic bifurcation' hypothesis in this case,[3] an alternative explanation is suggested: small urban places forming the centres of the above clusters evolved out of existing rural communities (Rehovot and Petakh Tikva), or were established to provide services for the local rural population (Netania), even before Tel Aviv reached a 'catastrophic bifurcation' size. In the 1956 map, however, two parallel processes are clearly evident – suburban sprawl around Tel Aviv, and consolidation of 'peripheral' clusters in the city's outer ring.

The formation of new settlement clusters may also be caused by social and economic needs, rather by service considerations. In particular, clusters of settlements may be formed to facilitate organisation and co-ordination of communal activities, such as the maintenance and operation of a complex irrigation system (Fedick, 1997).

Clusters of urban and rural settlements may also be nucleated around a common religious facility (such as a monastery or parish church), or be formed generically from settlements of tribal groups, tracing their former generations to a common ancestor (Oliver, 1997).

Aston (1999) describes groups of early settlements in Medieval England, which can be considered prototypes of contemporary urban clusters. Such estates were centred around head places or *caputs*, some of which were established on Roman and pre-Roman sites. Most caputs were in the lowlands, in valleys surrounded by fertile land, and many of them were in royal ownership or belonged to a bishop or an ancient abbey. In some cases, the caputs were the central places of administrative units known as hundreds. Around the caputs (called the Mayor settlements in Wales), there were dependent settlements whose population worked on the lord's land. The dependency of these settlements upon the caputs was indicated by the subsidiary status of their churches and by rents and services paid to the caput.

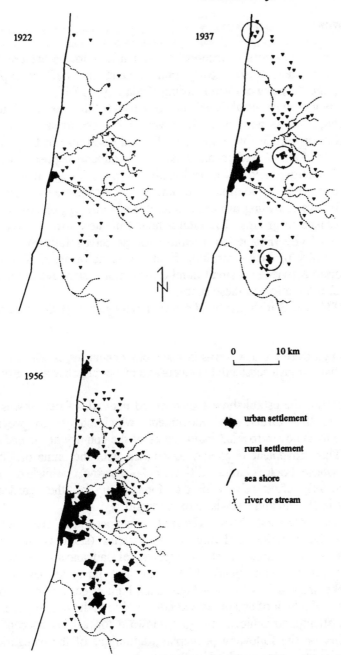

Figure 12.3 Changes of the settlement pattern around Tel Aviv, Israel in 1922-56

New Towns

Of the numerous factors in response to which new towns are created, the following two factors are clearly predominant: the *pull* of exploitable resources, and the *push* of overcrowding (Galantay, 1975).

The new towns established in response to the needs of resource exploitation, such as new industrial towns in the countries of the 'former Soviet orbit' or mining towns in Australia and elsewhere in the world, are as a rule 'stand-alone' settlements located near mineral deposits or a cheap source of energy, and a considerable distance away from existing population centres. In contrast, the new towns established in response to the push of overcrowding are often satellites of existing population centres and may cluster in groups. The establishment of these towns is most often a response of governments to a failure (or perceived failure)[4] of market forces to resolve problems resulting from over-concentration of population and economic activity in a small number of major metropolitan centres, by the 'natural bifurcation' of these centres.

In 1974, the British Central Office of Information (COI, p.1) proudly wrote:

> Although there are new towns in many other countries, nowhere have they been built in such substantial numbers as a matter of policy as in Britain.

In Britain, the establishment of a broad network of new towns traces its roots to the 'garden city' movement, which sought to provide an alternative to the overcrowded major cities of the country at the end of 19th century. This movement is closely associated with the name of Ebenezer Howard, whose book 'Garden Cities of To-morrow', published in 1898 (1985 reprint), effectively laid the foundation for the 'garden city' movement in Britain and elsewhere in the world.

In this influential book, Howard envisioned the new cities as combining the benefits of living in large cities (such as high wages, opportunities for employment, prospects of advancement) with the advantages of the countryside (fresh air and physical health), while avoiding the drawbacks of both – high rents, high prices and overcrowding in the city, and a lack of amenities and cultural life in the countryside.

In an attempt to achieve this goal, Howard formed his concept of the Garden City on the following principles (definitions of the categories and explanatory comments are added by the authors):

- *Land area and shape:* The city is built near the centre of a plot of land of 6,000 acres (approx. 24 km^2) and covers an area of 1,000 acres (approx.4 km^2). It has a circular form, with 1,240 yards (1,134 m) from its centre to the circumference;
- *Internal structure:* six boulevards – each 120 feet (40 m) wide – lead from the city centre to its perimeter and divide the city into six equal parts or wards. The centre of the city is occupied by a 5.5-acre (2.2 hectares) garden, surrounded by public buildings – town hall, theatre, library, etc. The rest of the central place is encircled by the 'Crystal Palace,' which is a winter-time recreation ground for the public;
- *Population size:* The city provides a place of residence for 30,000 people (excluding some 2,000 residents of the agricultural estate), which are settled in a total of 5,500 building lots having an average size of 20x130 feet (240 m^2);
- *Accessibility:* A circular 'Grand Avenue' is 420 feet (140 m) wide and divides the city into two unequal parts. This avenue is less than 240 yards (220 m) from the most remote lot;
- *Support services and facilities:* Factories, warehouses, dairies, markets etc. are all located on the outer ring of the town and face the railroad, which passes through the estate;
- *Further growth:* When the city reaches 32,000 residents, another similar 'garden city' is to be established with its own hinterland. The two cities are to be linked by a rapid transit, so they will be easily accessible from each other;
- *Clustering and inter-city links:* The cities are to be grouped into a cluster formed by one relatively big city of some 58,000 residents and a number of smaller towns (32,000 residents each), surrounding the central city and located along the circular railroad. The distance between each of these towns and the central city is not expected to exceed 3.5 miles (approx. 5.6 km) and can thus be covered in five minutes by train.

By 1903, Howard's ideas had been put in practice with the establishment of Letchworth Garden City – (56 km north of London). In 1920, another Garden City - Welwyn – had been established (COI, 1974).

According to the New Town Act of 1946, 12 new towns were designated in England and Wales and 2 in Scotland, each with its own development corporation financed by the government. Proposed ultimate population figures of these towns were set from 29,000 to 140,000.

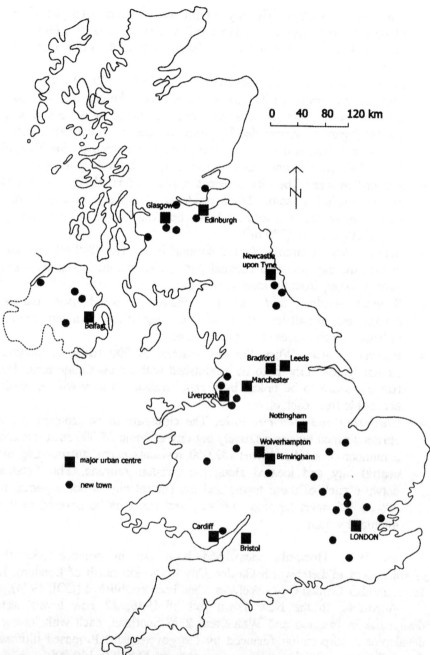

Figure 12.4 Location of new towns in the U.K.

Source: Compiled from COI (1974).

However, after 1961, target population figures for the towns were increased to 70,000 and 250,000 respectively (EB, 1999 – new town). In part, this change of policy was due to the fact the former thresholds were found to be insufficient for achieving a socio-economic 'take-off' and critical supporting service functions (Haughton and Hunter, 1994).

Table 12.1 Selected characteristics of new towns in the U.K.

Town	Year of desig- nation	Nearby city	Distance to nearby city, km	Population at designation	Ultimate population
Stevenage	1946	London	50	7,000	105,000
Crawley	1947	'	48	10,000	79,000
Hemel Hempstead	'	'	47	21,000	80,000
Harlow	'	'	40	4,500	90,000
Hatfield	1948	'	32	8,500	30,000
Basildon	1949	'	48	25,000	140,000
Bracknell	'	'	45	5,000	60,000
Corby	1950	Leicester	37	15,700	83,000
Skelmersdale	1961	Liverpool	21	10,000	80,000
Telford	1968	Birmingham	48	70,000	220,000
Redditch	1964	'	23	32,000	90,000
Runcorn	1964	Liverpool	23	28,500	100,000
Washington	1964	Newcastle	10	20,000	80,000
Milton Keynes	1967	London	81	40,000	250,000
Stonehouse	1973	Glasgow	13	7,900	70,000
Craigavon	1965	Belfast	48	40,000	180,000
Antrim	1965	'	28	7,000	50,000
Ballymena	1967	'	44	21,000	80,000

Source: Compiled from COI (1974).

By 1974, 33 new towns were designated in the U.K., with 21 new towns in England, 6 in Scotland, and 4 in Northern Ireland (COI, 1974). Most new towns were established so that their distance from a nearby urban centre (see Table 12.1) and from one another (see Figure 12.4) was practicable for daily commuting. This effectively created a number of new urban clusters.

The success of the British 'new town' movement, or at least a lack of obvious failures, encouraged other countries to follow suit. In Israel, for instance, more than 30 towns were established in the late 1950s-early 1970s, predominantly in the country's outlying areas (Shefer and Bar-El, 1993). From the outset, many of these towns were designated as potential service centres of a five-level urban-rural hierarchy, according to a popular town-planning concept of that period (Table 12.2).

Table 12.2 Hierarchy of settlements in Israel – theoretical concept

Type of settlement	Population size	Functional characteristics
Village, kibbutz or moshav	<500	
Rural centre	500-1,000	Economic, social, and cultural centre for 4-6 moshavs. Residents are craftsmen and service providers.
Rural-urban centre	6,000-12,000	Serves an area with a radius of approx. 10 miles, including 30 villages. Includes secondary schools, housing for farm labourers, rural-related industry, and some administrative services.
Medium-sized town	15,000-60,000	Regional centre for commerce, culture and administration.
Large city	100,000+	Major central functions of government, education and commerce.

Source: Strong (1971); cited in Altman and Rosenbaum (1975).

Another example of 'new town' planning is found in India, where a relatively large number of new settlements were established in the Rajasthan Desert along the Pakistan border. According to Saini (1980), the population of this settlement cluster is ultimately expected to reach 2-2,5 million people, settled in 1,200 new villages, 160 agro-service centres ('amenity villages') and 28 market towns of 20,000 residents each. In this framework, each village is expected to operate within a radius of 2.5 km;

an 'amenity village' has a service area of 6.5 to 8 km radius; and a market town is expected to serve seven amenity villages and forty-five basic villages within a radius of 20 km.

Our short review of new town policies would, of course, be incomplete without making a reference to the large-scale new town program of the former Soviet Union. This program underwent three distinctive phases:

- During the first five-year plan (1928-32), sixty new towns were built, primarily in the areas where settlement was sparse. Among the new towns established during this period were Karaganda in Kazakhstan, Magnitogosk and Stalingrad (Volgograd) in Russia, and Zaporizhzhya in Ukraine, which all subsequently developed into large population centres of their geographic regions;

- The relocation of industries from the European part of the country during World War II gave another boost to the establishment of new towns. Thus, between 1942 and 1944, sixty-seven new towns were built and numerous existing small settlements were considerably expanded. These included mining centres near the Polar Circle (Vorkuta, Norilsk, Dudinka, etc.), industrial towns in Siberia and Ural, and new towns created around railroad stations where trains evacuating population and plants from the European part of the country could be unloaded;

- After WWII, the construction of new towns continued. Thus, during the Cold War, numerous new towns were constructed around classified military installations in the European part of the country as well as in more geographically remote areas – in Ural and Siberia. Many of these 'classified' towns (such as Krasnoyarsk-26 in the Krasnoyarsk region of Russia) subsequently grew into major urban centres of some 100,000+ residents. In the 1970s – early 1980s, dozens of new towns were built around the newly constructed Baikal-Amur main railroad (BAM),[5] one of the major infrastructure projects of the Soviet era (Galantay, 1975; Portnov, 1992; Show, 1987).

Notes

[1] The notion of a standard housing unit is commonly used by national statistical services as a mean of calculating the cost of living index. A common type of housing built in the area may represent such a standard unit, which, depending on the local conditions, may be represented either by a single-family house or by a standard flat in an apartment block.

[2] The maps are compiled from 'Atlas of Israel' (1956; Department of Surveys, Jerusalem).

[3] It is worth noting that in 1937, the population size of Tel Aviv was less than 110,000 residents - clearly not the size at which 'catastrophic bifurcation' is likely to occur.

[4] As Hirschman (1958) notes, governments often favour large-scale development projects, such as new towns, large-scale communication and transportation facilities, irrigation and drainage systems, which are perceived as 'sound' goals for spending the taxpayers' money. He also argues that planners often claim for such projects 'overriding and fundamental importance,' since 'alternative and possibly more desirable uses of public funds are simply not within the horizon of the planners' (pp. 85-86).

[5] The BAM railroad *(Baikal-Amur Magistral)* was constructed between Ust-Kut, on the Lena River, and Komsomolsk-na-Amure, on the Amur River. It covers a distance of some 3,200 km and was completed in the 1980s (EB, 1999 – Siberia).

13 Benefits and Drawbacks of Clustering

Non-linear relations among variables are commonplace in socio-economic and regional sciences. A good example of such non-linearity is the Environmental Kuznets Curve (EKC), which points to an inverted U-shape relation between an environmental impact of society on its natural environment and per capita income. This function implies that, upon reaching a certain level of wealth, economic growth leads to amelioration of the negative environmental impacts of the early stages of economic development (Perman and Stern, 1999). Another non-linear relationship between socio-economic variables is Weber's agglomeration function. This function also has an inverted U-shape, indicating that the initial benefits of industrial concentration may be reduced as a certain critical point of concentration is reached, and diseconomies of further concentration ('centrifugal forces') – the cost of congestion, and the bidding-up prices of land and labour - come into play (Krugman, 1995; 1999).

Is the relationship between urban growth and concentration of towns in clusters different? Is the relationship between these two factors linear? In other words, is clustering *always* conducive to the sustainable growth of urban places?

In this chapter, we shall attempt to answer these important questions, providing a variety of theoretical considerations. Part IV of this book is an attempt to validate these relationships by means of a number of case studies. To distinguish between different location situations, the discussion will focus separately on sparsely populated peripheral areas and on densely populated central regions.[1] It will be argued, in particular, that in sparsely populated peripheral areas, the presence of small neighbouring urban communities may increase their chances to attract potential migrants and private investors due to larger opportunities for socio-economic interaction and information exchanges. On the other hand, in core areas, where a major metropolitan centre dominates social-economic life, dense clusters of small urban localities may effectively reduce the rate of migration and investment flow to a given town due to diseconomies of agglomeration and inter-town competition for potential investors and migrants.

Peripheral Areas

As we noted in Chapter 2 of this book, the considerable distances often found between established urban localities in peripheral areas are likely to cause a shortage of joint intra-regional educational and recreational infrastructure, and to limit job opportunities. The latter may have immediate implications for the *local residents* of spatially dispersed peripheral towns. For example, employees of an industrial enterprise shut down in a central, densely populated district may find similar jobs in the same city or in adjacent towns, to which they can commute daily without changing their place of residence. Under similar circumstances, employees of a company shut down in a small, peripheral community may not be able to find any alternative employment within commuting range from their homes and thus may have to leave the area for another district where similar employment is available. Being part of a cluster of towns may thus provide a wider choice of employment opportunities for the residents of peripheral communities, creating an emergency buffer and limiting emigration when economic circumstances become unfavourable (Figure 13.1).

Clustering of urban communities in thinly populated peripheral regions may also have a positive effect on the attractiveness of a geographic area to *migrants from other regions*. As postulated by the competing destination model of inter-area migration (see Chapter 11 for a more detailed discussion), migrants from distant regions often consider clusters of towns as potential destinations, and then choose among individual urban locations in the preferred cluster. Given this tendency, migrants may, for instance, consider a cluster of small towns, located within commuting range from one another, as a single spatial unit of a larger size, assuming that it may provide a better choice of socio-economic opportunities (Figure 13.1). Migrants opting for a cluster of adjacent towns may, for instance, be attracted by a choice of schools for their children - a choice which may not be available in individual, isolated towns. Furthermore, if the overall population size of the settlement cluster is sufficiently large, it may justify the establishment of a college or a hospital. Each of these functions, as argued in Chapter 3, is of great value in enhancing the attractiveness of urban places to prospective migrants.

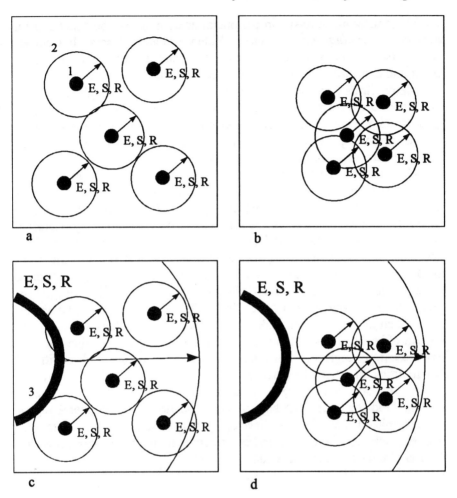

Figure 13.1   Clusters of towns in a peripheral (a, b) and centrally located region (c, d)

1 – small town; 2 – range of daily commuting; 3 – principal city; E, S, R – employment, services, and recreation. The diagram shows that clustering of small towns in a sparsely populated peripheral region (a, b) may provide a wider choice of employment, services and recreational opportunities for its residents as well a bigger number of consumers and additional opportunities for cooperation among firms. On the other hand, further clustering may have adverse effects on the development of individual towns in a centrally located region in which urban life is dominated by a major population centre (c, d), because of competition between the towns and the metropolitan centre and among the towns themselves.

The clustering of towns in peripheral areas may also be beneficial for *firms and individual entrepreneurs*. Within a cluster of small but closely located towns, entrepreneurs may expect to find a larger pool of skilled labour and consumers, compared with that available in a single-town.

Many firms, particularly those oriented towards high-technology production, are attracted to towns having a college or a university campus. Apart from a supply of college graduates, a college or university may provide a base for cooperation in research through the joint use of laboratory facilities and communication networks.

The establishment of a new industrial enterprise in a given urban cluster may, in turn, trigger a chain reaction leading to further concentration of firms, an effect which Myrdal (1958) called the *process of cumulative causation*.[2] Indeed, recent studies of industrial agglomeration indicate that clustering of industries is a cumulative process which is conducive to an increase in the efficiency of production, growth in competitiveness, and an overall improvement of the economic development of the area (see *inter alia* Shilton and Craig, 1999; Rogerson, 1998; Walcott, 1999; Swann *et al*, 1998; Fik, 1991; Foss, 1996; Saxenian, 1996; Shelburne and Bednarzik, 1993). According to these studies, the positive effect of industrial clustering is attributed to information sharing, joint research, high order capabilities of networking, and additional opportunities for international trade.

As the size and number of urban places in a settlement cluster increases and the overall density of the urban field in a peripheral region rises, peripheral localities may develop an enhanced capacity for retaining their existing population, be more attractive to migrants and enjoy the benefits of industrial concentration.

Core Areas

The situation may be somewhat different when urban clustering takes place in densely populated core regions. In these areas, diseconomies of over-concentration, such as road congestion, high land and labour prices, and depletion of recreation resources[3] may become increasingly evident as the density of the urban field increases.

These diseconomies may, however, be especially detrimental for small towns in core areas. Because of their proximity to large population centres, these towns may suffer from the adverse effects of over-concentration of population and economic activity in the region. Concurrently, they have less to offer potential investors and migrants in terms of infrastructure, cultural and recreational opportunities, compared to bigger cities in the region (Figure 13.1). The bulk of inward investment may thus be directed to the metropolitan core, while centripetal migrants may 'bypass' these small towns and concentrate in larger population centres. Furthermore, small towns in core regions may not be particularly attractive to 'centrifugal migrants' either, who often prefer cheaper housing and better recreational opportunities found in more remote locations. Thus, a further increase in the density of urban clusters in core areas may become clearly disadvantageous for small, individual urban settlements.

In addition to the negative consequences of high densities and the drawbacks of over-concentration, small urban places in centrally located regions may also suffer adverse effects from inter-town competition. As the number of small towns in the core (N) which provide a similar range of functions and services increases, each of these towns is likely to attract a smaller share of migrants (M) and investments (I) directed to the region. In other words, we may expect that $(M+I)/N \rightarrow 0$ as $N \rightarrow \infty$.

The combined effect of these processes - diseconomies of concentration, growing competition between towns and the adjacent metropolitan centres, and competition among adjacent towns themselves – leads to the conclusion that increased clustering in a core region is likely to have an adverse effect on the development of individual urban communities.

The overall relationship between clustering of the urban field and development of towns can thus be summarised as follows: clustering enhances the initial development of individual towns in a region, but further clustering may lead to the negative consequences of over-concentration and a decline in the capacity for further growth.

Notes

[1] The core-periphery dichotomy, which we use in the present discussion was also described in some detail in an endnote to Chapter 2 of this book.

[2] According to Myrdal's theory, a single socio-economic incident may trigger a wide range of events, affecting further development of a region or a community as a whole. For example, a decline in one sector of a regional economy may have direct effects on the income of workers employed in this sector, and thus on demand created by them, leading to indirect effects on the performance of other sectors which provide services to the local population. As a result, the region may suffer a general decline leading potential investors and migrants to look for alternative, more prosperous, locations. Myrdal also assumes that this sequence of cumulative causation works in a similar way if the initial change is positive. For instance, a decision to locate an industry in a particular location may give a

spur to its general development, resulting in an increase in employment opportunities and higher average incomes. Consequently, local businesses can expand their activities in line with increasing demand for their products and services. Labor, capital and enterprise will also be attracted from outside to take advantage of expanding opportunities. This process creates, according to Myrdal, external economies favourable to sustaining development. In this conceptual framework, Myrdal distinguishes between two types of processes: 1) The *backwash effect,* through which more developed regions develop further at the expense of less developed areas, and 2) The *spread effect,* which works in the opposite direction, causing expansion from growing centres to other areas through demand for their products and through spill-over of population.

[3] Krugman (1995; 1999), who calls these factors 'centrifugal forces' of dispersion, discusses in detail forces of over-concentration and their concomitant diseconomies.

14 The Index of Clustering as an Integrated Measure of Urban Location

In previous chapters, we discussed various measures of urban location: population density, remoteness, isolation, and various agglomeration indices. None of these measures can, however, describe comprehensively the location of a town in the general setting of urban places.

For instance, *population density* is an important regional development datum whose significance is traditionally advocated by location economics and population studies (Levy, 1985; Smith, 1975; MacKellar and Vining, 1995). In many countries, this indicator of urban growth is included in the list of major time-series data monitored by the national statistics (ICBS, 1951-98; SN, 1994).

However, mean density figures for a given region often hide significant variations in the local distribution of population. For instance, the entire population of a region may be concentrated in one major population centre, or it may be scattered in a dozen small towns and villages. The mean density figure for both regions might be the same, though these two situations are very different. The usefulness of mean density figures is thus limited, unless the scale of the statistical areas is sufficiently detailed to allow a spatial analysis of the region in question.

Percentage of the population living in localities of certain size is another indicator of regional development frequently used in urban and regional studies, particularly those dealing with city-size distribution (see Chapters 3-5 of this book and also Zipf, 1949; Soen, 1977; Carroll, 1982; Alperovich, 1993; Woldenberg, 1979; Krakover, 1998b). The applicability of this indicator to a geographic region also appears to be restricted. Knowing, for instance, that 50 per cent of a region's population live in urban settlements of 50,000-100,000 residents tells us little about actual patterns of urbanisation in the area. Indeed, all these towns may form a single

205

territorial contiguity or they may be dispersed at considerable distances from each other. From the standpoint of the present analysis, these two cases represent completely different situations, while the size-distribution index treats them alike.

Indicators of *remoteness and isolation* are two other measures considered, in some detail, in the previous chapters. We may recall that the latter measure (isolation) is determined by the location of the town in relation to other urban localities within a region, while remoteness measures the distance from the town in question to the closest major population centre of the country.

Although these two measures are undoubtedly informative indicators of urban location, considering each of them separately may also be misleading. For instance, the lack of neighbouring urban communities (isolation) may have a different effect on the development of a centrally located town compared to a peripheral town. In the latter case, the lack of opportunities for urban interaction may reduce substantially the number of employment opportunities available to its residents within the distance practicable for daily commuting, and the level of services and facilities they can use without recourse to long-distance travel. However, if a centrally located town has no other urban places of similar size in its vicinity, this relative isolation may be compensated, at least partially, by its proximity to a major urban centre. The effects of remoteness and isolation should thus be considered in combination and measured by an integrated location index, whose values should vary as a function both of remoteness from the largest population centres and of intra-regional patterns of urban settlement.

Index of Clustering

An integrated indicator of the location of towns - the Index of Clustering (IC) – can be expressed as a simple ratio (Figure 14. 1A):

$$IC = IS / IR,$$

where IS and IR are respectively spatial isolation (defined here as the number of towns located within a practical range for daily commuting, including the town in question), and an index of remoteness [the distance from a given settlement to the closest major urban centre, in kilometres] (Portnov and Erell, 1998b).

The index of clustering has high values in centrally located areas, where distances from major population centres are small (IR→0) and the urban field is dense (IS→∞); It has low values in more remote peripheral areas, where distances from major population centres are large (IR→∞) and the pattern of urban settlement is diffuse (IS→0).

The index in question does, however, have two obvious drawbacks:

- First, it ignores the population size of the communities forming a cluster of urban settlements;
- Second, it is based on aerial distances between towns, which are easy to measure but may sometimes be misleading. For instance, if a mountain chain or fjord separates towns, social and functional links between them may be severely restricted despite close aerial proximity (Chapter 1). Local commuters are well aware of these geographical obstacles and of the additional time required to overcome them. If the extent of the infrastructure and quality of service are more or less uniform throughout the area under study, then road distance may be a more accurate measure.

The original Index of Clustering (IC) may thus be modified accordingly. For instance, the numerator of the above ratio (isolation) may be measured in two different ways:

1) The *number* of other towns located within a practical range for daily commuting, including the town itself (IC1), as suggested originally, and
2) The *total population* of all towns located within a commuting range from the urban place in question (IC2).

In addition, remoteness (the denominator of the ratio) may be measured by *road distances* rather than by aerial distances (Figure 14.1B).

One comment is important. The distance practicable for daily commuting depends on various factors. These include the overall population size of a country, its geographic extent, historical patterns of urban development, location of services and facilities, quality of transportation, level of motorisation etc. It may also differ across various geographic areas of a given country, depending on the local density of population and road infrastructure. We may recall that this issue was discussed in some detail in Chapter 1, in which distances practicable for daily commuting in selected countries were compared. These distances vary from 20-30 km in small and densely populated Israel to 80-100 km for the U.S.A. and Australia.

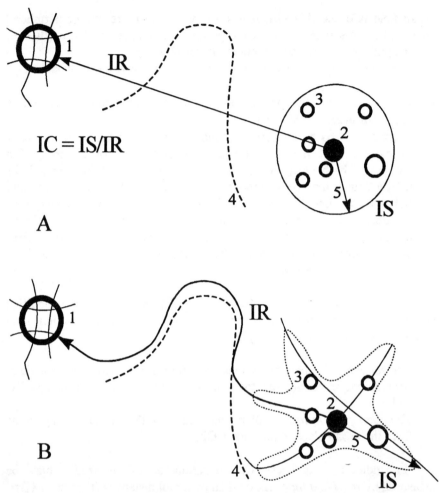

IC = IS/IR

A

B

Figure 14.1   Index of Clustering (IC) as the ratio between Index of Isolation (IS) and Index of Remoteness (IR)

A – IC derived from aerial distances; B – IC derived from road distances;

1 – major urban centre; 2 – subject town; 3 – adjacent urban localities; 4 – dominant landscape feature (fjord, mountain chain, etc.); 5 – distance practicable for daily commuting.

The proposed index has high values in centrally located geographic areas, where urban settlement is dense and distances to major urban centres are small. Concurrently, the values of the index in question are small in more remote peripheral areas, where urban settlements are scattered and distances to major population centres are relatively large.

Range of Values

Although both indices of clustering (IC1 and IC2) have high values in central, densely populated areas, and lower values elsewhere, the difference between the two indices is nevertheless substantial.

For instance, let us consider two clusters of towns, one of which is located in close proximity to a major population centre of the country (Town 3; Cluster 1),[1] while the second cluster (Cluster 2) is situated in a geographically remote area and comprises equally small urban places (Table 14. 1).

Table 14.1   Example of location indices for two clusters of towns

Town/Index	Cluster 1	Cluster 2
Town 1 (subject town)	20,000*	20,000*
Town 2	45,000*	15,000*
Town 3	65,000*	20,000*
Town 4	45,000*	15,000*
Town 5	9,000*	9,000*
IS1	5	5
IS2	184,000	79,000
IR (subject town)	20	120
IC1	0.20	0.04
IC2	9.20	0.66
IC2/IC1	46.00	15.84

* Population size, number of residents;
IS1 = Index of Isolation (1) – number of other urban communities within commuting range;
IS2 = Index of Isolation (2) – overall population size of urban communities located within commuting range, including the subject town;
IR = Index of Remoteness (road distance from the subject town to the closest major urban centre of the country), km;
IC1 = Index of Clustering (1) (IC1 = $IS1*10^{-3}/IR$);
IC2 = Index of Clustering (2) (IC2 = $IS2*10^{-3}/IR$).

Although both clusters include the same number of towns (5), the resulting values of IC1 are different – 0.20 for the subject town located in the centrally located cluster (Cluster 1) compared with 0.04 for the subject town which is a part of the more remote Cluster 2.

The difference between the values of IC2 is even larger: 9.2 (Cluster 1) vs. 0.66 (Cluster 2). Notably, the ratios between the two indices (IC2/IC1) differ substantially: 46.0 for Cluster 1 and 15.84 for Cluster 2.

This difference is caused by the fact that in the calculation of IC1, towns of different population size are treated alike. Therefore, the presence of large towns in Cluster 1 (Towns 2, 3 and 4) had no effect on the value of the resulting index, while in the calculation of IC2 (which takes into account the total population size of an urban cluster), the presence of these large towns affected the results and was reflected in the different ratios between IC1 and IC2 in the clusters.

Since there are two versions of the index of clustering, it may well be asked – is there any advantage of one over the other?

The answer to this question is not straightforward. IC2, used separately from its IC1 'twin,' may misrepresent differences in the actual pattern of settlements within a cluster, since under different circumstances, IC2 may return identical values. For instance, the subject town may have five relatively big urban localities within the commuting range or be surrounded by ten smaller urban places of the same overall population size. Assuming that the distance from the subject town to the closest major urban centre in both cases is the same, the values calculated for IC2 will be the same, although the urban field is quite different. The choice of the more appropriate index may be left to the planner, or they may be used in conjunction, which may increase the accuracy of results.

An alternative approach is to use an integrated index that may, for instance, be obtained by multiplication of two location measures in question:

$$IC3 = IC1 * IC2$$

Using data from Table 14.1, we can calculate the values of the integrated index under consideration. For centrally located Cluster 1, this index is equal 1.84 [0.2*9.2], while for peripheral Cluster 2, its value is substantially lower: 0.04*0.66=0.03.

Variability of IC within Urban Clusters

The values of the above location indices (IC1-IC3) are generally not identical for all of the urban localities within any given cluster of towns. Figure 14.2 helps to illustrate the nature of this intra-cluster variation.

When the index of clustering is calculated for the subject town in Figure 14. 2A, the whole set of towns forming the cluster and falling within this town's commuting range is included. The overall population size of the settlement cluster of which this town is a part, is thus: IS2 = 16.2+15.5+ +60.0+14.5+5.5 = 111.7 (see Figure 14.2, year *i*).

If the town in question is, for instance, 200 km away from the closest urban centre of the country, this would result in an IC2 for this town of 0.56: 111.7/200 = 0.56. Another town, which is a part of the same settlement cluster (Figure 14.2B) but which is situated close to the cluster's margin, beyond commuting range from the most of the its other 'members,' would have a substantially lower value of IS2: 60.0+14.5 = 74,5. Assuming that IR for this town is also 200 km, IC2 for this town amounts to only 74.5/200 = 0.37.

Unlike IC1, which is calculated using the overall *number* of urban places located within the commuting range from a given town (including the town in question itself), the values of both IC2 and IC3 are subject to changes in the population size of the cluster's 'members.' For instance, if population figures for the year *i+n* are used instead of those for year *i*, the value of IC2 for the subject town in the above example will change to: (28.5+24.5+85.5+18.9+7.5)/200=0.82 (Figure 14.2A), compared to 0.56, calculated for year *i*.

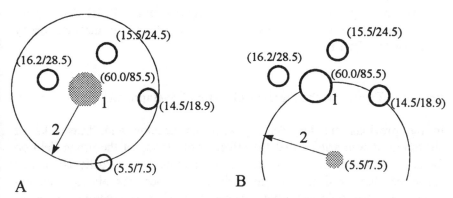

Figure 14.2   Variations of the estimation base of IC within a cluster of towns

1 – subject town; 2 – commuting range. Figures in parentheses indicate population size of the town in the year *i* and year *i+n*, respectively.

The index in question is thus not a simple measure of location. Despite the relative simplicity of its calculation, this index reflects both physical parameters of the urban field (remoteness and isolation), and population dynamics of urban communities, as reflected in changes of their population size.

Weighting of Components

It is worth noting that in the calculation of the proposed index of clustering (IC=IS/IR), its two components – *remoteness and isolation* - are considered to have *equal weighting*. However, in some countries or regions, the index of isolation (IS) may, for instance, have a more substantial effect on the patterns of urban growth compared to that of remoteness, or vice versa. In order to take these local characteristics into account, the above method of calculating IC may be adjusted as follows:

$$IC=IS^{\alpha}/IR,$$

where α is a power variable ($\alpha>0$), which is subject to calibration under local conditions. If $0<\alpha<1$, then a larger weight is assigned to the effects of IR (remoteness) than to those of isolation. If $\alpha>1$, then isolation will have a greater effect.

When $\alpha=1.0$, IC is calculated in its original form – IS/IR. As we may recall, such a power transformation is often found in distance decay functions (see Part I).

Predicted Effects on the Patterns of Urban Development

In the previous chapter, dealing with the benefits and drawbacks of clustering, it was argued that the effect of clustering of the urban field on the development of towns may *not* always be positive. In particular, it was suggested that, if density of the urban field increases above a certain quantitative threshold, a further concentration of urban communities might become detrimental for each of them due to overpopulation and inter-town competition for potential migrants and investors. Figure 14.3, showing the likely effect of clustering of the urban field on the attractiveness of individual urban localities in centrally located and peripheral regions illustrates this point.

One additional comment is also important. The relationship between the index of clustering and remoteness may sometimes be non-linear. For instance, when moving towards densely populated core areas through areas of transition lying between separate clusters of towns (where only scattered urban communities are found), the values of the index of clustering may increase while the actual density of the urban field may at some point, decline. This may require modification of the relatively simple inverted U-shaped relationship between clustering of the urban field and attractiveness of towns in terms of population movement (see Figure 14.3). For instance, the relationship between these two factors may form a relatively complex wave-like curve with decreasing amplitude, such as that described by the *Bessel* function (see Figure 14.4).

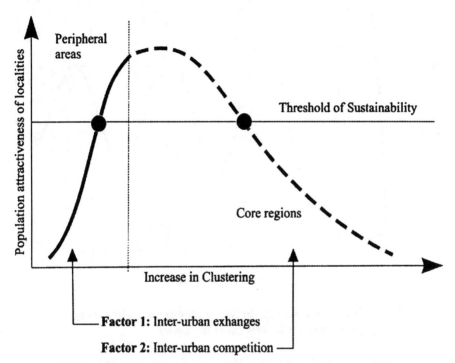

Figure 14.3 The expected effect of clustering on socio-economic development of centrally located and peripheral towns

The effect of clustering on urban development is expected to be twofold. In peripheral areas, an increase in the density of the urban field may improve the chances of individual localities to achieve sustainable urban growth due to a wider choice of service and employment opportunities. In contrast, in core areas, dense urban field may reduce the chances of individual communities to attract migrants and private investors due to inter-town competition and overcrowding.

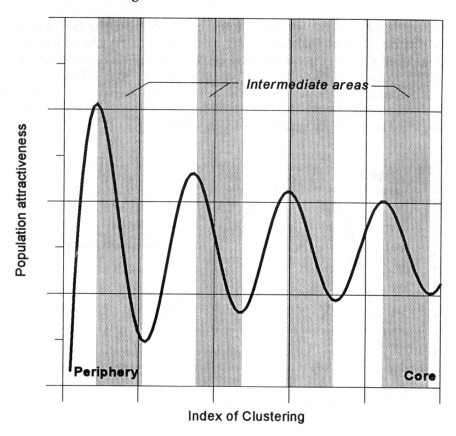

Figure 14.4   Interrelationship between Index of Clustering and the population attractiveness of towns

The functional relationship between the index of clustering and the population attractiveness of a town may form a complex wave-like curve with decreasing amplitude, similar to that known as the *Bessel* function. Periodic 'depressions' on this curve presumably correspond to thinly populated 'intermediate' areas between clusters of towns, which are found both in peripheral regions and in centrally located geographic areas.

In such a function, periodic 'depressions' on the curve may correspond to thinly populated, 'intermediate' areas which separate individual clusters of towns, in both peripheral and centrally located regions.

Note

[1] As mentioned previously (see the section of this book on city-size distribution), the choice of major cities is somewhat arbitrary. The services provided by cities of a particular population size may vary from country to country, depending on local economic and social patterns as well as on transportation infrastructure. A functional definition is, however, the most appropriate one in this context.

PART IV
CASE STUDIES

Towns are...'villages which succeeded'

F. Hudson, *A Geography of Settlements*

15 Selection of Case Studies

In order to confirm our hypothesis that the status of a town within the general setting of urban places is inter-related with the degree of sustainability it exhibits in its population growth and economic development, three tests must be met. These are: 1) The presence of reliable indicators of sustainability and location, in relation to major population centres of a country and to other urban places in the region; 2) The existence of comparable cases; and, lastly, 3) The availability of reliable and comparable sources of data.

Indicators of Location and Growth Sustainability

In the previous chapter, we introduced the Index of Clustering (IC), which is calculated as the ratio of two variables:

i) *Density of the urban field* in the region, measured as either the overall number of urban places located within commuting distance from a given town, or as the total population of the same area, and

ii) *The town's remoteness* from the closest major urban centre of the country, measured by either road distance or in estimated travel time.

Unlike other measures of location, such as socio-economic potential, agglomeration indices, aerial distances, densities, etc., the index in question reflects more accurately and reliably the town's location both in relation to other urban places within a region (intra-regional isolation) and relative to the principal cities of a country (remoteness). It is also important that, despite the relative simplicity of its calculation, the index in question takes into account the existing commuting patterns in a given country (commuting range), and the dynamic of population change around the urban place in question. The latter is reflected by the changing population size of the urban field of an urban place, whose relative location is to be estimated. These advantages seem to justify fully our choice of this index as an integrated *measure of urban location* for the following analysis.

The other element of our thesis requiring validation is the *measurement of sustainable growth of towns,* whose dependence on location factors is to be evaluated. In Chapter 9, we introduced an indicator of sustainable urban growth – the ratio between migration balance (MB) and natural growth (NG), which we called the MB/NG index. Compared with more direct indicators of population change in urban communities, such as overall growth, migration balance, etc., the index in question has a number of important advantages, namely simplification of cross-country comparison, comprehensiveness and the ease of interpretation.

The MB/NG index may be considered a *general* measure of sustainable urban growth, since enduring attractiveness of urban places implies sound economic development and other essential preconditions for sustainable urban growth. However, in the following analysis this indicator will be supplemented by more traditional measures of the socio-economic sustainability of urban places. These are the rates of unemployment and private construction, and home ownership patterns. These indicators, in addition to the MB/NG index, will be used to compare the development of different towns, where the availability of appropriate data makes such an analysis feasible.

Suitable and Comparable Cases

Since the present analysis attempts to investigate the effect of clustering on the development of towns in regions with different spatial characteristics, case studies will be carried out in countries with uneven patterns of population distribution and development.

In the following chapters of this section of the book (Part IV), three such case studies will be reported – Israel, Norway, and New South Wales (NSW is one of six states comprising the Commonwealth of Australia[1]). Although Israel, Norway and NSW differ substantially with respect to a number of indicators, such as land area, the overall rate of population growth, population density, etc. (see Table 15.1), all of them are characterised by large internal variations, particularly with respect to their population distribution.

Table 15.1 Selected socio-economic indicators of Israel, Norway, and New South Wales (NSW), Australia

Indicator	Israel	Norway	NSW
Population size [1,000][a]	6,000	4,400	6,400
Land area [km^2]	21,946	324,220	800,640
Overall population density per km^2	246	14	8
Population density in the most populated district[b] per km^2	6,717	1,144	328
Population density in the least populated district[c] per km^2	33.6	1.7	0.3
Overall population growth rate [%]	2.1	0.5	1.2
GDP [$US per capita][d]	18,100	24,700	22,260
Unemployment rate, per cent[e]	8.7	2.6	10.0
Net immigration rate, per 1,000 residents[f]	10.5	1.7	1.2
Interregional inequalities:[g]			
– population density	2.15	3.06	4.07
– average income[i]	0.16	0.12	0.13
– persons with higher education	0.48	0.24	NA

Compiled from: CIA (2000); ICBS (1998), SN (1999), and Australian Bureau of Statistics (1999).
[a] As of 1999; [b] the Oslo county in Norway; the Tel Aviv district in Israel, and Sydney Metropolitan Area in NSW; [c] The Be'er Sheva sub-district in Israel, the Finnmark county in Norway, and Broken Hill SLA in New South Wales, Australia; [d] as of 1998; [e] as of 1998 for Israel, 1997 for Norway and NSW; [f] including foreign immigrants to NSW (as of 1986-91); [g] calculated by the authors using the coefficient of variation (coefficient of variation = as inter-area standard deviation divided by the mean); [i] income per employee in Israel in 1995, income per taxpayer in Norway in 1997, and income per capita in NSW in 1991.

Thus, for instance, in the Tel Aviv district of Israel, the overall density of population exceeds 6,700 residents per km^2, while in the Be'er Sheva sub-district, this indicator is almost 200 times lower – only 34 persons per km^2.

In Norway, the ratio between the population densities in the most populated region, the Oslo county, which has 1,150 residents per km^2, and that of the least populated area, the Finnmark county, with only 1.7 residents per km^2, exceeds 600. Such a ratio is far greater for NSW – disparity in densities across geographic subdivisions of this state exceeds 1,000.

In order to avoid, as far as possible, problems resulting from lack of comparability of the towns in the sample, the following criteria were proposed:

- Population size of 10,000-50,000 residents (From the outset, the sample was restricted to small and medium-size towns and excluded rural settlements and large cities, whose development patterns are assumed to be quite different);
- Predominantly urban character of development. (While in Israel, local municipalities are either urban or rural, communities in Norway and Statistical Local Areas (SLAs) in NSW may consist of both urban and rural localities. In order to allow comparison, the sample of municipalities in Norway and NSW included only those in which the town forms the majority of the local population - see Table 15.2);

The number of towns included in each study and their basic characteristics are reported in Table 15.2, which shows that the samples generally satisfy the above criteria. A detailed list of the towns included in the study is given in Appendices 2-4, along with their development characteristics).

Table 15.2   Selected characteristics of the sets

Indicator	Israel	Norway	NSW
Overall size of the sample[a]	15	26	30
Population range [1,000 residents]	18-40	13-58	9-50
Period covered by the study	1970-94	1970-97	1980-91
Average per cent of population in towns of the above population size[b]	100	81	70
Sample split-up:			
Core towns[c]	5	6	6
Peripheral towns (I)[d]	5	7	15
Peripheral towns (II)[e]	5	10	-
Small regional centres and other special cases[f]	-	3	9

[a] number of municipalities in Israel and Norway, and the number of SLAs in NSW; [b] in NSW, percentage of population of Statistical Local Areas (SLAs) residing in towns of the above population size; [c] towns located within commuting range from one of the principal cities of the country; [d] distinguished by somewhat higher values of the index of clustering; [e] have lower values of clustering; [f] small administrative, cultural and educational centres of peripheral regions in Norway, coastal towns in NSW.

Comparable and Reliable Data Sources

For any given town, indicators of socio-economic performance may vary over a wide range in a short period of time. For instance, in a given year, a town may attract more migrants than in any number of previous years, while in the following year, the net migration balance of the town may become negative. Similar short-term fluctuations occur in other time-series data – unemployment rates, construction, etc. (see *inter alia* Balchin, 1990; Armstrong and Taylor; 1993; Diamond and Spence, 1983; Portnov and Pearlmutter, 1999a). To reduce the effect of such short-term fluctuations on the outcome of the analysis, long-term averages are required. Thus, it was important that the countries included in the sample (Israel, Norway and NSW) have comparable sets of long-term statistical data.

Another important issue to be considered is the effect of exogenous factors. For instance, if foreign immigration to a country fluctuates considerably from year to year (which is the case for Israel), the varying number of newcomers may complicate the temporal comparison and bring an undesirable bias into estimates of population growth of towns. To deal with such fluctuations, a procedure of normalisation may be used. For instance, the annual immigration component for a town may be normalised relative to the average annual immigration to the country for the entire time-span in question.

Other externalities imposed upon towns, apart from their location, are climate, overall employment situation, availability of services, etc. (see Chapter 10 of this book for a more detailed discussion). Unless properly controlled, these factors may mask the actual effects of a town's location. To deal with such potential problems, a multi-variant analysis technique, such as multiple regression analysis, should be used to confirm that location factors *do have* a statistically significant effect on the development of the towns included in the study.

Finally, it should be kept in mind that the effect of some of the factors influencing the long-term patterns of development of towns may be time-lagged, since it is the perception of reality, rather the actual conditions, which affects the decision making process of individuals (Portnov and Erell, 1998a). This is particularly true if the relevant information is not easily available, e.g. through first hand knowledge. Thus, for instance, potential migrants and investors often become aware of changes in conditions at distant destinations long after they have actually occurred. Therefore, the values of some of the explanatory variables (specifically, housing, employment, and services) should be lagged in order to reflect this process.

Note

[1] The urban settlement pattern in Australia is characterised by the nuclei of towns scattered around spatially dispersed principal cities – Sydney, Melbourne, Brisbane, Canberra, Perth, and Adelaide. Partly due to the large landmass of the country (some 7.7 million km^2) and to the concentration of nearly all fertile land along the ocean coast, some of these urban concentrations are thousands of kilometres apart, and their local climatic, geographic and socio-economic conditions are very different. In order to provide a settlement sample whose size is comparable to that in the other countries included in the study (See Table 15.2), and to minimise the possibility of errors introduced by a comparison of towns exposed to very different conditions, it was decided to select only one region of the Australian continent for the case study. New South Wales (NSW) was deemed appropriate since it has a population size comparable to those of the two other countries included in the study area (6.4 million residents). NSW also has the largest number of towns of any state in the Commonwealth (41 towns of 9,000+ residents). It has an uneven population distribution, with relatively dense population near the coast and sparser population in the dry interior. Each of these factors is extremely important for the present analysis, which required a relatively large number of diverse towns.

16 Israel – Case Study[1]

To study the effect of towns' location on their long-term socio-economic performance, the towns for the analysis were divided into separate sets, using the values of the Index of Clustering (see Chapter 14 of this book for a more detailed discussion) as the criterion for allocation:

- Set 1: Towns located within commuting distances of Tel Aviv;
- Set 2: Small towns in the Northern district (Galilee), where the closest city is Haifa, and
- Set 3: Towns of the Southern district, where the major centre is Be'er Sheva (Negev).[2]

A total of 15 towns were included in the sample (see Figure 16.1 for the location of towns and Appendix 2 for the towns' main development characteristics).

All the towns included in the sample were established within a relatively short period of time in the 1950s-early 1960s, as part of the large-scale 'development town' program of the government of Israel (see Figure 16.2). All else being equal, they are presumed to be at similar stages of their development.[3]

The relatively small size of the sample – 15 towns - was due to the absence of other settlements of comparable size, particularly in the Negev region. The need to establish sufficient socio-economic similarity of the settlements investigated, especially concerning their ethnic makeup, further restricted the sample size.

As mentioned in the previous chapter, the division of the samples into three homogeneous sets was considered to be essential in order to verify our initial hypothesis that specifics of location should have a substantial effect on the patterns of population growth of towns. It was also important to investigate whether proximity to major population centres may reverse the advantages of urban clustering, as hypothesised in Chapter 14 (see Figures 14.3-14.4).

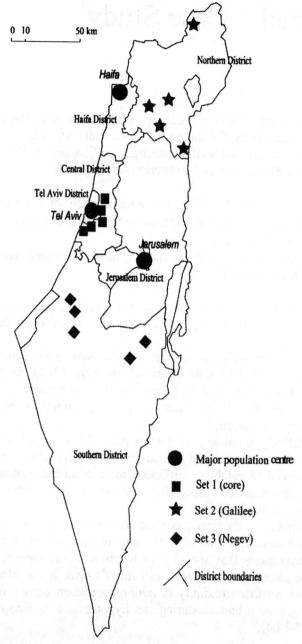

Figure 16.1 Location of towns included in the research sets in Israel

Variables and Data Sources

Twelve biannual points in time - 1970 through 1994 - were selected for the case study, using fully comparable and complete sets of data, which resulted in a total of 180 valid observations for the 15 towns in the sample. The time-series data for the analysis were drawn from the annual publications of Israeli Central Bureau of Statistics, 'Local Authorities in Israel: Physical Data' (ICBS, 1965-1997).

Dependent Variable

The original MB/NG index was used as an integrated indicator of sustainable population growth of the towns in the sample. This indicator has several drawbacks (see Chapter 9 of this book), but the interpretation of the results in the case of Israel was relatively simple, since all towns included in the study appeared to have only positive rates of natural growth throughout the' whole period. However, the use of the original MB/NG index may be somewhat problematic for a comparative analysis with other countries, particularly with Norway, in which many urban localities exhibit negative rates of natural growth. With due respect for this, it was decided to rank the cases included in the research samples using a 4-point categorical scale, as proposed in Chapter 9: +2.0 (sustainable growth), 0.5 (transitional growth), -0.5 (transforming growth), and –2.0 (decline).

Although such a scale does not reflect small differences among individual longitudinal values of the MB/NG index in a given year, it performs well with long-term averages. For instance, if the average value of this index for a given town over a 10-year period equals 1.5, its population growth during this period was due mainly to the town's attractiveness to migration (MB/NG>1). This, as suggested, is indicative of sustainable growth. Concurrently, an average of –1.5 on the revised scale indicates an absolute decline in population. In other words, the suggested categorical values, averaged over a period of several years, do not deviate from the original MB/NG scale and are still easy to interpret (see Table 9.1 in Chapter 9).

Explanatory Variables

The effect of a town's location, given by the Index of Clustering (IC), on the sustainability of its population growth, as measured by the MB/NG index, was compared with the effects of several other factors affecting development: housing, employment, employment growth, services, and population size (We shall not repeat the arguments concerning the importance of these factors, which were established in Chapter 10, but rather turn directly to the proxies chosen to measure their effects):

- *Housing.* The annual rate of new housing construction ['000 m^2 of floor area per annum] was chosen to reflect the condition of the housing market in the localities;
- *Employment.* Annual changes in unemployment in a community [%], were selected to reflect changes in the job market;
- *Services.* In the absence of detailed data on specific services, the average number of pupils per class in elementary and secondary schools was used as an indicator of the quality of educational facilities in a town;
- *Population size* was measured in thousands of residents residing in a town at the end of a given year;
- *Climate.* In Israel, over-heated conditions are often perceived as a major cause of thermal discomfort (Portnov and Erell, 1998a). Therefore, the mean annual number of days with heat stress was used as an index of climatic harshness (Bitan and Rubin, 1991);
- *Sets.* The allocation of a given town to a specific set of localities was represented by a categorical variable whose values correspond to a corresponding set number - 1 through 3. (The introduction of this factor as independent variable was designed to test whether homogeneous sets actually differ with respect to their long-term development trends);
- *Location.* The combined effect of remoteness and isolation was measured by the index of clustering. The practical range for daily commuting in Israel was assumed to be 20 km. (For a definition of this index and its use, see Chapter 14 of this book).

Analysis Technique

Statistical significance of the factors influencing the sustainability of population growth, indicated by the MB/NG index, was identified and measured by Multiple Regression Analysis (MRA). In particular, three functional forms of regression models – a double linear form, linear-log, and double-log form – were tested.

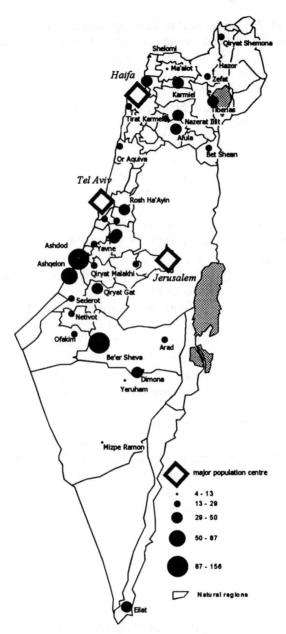

Figure 16.2   Location and population size of development towns in Israel (thousands of residents, as of 1997)

Although the double-linear form appeared to provide the best fit in most cases, our reluctance to use this functional form was due to consideration of homogeneity of variance. On the other hand, a logarithmic transformation helped us to ensure the homoscedasticity of errors. The Hartley's F-Max test for violations of the similarity-of-variance assumption confirmed that variances are indeed homoscedastic. Therefore, in the following discussion, linear-log models, providing the second best fit, are reported. The collinearity of explanatory variables was also tested. The collinearity statistic, reported in Table 16.1, indicates that the collinearity among the variables is within tolerable limits (Tol.>0.3).

Two additional considerations also deserve a note.

In Israel, the overall rate of foreign immigration has been subject to substantial annual changes, varying from 9,500 immigrants in 1986 to about 199,500 immigrants in 1990 (ICBS, 1998 – Statistical Abstract of Israel). Since the rate of immigration to a particular community is a key component of its migration balance (MB), it may be expected that the above fluctuations in the overall number of new immigrants affect directly the values of the suggested indicator of sustainability (the MB/NG index). In order to reduce the impact of the annual fluctuation in the rate of foreign immigration on the outcome of the analysis, initial immigration data for each community were normalised, as suggested in Chapter 15 of this book, using the average annual immigration to the country for the entire time-span in question (42,000 new immigrants per annum) as the conditional base line.

As argued in Chapter 15, the effect of some of the factors influencing population growth of towns is normally time-lagged, since it is the perception of reality, rather the actual conditions, which affects the decision making process of individuals. With due regard for this, the values of some of the explanatory variables (housing, employment, and services) were one-year lagged in order to reflect this process.

Research Results

Influencing Factors

The results of multiple regression analysis are given in Table 16.1. Though the model fit is not exceptionally high ($R^2=0.407$), this may be attributed to a relatively large number of observations (180). At the same time, it is worth noting that three out of seven explanatory variables included in the analysis appeared to be highly significant statistically (T>3.0; P<0.01), and all of these significant variables exhibit the expected signs. The dominant factors affecting the structure of population growth (P<0.01) are *housing, clustering,* and *climatic harshness.*

Table 16.1 **Factors affecting the structure of population growth (the MB/NG index) of selected towns in Israel (MRA – linear-log form)**

	B[a]	T[b]	Significance[c]	Tolerance[d]
Population size	-0.064	-0.236	0.814	0.647
Services	0.311	1.309	0.193	0.584
Unemployment change	0.027	0.111	0.912	0.936
Housing	0.632	3.169	0.002	0.849
Index of clustering	0.199	3.064	0.003	0.349
Climate	-1.727	-4.295	0.000	0.606
Sets	0.094	0.270	0.788	0.307
Constant	3.124	0.964	0.337	
No of observations	180			
R^2	0.407			
F	9.722			
Durbin-Watson	2.259			

[a] Unstandardised coefficients; [b] t-statistic; [d] significance of t-statistic (probability of occurrence by chance); [d] statistic used to determine how much the independent variables are linearly related to one another (multicollinearity), and is the proportion of a variable's variance not accounted for by other independent variables in the equation.

It appears that, contrary to our initial assumption (see Chaps. 13-14), grouping a number of small urban centres may improve their chances of achieving sustainable population growth not only in peripheral areas, but in densely populated core areas as well, as long as the value of the index of clustering increases. This unexpected result warranted further testing. To this end, the long-term averages of the MB/NG indices were plotted against two indices of clustering - IC1 and IC2. (The definitions of these indices were introduced in Chapter 14 of this book, which dealt with indices of clustering as integrated measures of urban location.)

Clustering vs. MB/NG Index

The relationship between the suggested measure of sustainable population growth, the MB/NG index, and that of the settlement location, as described

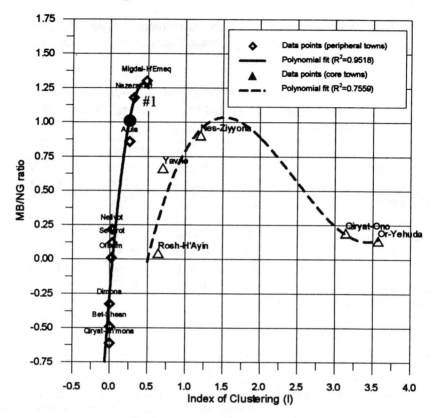

Figure 16.3   Sustainability of population growth (the MB/NG index) as a function of towns' location (IC1)

Each symbol represents twelve-year averages computed for the selected localities (Sets 1 through 3). The filled dot (#1) corresponds to the point beyond which migration balance (MB) tends to become the predominant source of a town's population growth.

by the indices of clustering (IC1 and IC2), is shown in Figures 16.3 and 16.4.

The models appear to be good fits (R^2=0.76-0.95) and are relatively easy to interpret. The graphs show that, fully in line with our initial assumptions (see Chaps. 13 and 14), the sustainability of population growth of towns increases initially with increasing values of the index of clustering. In particular, when the value of this index is greater than 0.25 (IC1, Figure 16.3) or 3.5 (IC2, Figure 16.4), respectively, migration becomes the major component of a town's population growth. This transition from less sustainable growth (MB/NG<-0.5) to more sustainable

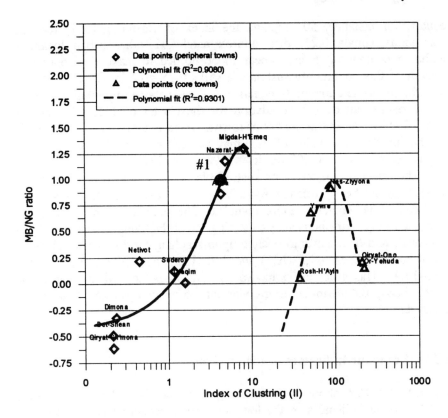

Figure 16.4 Sustainability of population growth (the MB/NG index) as a function of towns' location (IC2)

See comments to Figure 16.3.

development (MB/NG>1.0) is clearly seen in Figures 16.3-16.4 (peripheral communities). Thus, when the values of IC1 increase from 0.0 (Qiryat Sh'mona) to 0.5 (Migdal-H'Emeq), the respective multi-year averages of the MB/NG index grow from −0.6 (transforming growth) to 1.3 (sustained growth). In terms of IC2 (Figure 16.4), this transition takes place in the interval of 0.1-8.0.

While the first index (IC1) helps to identify the absolute number of towns forming such a sustainable urban cluster, the latter index (IC2) indicates the cluster's population size. Let us consider an example. If the distance from a particular town to the closest major city of the country equals, for instance, 50 km, and the index of clustering (IC1) for this community equals 0.25, then approximately 12 other urban localities within a commuting range appear to be needed to make the population growth of this community sustainable (50 x 0.25 = 12.5). Concurrently, if IC2 for the same community equals 3.5, then sustained population growth would require an overall population for the cluster of 175,000 residents (50x3.5=175). A similar cluster of towns, which is more remote (100 km), but having the same value of IC2, may become sustainable once the total population exceeds 350,000 residents (100x3.5=350).

The effect of clustering on sustainable population growth of centrally located towns (Set 1: Rosh-H'Ayin, Yavne, Nes-Ziyyona, Qiryat-Ono and Or-Yehuda) is, however, more complex. The population of these towns grows initially with increasing clustering (Rosh-H'Ayin, Yavne, and Nes-Ziyyona), and then starts to decline upon reaching the following values of the location indices – 1,5 (IC1) and 100 (IC2), respectively (see Figures 16.3-16.4). This inflection point was, in fact, hypothesised in Chapter 14 of this book, and attributed to growing inter-town competition for potential migrants.

IC vs. Economic Indicators of Urban Growth

Figures 16.5-16.6 show the relationship between the index of clustering and two other indicators of the long-term socio-economic performance of towns, namely the average annual rate of private construction (Figure 16.5), and unemployment (Figure 16.6).

The use of the latter indicator - private construction - deserves a note. Unlike that of public construction, which is often affected by political and ideological considerations rather than by market demand (see Portnov and Pearlmutter (1999b) for a more detailed discussion), the intensity of private construction in the locality is a better indicator of the local 'investment climate' and of the attractiveness of the town to private investors in general.

As Figure 16.5 shows, the rate of private construction in the towns grows initially as clustering of the urban field increases (Sederot, Netivot, Arad, Yavne, Migdal H'Emeq, Afula, Rosh H'Ayin). Then, upon reaching a certain threshold (IC1=1.0-1.5), the rate of private construction starts to decline (Nes Ziyyona, Qiryat Ono and Or Yehuda). We may recall that the ∩-shaped functional relationship between the index of clustering (IC) and the socio-economic development of urban communities was, in fact, predicted in the previous discussion. It was assumed, in particular, that an

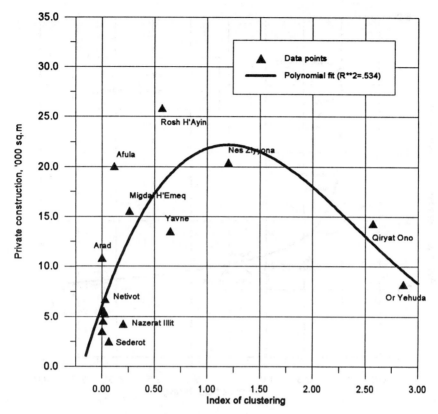

Figure 16.5   **Index of clustering vs. the rate of private construction in selected towns**

Each symbol represents a twelve-year average for a locality. As the diagram indicates, the per capita rate of private construction increases initially in line with increasing values of the index of clustering. Then, after reaching a certain threshold (IC=1.0-1.5), the per capita rate of construction starts to decline. Apparent reasons are inter-town competition for potential investors and adverse effects of excessive agglomeration – high land prices, environmental degradation, etc.

increase in urban clustering may have a positive effect on the socio-economic development of peripheral localities, while in densely populated core areas, the dense patterns of urbanisation may have an adverse effect on the socio-economic development of individual towns due to 'inter-town competition' for potential investors and migrants.

The relationship between the index of clustering (IC1) and the local unemployment rates appears to be more straightforward. As Figure 16.6 shows, the employment situation in the localities tends, in general, to

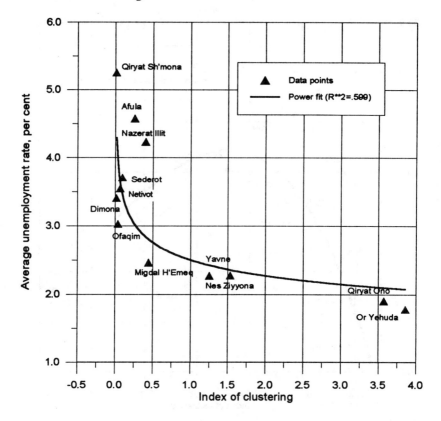

Figure 16.6   Index of clustering vs. average per cent of unemployed in selected urban localities

Each symbol represents a twelve-year average for a locality. As the diagram shows, the extent of unemployment in a community tends to decline as the clustering of the urban field increases. It appears that the population of denser urban clusters generally creates more opportunities of employment with a daily commuting range. At the same time, the population of isolated towns may have fewer opportunities for alternative employment within a daily reach and may thus be more vulnerable to adverse economic changes in the localities.

improve, as the density of the urban field (as indicated by IC1) increases. The nature of this relationship is rather simple: The population of a town surrounded by a number of other urban communities may have more opportunities for employment; if employment is not available in the town in question, it may be found in one of the adjacent urban places within the spatial range practicable for daily commuting.

Notes

[1] The present chapter is partly based on Portnov *et al* (2000).

[2] The majority of urban settlements in Israel is concentrated along the Mediterranean coast, or in close proximity to its major metropolitan centres - Tel Aviv, Jerusalem, and Haifa (see Figure 16.1). The overall population of these urban centres along with their immediate hinterland (i.e. the Tel Aviv, Central, Jerusalem, and Haifa districts) amounts to over 3.5 million residents, or nearly 70% of the country's population. The concentration of the country's population and lack of development in outlying regions create significant problems for national security as well as for maintaining the future capacity for absorption of immigrants. Realising the extent of these problems, government and planning officials in Israel have favoured at various times the implementation of a policy promoting dispersal of the population to the peripheral regions of the country. While from the early 1950's to late 1960's, this policy was sustained primarily by directing new immigrants to sparsely populated areas of the country (Fialkoff, 1992), it was gradually replaced by geographically selective 'aid programs', which provided financial incentives to builders and buyers in specified development areas. The subsequent population growth of settlements in these development areas was generally slower than initially expected (Newman *et al*, 1995). Moreover, the pattern of growth did not exhibit (at least at first glance) any direct relationship with the settlements' geographic location either in the peripheral areas or in the central districts of the country. This irregularity prompted in recent years a fairly heated discussion about the nature of the factors determining population growth patterns of urban settlements located in various regions of the country.

[3] For a detailed discussion of the population dispersal policy in Israel and its implications for subsequent patterns of internal migration see Portnov and Etzion (2000).

17 Norway – Case Study[1]

Although the landmass of Norway is not exceedingly large (323,900 km²), the country stretches for nearly 2,000 km from north to south, and its settlement pattern is extremely diverse. Unlike Israel, where only three sets of towns were formed, in Norway, large distances and different functions of towns made it possible to form four sets of towns for the subsequent analysis (see Figure 17.1):

- *Set 1* included urban municipalities located in the Østfold, Buskerud and Akershus counties, within commuting distance from Oslo;[2]
- *Set 2* (Periphery I) consisted of a group of towns located mainly along the Oslo fjord in the Vestfold, Telemark, and Østfold counties. Although these municipalities are parts of the south-east core region of the country, they are located beyond distances practicable for daily commuting to Oslo (assumed to be less than 60 km);
- *Set 3* (Periphery II) included more remote towns in the Hedmark, Oppland, Troms, Møre og Romsdal, and Nordland counties;
- *Set 4* consisted of small educational and economic centres of Northern Norway – Alta, Bodø, and Tromsø (According to the Standard Classification of Municipalities (SN, 1994), these communities are defined as central and less central service industry municipalities (Classes 6 and 7) in which service industries employ more than twice as many people as production industries.

These four sets cover 26 towns of the country (see Figure 17.1). The full list of towns included in the samples and their main development characteristics are given in Appendix 3. The data for the analysis were obtained from the Municipality Database maintained by the Norwegian Social Science Data Services, Bergen (NSD), and include 28 annual observations for each of 26 municipalities included in the sample, over the period 1970-1997, i.e. a total of 728 observations.[3] However, the analysis was somewhat restricted by the lack of annual data for housing, which are reported in Norway only in Censuses of Population and Housing held each ten years. The overall number of fully documented observations for Norway was thus 52 - two for each of 26 towns.

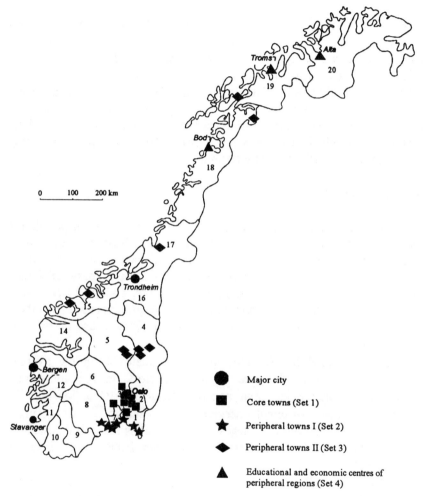

Figure 17.1 Location of towns included in the research sets in Norway

Counties: 1- Østfold; 2 – Akershus; 3 – Oslo; 4 – Hedmark; 5 – Oppland; 6 – Buskerud; 7 – Vestfold; 8 – Telemark; 9 – Aust-Agder; 10 – Vest-Agder; 11 – Rogaland; 12 – Hordaland; 14- Sogn og Fjordane; 15 – Møre og Romsdal; 16 – Sør-Trødelag; 18 – Nordland; 19 – Troms; 20 – Finnmark (County #13 is notably missing. This is due to a merge between two counties in the 1970s, upon which one larger county – Hordaland – was formed).

Components of the Model

Dependent Variable

Like the case study of Israel (see Chapter 16 of this book), long term-averages of migration and natural growth were calculated for each municipality in the sample. These values were used to calculate the MB/NG index. The original values were subsequently transformed into a 4-point categorical scale: +2.0 (sustainable growth), 0.5 (transitional growth), -0.5 (transforming growth), and -2.0 (decline). Although this scale does not reflect small differences among individual longitudinal values of the MB/NG index in a given year, it performs well with long-term averages and is still easy to interpret.

Explanatory Variables

The effects of *remoteness* and *isolation* on the sustainability of population growth of towns in Norway, as measured by the MB/NG index, were compared with the effects of other factors presumed to have an effect. These factors were similar to those used in the case study of Israel: housing, employment, employment growth, services, and population size. Below we shall outline only differences in the proxies used for these factors' estimation, as compared to those used in the Israeli case study:

- *Housing:* Availability of housing was estimated from the average annual increase in the size of housing stock in the community compared to the previous year, as a percentage of existing housing;
- *Services:* Two different service-related indicators were used: a) number of students in colleges and universities per 1,000 residents, and b) number of effective hospital beds per 1,000 residents of the municipality;
- *Climate:* Two climatic indices - average annual precipitation [mm] and mean temperature in January [^{0}C] - were considered as proxies for climatic harshness in Norway. In the following discussion, only the better performing indicator – precipitation – is reported;
- *Sets:* Although this variable was included initially in the multiple regression analysis (MRA), as it was in the case study of Israel, we omitted it subsequently from the equation due to its strong collinearity with another explanatory variable – the index of clustering – which appeared to have better statistical performance;

- *Index of clustering:* In estimating this index, the practical range for daily commuting, based on actual commuting patterns in Norway, was assumed to be 60 km (compared to 20 km in Israel).

General Model

Results of the multiple regression analysis are shown in Table 17.1. The model fit appears to be reasonably high ($R^2=0.725$), and nearly half of explanatory variables are not only statistically significant ($T>2.0$; $P<0.05$) but also exhibit the expected signs. The dominant factors affecting the structure of population growth ($P<0.05$) are *housing, clustering,* and *hospital services.*

Table 17.1   Factors affecting the structure of population growth (the MB/NG index) of selected municipalities of Norway (MRA – linear-log form)

Factor	B[a]	T[b]	Significance	Tolerance[c]
Population size	-0.167	-0.464	0.650	0.433
Hospitals	0.104	2.171	0.048	0.671
Educational services	0.081	1.132	0.277	0.241
Unemployment change	-0.087	-0.166	0.870	0.376
Housing	2.634	4.037	0.001	0.456
Index of clustering	0.381	2.694	0.017	0.329
Climate	-0.243	-0.553	0.589	0.315
Constant	-0.488	-0.159	0.876	
No of observations	52			
R^2	0.725			
F	5.267			
Durbin-Watson	2.016			

[a] Unstandardised coefficients; [b] t-statistic; [d] significance of t-statistic (probability of occurrence by chance); [c] a statistic used to determine the extent to which the independent variables are linearly related to one another (multicollinearity), and is the proportion of a variable's variance not accounted for by other independent variables in the equation.

Since the sign of the clustering variable is positive, it appears that, like in Israel, grouping a number of small urban centres may improve their chances of achieving sustainable population growth, in core areas as well as in peripheral areas. As in the previous case study, this result warranted

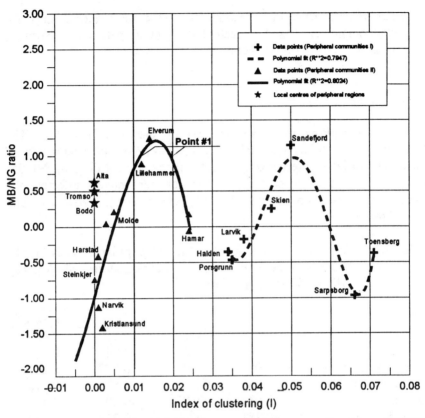

Figure 17.2   **Sustainability of population growth (the MB/NG index) as a function of communities' location (IC1)**

Each symbol represents 28-year averages (1970-1997) computed for the selected localities (Sets 1-4). The filled dot (#1) corresponds to the point beyond which migration balance (MB) tends to become the predominant source of a community's population growth.

further testing. To this effect, the long-term averages of the MB/NG indices were plotted against the two indices of clustering - IC1 and IC2 (See Chapter 14 of this book for a more detailed discussion).

Clustering vs. MB/NG Index

As Figures 17.2-17.3 show, the relationship between clustering of the urban field (IC) and the degree of sustainability exhibited by urban communities in Norway in their population growth (the MB/NG index) is neither linear nor proportional. In less densely populated areas, the values

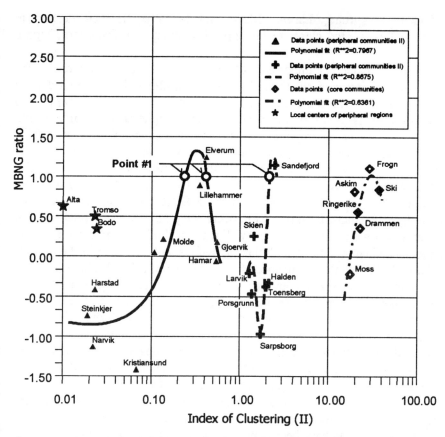

Figure 17.3 **Sustainability of population growth (the MB/NG index) as a function of communities' location (IC2)**

See comments to Figure 17.2.

of the MB/NG index tend to increase initially in line with growth in clustering, but when the urban field becomes relatively more dense and inter-town competition increases, the attractiveness of individual towns starts to decline.

This trend is observed in virtually all of the sets of towns included in the study. For instance, in Set 3, sustainability of population growth increases initially when IC1's values (Figure 17.2) grow from 0.001 to 0.015 (Kristiansund, Narvik, Steinkjer, Harstad, Molde, Lillehammer and Elverum), then it drops when a threshold of 0.015 is passed (Gjøvik and Hamar). In Set 2, values of IC1 (Figure 17.2) increase from 0.035 to 0.05

(Halden, Porsgrunn, Larvik, Skien and Sandefjord), then decline in communities located closer to the core (Sarpsborg and Toensberg; Figure 17.2).

One comment is important: Moving closer towards core areas, the values of the index of clustering may increase, although the actual density of the urban field may, at some point, decline. This may happen in transition areas lying between clusters of peripheral communities and densely populated metropolitan areas. In these areas, the values of the MB/NG index appear to grow again in line with increasing values of the index of clustering (Halden-Porsgrunn-Larvik-Skien; Figure 17.2). Consequently, as hypothesised in Chapter 14 of this book, the relationship between the index of clustering and the MB/NG index forms a complex wave-like (M-shaped) curve with decreasing amplitude, similar to that which is known as the *Bessel curve*. 'Fragments' of this curve are found in Israel (see Chapter 16), though the relatively small land area of the country apparently limited the occurrence of a wide range of possible situations.

Three peripheral communities of Norway – Alta, Tromsø and Bodø – deviate clearly from the general trend (Figures 17.2-17.3). These remote communities have low values of the index of clustering, but have substantially higher values of the MB/NG index than would have been expected. A possible explanation for this discrepancy may be that the communities in question are educational, administrative, cultural and economic centres of their respective regions. The presence of colleges, hospitals, and other unique regional functions may increase the attractiveness of these communities to residents of surrounding areas, beyond what would have been expected from spatial considerations alone.

Although it is clear that clustering of the urban field is not the only factor affecting population growth of these towns, the unexpected 'surplus' in this particular case is likely to be at the *expense of more remote and less developed towns in the surrounding areas*. This assumption appears to be supported by the fact that net out-migration from the above communities to the Oslo-Akershus region is compensated for by a net migration gain from surrounding areas (see Table 17.2).

The point of inflection at which the MB/NG index reaches the 1.0 threshold (see Point #1 in Figures 17.2-17.3) is important. This threshold indicates that migration becomes the predominant component of a community's population growth. As Figures 17.2-17.3 show, a peripheral urban community in Norway appears to reach this threshold at the following ranges of clustering: 0.01-0.02 (IC1) and 0.3-0.5 (IC2), respectively. Therefore, if the road distance from an urban community to the closest major urban centre of the country equals, for instance, 200 km, the overall size of the urban cluster required to achieve sustainable population growth is approximately 60,000-100,000 residents (200x0.3x 1,000=60,000; 200x0.5x1,000=100,000).

Analogously, the growth of a similar cluster of towns in Norway located 500 km from the nearest major city may become sustainable once its population exceeds 150,000 residents. Not surprisingly, these absolute thresholds are much lower than those found in smaller and more densely populated Israel (see Chapter 16).

Table 17.2   Net migration in selected municipalities of Norway in 1990, 1993 and 1997, persons

'Source' municipality/ migrants' destinations	1990	1993	1997
Bodø			
North of Norway	253	358	455
Nordland	216	311	314
Akershus/Oslo	-95	-83	-208
Abroad	-30	59	166
Tromsø			
North of Norway	458	597	466
Troms	333	358	179
Akershus/Oslo	-60	-129	-462
Abroad	-55	164	126
Alta			
North of Norway	95	61	91
Finnmark	68	130	112
Akershus/Oslo	9	-24	-71
Abroad	105	95	20

Notes

[1] The chapter is partially based on Portnov *et al* (2000).

[2] The concentration of population and economic activity in the core areas of Norway is clearly evident. Two counties – Oslo and Akershus - form the core region of Norway (see Figure 17.1). They occupy only *two* per cent of its land area but are home to more than 20 per cent of the country's population and generate almost 30 per cent of the overall taxable income (SN, 1997-1999). Concurrently, three large counties of North Norway – Nordland, Troms and Finnmark, – which together account for about 35 per cent of Norway's total area, have less than 11 per cent of the country's population and generate only 9 per cent of the overall taxable income *(ibid.)*. Not surprisingly, the core areas of

the country have a much higher intake of migrants (Rees *et al,* 1998; Portnov *et al,* 2000; SN, 1997; Stambøl, 1991).

[3] In Israel, local municipalities are either urban or rural; In Norway, however, municipalities may consist of both urban and rural localities. With this in mind, the sample of municipalities in Norway included only those in which a town of 10-50,000 residents forms the majority of the local population (see Appendix 3).

18 Australia – Case Study[1]

New South Wales (NSW), selected for the present case study (see Chapter 15 for a more detailed discussion of the reasons and considerations for its selection), is located in the south-eastern part of the Australian continent. It is the most populated state of the Australian Commonwealth (6.3 million residents, as of 1997), and one of the most industrialised and urbanised ones (ABS, 1999).

NSW was the first state settled by the Europeans. Sydney, its capital, (3.3 million residents, as of 1996), was established in 1788, when British ships landed 1,373 people at Port Jackson, including 732 convicts. The settlement was later named after Lord Sydney, Secretary of State for Home Affairs, who authorised the colonisation of the continent. The development of settlements in the continental part of NSW began when gold was first discovered in 1851 at Bathurst, some 160 km west of Sydney. Following this discovery, numerous tent cities of prospectors were established, some housing as many as 40,000 people. Most of these tent settlements later disappeared as prospectors moved to the next gold field (AEW, 2000).

Presently, urban development in NSW is concentrated predominantly along its ocean coast, with most coastal settlements exhibiting higher rates of population growth and more dynamic economies than those in inland areas (see Table 18.1). At least in part, these differences are due to the continuous decline of the 'traditional' inland economy, based on mining and agriculture, and the development of the 'new economy' based upon information technologies, leisure activities and tourism.

Because of these differences between coastal and inland settlements in NSW, a simple division of town sets into categories based on the values of the index of clustering was considered insufficient for the present case study. The settlement sample was therefore divided into three subgroups, with a clear separation of coastal towns into an individual set (see Figure 18.1; Appendix 4):

247

Table 18.1   Development characteristics of selected inland and coastal Statistical Local Areas (SLAs) of NSW*

Group of SLAs	Immigration in 1991	Migration balance 1981-86	Migration balance 1986-91	Income change in 1986-91 [%]
Inland SLAs:				
Grafton	758	3,490	-371	26.0
Casino	444	-420	-191	31.3
Muswellbrook	1,002	554	-364	13.8
Armidale	2,496	-285	87	23.2
Bathurst	2,353	1,586	840	28.6
Orange	2,712	-336	-393	25.1
Tamworth	1,912	-565	-626	22.5
Inverell	236	-595	-676	28.9
Albury	4,005	605	-278	19.2
Parkes	682	-989	-645	29.9
Dubbo	1,845	396	677	27.6
Wagga Wagga	3,905	-582	1,193	25.6
Moree Plains	867	-1,188	-1,352	24.5
Griffith	3,303	-770	-1,145	26.2
Broken Hill	1,182	-3,017	-1,731	24.5
Average:	1,847	-141	-332	25.1
Coastal SLAs:				
Ballina	2,868	3,066	4,384	40.4
Eurobodalla	3,435	3,630	4,158	29.3
Tweed	4,732	4,323	6,491	31.9
Hastings	5,197	4,978	5,745	36.0
Port Stephens	4,943	4,406	4,155	27.8
Kiama	2,094	1,170	1,460	29.3
Coffs Harbour	6,120	4,864	5,083	31.8
Greater Taree	2,961	2,194	2,833	27.2
Average:	4,044	3,579	4,308	31.7

Source: Compiled from publications of Australian Bureau of Statistics; *SLAs listed are those with predominantly urban population living in towns of 9,000-50,000 residents.

- *Set 1* (core towns) included inland towns located within commuting distance from one of the major urban centres of the region – Sydney, Canberra, Newcastle, or Wollongong;

- *Set 2* (inland peripheral towns) consisted of a group of towns located in the continental part of the state, beyond distances practicable for daily commuting to the principle cities (assumed to be approximately 100 km – see Chapter 1 for a more detailed discussion);[2]
- *Set 3* (coastal towns) included towns of the coastal plain located beyond commuting distance from the principle cities, estimated at about 100 km.

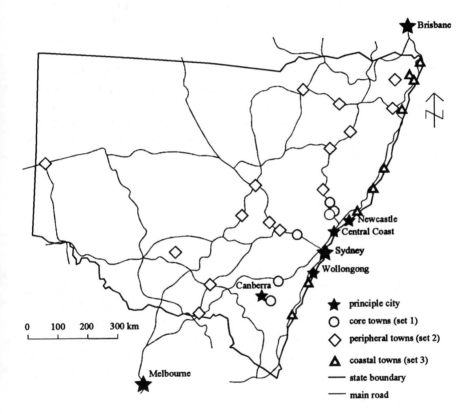

Figure 18.1 NSW: Location of the towns included in the sets

Three separate sets of towns are formed: core towns, located within commuting distances form one of the major population centres of the state (Set 1); inland peripheral towns, located beyond the commuting range from the principle cities (Set 2), and coastal towns (Set 3). The grouping of the coastal towns into a separate set was due to evidence that these towns tend to exhibit more dynamic economies than their inland counterparts, and attract many more migrants.

The full list of towns included in each of the sets and their selected development characteristics are given in Appendix 4.

Data for the analysis were obtained from the publications of Australian Bureau of Statistics reporting the results of the quinquennial Census of Population and Housing[3]. In particular, data from two census enumerations (1986 and 1991) were used for the analysis.

The analysis was restricted to Statistical Local Areas (Census Local Government Areas prior to 1986), which is the finest spatial grid for which migration and other population data are reported in the local census enumerations.

From the outset, our analysis was limited to investigating patterns of population growth in urban settlements of a particular population size – 10,000-50,000 residents. In particular, only SLAs in which a central town of the above size forms the majority of population were included in the sample (Appendix 4). The procedure for pre-selection of urban localities, used in Norway (see Chapter 17 of this book), was applied to the present case study as well.

Components of the Model

Dependent Variable

As in the previous cases studies (see Chapters 16 and 17 of this book), the MB/NG index was used as to measure sustainable population growth of towns. However, lack of comparable data in NSW required readjustment of the index. In particular, there are neither direct figures for natural growth (NG) at the SLA level, nor separate figures for foreign immigrants.

In view of these limitations, the closest approximation of the missing values of NG we could get was as follows: First, the rates of overall growth (OG) were calculated based on the difference between population sizes of an SLA in the 1991 and 1986 Census counts. Then, the rates of NG were estimated by subtracting the net balance of internal migration (IN), and the change in the number of foreign-born residents (ΔFB) from the rates of overall growth: $NG=OG-(IN+\Delta FB)$.

Calculating the rates of natural growth in this manner is not, however, sufficiently accurate. First, the change of the number of foreign-born residents *is not* identical to the balance of external migration, since the former indicator (ΔFB) includes not only external migration but also the natural change in the immigrant population (mortality rates). In addition, the census includes temporary residents and visitors in the localities, and excluded those absent from home at the time of the census count. This creates large errors in towns with a large transient population, such as resort towns.

Due to these limitations on the input data, we were reluctant to calculate the values of the MB/NG index directly, as the ratio between migration balance (MB) and natural growth (NG), and, therefore, opted for a more complicated procedure, using a hyperbolic tangent transformation (tanh2), described in detail in Chapter 9 of this book. This procedure requires two inputs – the rate of overall growth (MB+NG) and the sign (rather than actual values) of the natural growth – and thus permits a certain degree of elasticity concerning the inputs. The resulting scale of the transformed index does not, however, deviate from the original one (see Table 9.1 in Chapter 9) and is thus still easy to interpret and compare with the results of other case studies.

Explanatory Variables

Like the case studies of Israel and Norway (see Chapters 16 and 17), the NSW study included the following major aspects of the towns' development: employment, location, personal incomes, and climatic conditions. In addition, an indicator of proximity to the coast was included as a separate variable, while 'housing construction' and 'service' variables, used in other case studies, were omitted from the present analysis due to a lack of data. The list of explanatory variables in the current study was as follows:

- *Unemployment.* The index chosen to reflect the condition of the employment market was the average annual change in the per cent of unemployed in a community [%];
- *Population size* was measured in thousands of residents in an SLA at the beginning of the given inter-census period;
- *Climate.* Two climate-related variables – the average annual amount of precipitation [mm] and the mean temperature in July [°C] - were included initially in the analysis. (In the following discussion, only the better performing variable – precipitation – is reported);[4]
- *Proximity to the coast.* This variable was estimated as the minimal road distance from the central town of the SLA to the ocean coast, in km. (As mentioned in the previous discussion, in-land and coastal communities of NSW are expected to differ substantially in their patterns of population growth);

- *Per capita income* was measured in AUD$ as an indicator of the overall material standard of living;
- *Location.* Like in other case studies, the combined effect of remoteness and isolation of towns was measured by the Index of Clustering (for definition of this index and the discussion of its performance, see Chapter 14).

Influencing Factors

Multiple regression analysis (MRA) was used to identify and measure the statistical significance of the factors affecting the population growth of towns (as estimated by the MB/NG index). The results of the analysis are reported in Table 18.2.

Table 18.2   Factors affecting the population growth of towns (MRA – linear-log form)[a]

Variable	B[b]	Beta[c]	T[d]	T Sig[e]	Tolerance[f]
Coast proximity	-0.240	-0.670	-3.426	0.002	0.280
Index of Clustering	-0.143	-0.394	-2.200	0.038	0.333
Per capita income	-0.013	-0.011	-0.056	0.956	0.272
Population size	0.727	0.471	3.589	0.002	0.620
Rainfall	0.265	0.328	2.171	0.041	0.469
Unemployment	-0.328	-0.320	-1.678	0.107	0.293
Constant (B_o)	-6.595		-2.799	0.010	
R^2	0.754				
F	11.758[g]				
Number of cases	29				

[a] Dependent variable: the MB/NG index (adjusted hyperbolic tangent transformation (tanh2)– see Chapter 9 for more detail); [b] unstandardised coefficients; [c] standardised coefficients; [d] *t*-statistic; [e] significance level of *t*-statistic; [f] a statistic used to determine the extent to which the independent variables are linearly related to one another, and is the proportion of a variable's variance not accounted for by other independent variables in the equation; [g] indicates a 0.0001 two-tailed significance level.

As the table shows, four factors appear to be statistically significant (T>2.0; P<0.5) in this context. The factors are ranked according to the values of their standardised regression coefficients: *proximity to the coast, population size, index of clustering,* and the *amount of rainfall*.

Notably, three out of four statistically significant factors exhibit the expected signs. The sustainability of population growth of towns (as measured by the MB/NG index) appears to decline as distance from the ocean coast increases (B=-0.240; T=-3.426), and grow in line with increasing population size of the communities (B=0.727; T=3.589) and the amount of rainfall (B=0.265; T=0.171). These trends are, in general, not surprising. A similar link between population size and growth trends was also reported in the previous case studies. A somewhat stronger population growth potential of coastal towns in NSW was also predicted in the previous discussion. The average annual rainfall of some 600-1400 mm observed in the area does not apparently result in discomfort; however, greater rainfall allows more intensive and productive agriculture, an important source of income of many inland communities in the past, and still significant today.

A decline of the MB/NG index in line with increasing values of the index of clustering (B=-0.143; T=-2.200) is, however, more surprising, since in the previous case studies (see Chapters 16 and 17 of this book), we found that urban clustering was, in general, conducive to sustainable population growth of towns, though this relationship was not linear. This finding clearly warrants a further discussion.

Population Growth vs. Index of Clustering

The relationship between the suggested measure of sustainable population growth, the MB/NG index, and that of the settlement location, as described by the index of clustering (IC2), is shown in Figure 18.2.

If the coastal towns of NSW (whose names are shown in *italics* in Figure 18.2) are not considered, the relationship between the MB/NG index and the index of clustering is strikingly similar to that found in Israel and Norway (see Figure 16.4 in Chapter 16 and Figure 17.3 in Chapter 17).

In particular, the sustainability of population growth of towns in NSW increases initially with increasing values of the index of clustering (Moree, Inverell-Griffith, Parkes, Tamworth, Dubbo and Armidale; see Figure 18.2). Then, when the value of the index of clustering (IC2) reaches 0.2-0.3 (Wagga-Wagga, Bathurst, Orange and Albury-Wodonga), the MB/NG ratio approaches 1.0, which indicates that migration is close to becoming the major component of a town's population growth.

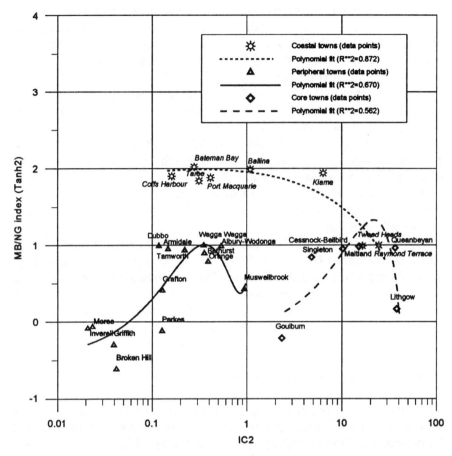

Figure 18.2   Sustainability of population growth (the MB/NG index) as a function of towns' location (IC2)

Each symbol represents a five-year average for 1986-91. The polynomial regression lines for towns comprising separate sets are fitted separately (coastal towns, core towns and peripheral towns).

After reaching the above threshold of clustering (IC2=0.2-0.3), the values of the MB/NG index appear to drop again (Muswellbrook and Goulburn), implying that the growth of these towns tends to become less sustainable, depending more on natural causes (fertility-mortality rates) than on a town's ability to attract migrants and retain current residents (migration balance).

However, the MB/NG index starts to increase again when IC2 reaches about 2.0-10.0 (Singleton, Cessnock-Bellbird and Maitland). After peaking at around 20.0-30.0 on the IC2 scale, the values of the MB/NG index drop again (Queanbeyan and Lithgow), which implies a less sustainable growth in these core communities.

Across the entire range of IC2's values, these fluctuations thus result in the M-like (Bessel-type) curve, similar to that we witnessed in Norway and, to some extent, in Israel (see Chapters 16 and 17). In all these cases, the clustering-sustainability relationship is as follows: initial increase in sustainability in line with increasing clustering, followed by a decline in growth sustainability, another increase, etc. The nature of these fluctuations has already been discussed in the previous chapters (Chapters 15-17). A possible occurrence of this phenomenon was predicted in Chapter 14 of this book, in which such fluctuations were attributed to the presence of thinly populated 'intermediate' areas between clusters of towns, which are found in both peripheral and centrally located geographic areas.

It is worth noting that the peripheral coastal towns of NSW (Set 3) clearly 'depart' from the above M-like trend line. These towns (Batemans Bay, Taree, Coffs Harbor, and Port Macquarie), which are beyond the range of daily commuting from established urban centres, appear to have considerably higher values of the MB/NG index than their inland 'counterparts' with similar values of the index of clustering (Tamworth, Bathurst, Orange and Wagga Wagga; see Figure 18.2).

We may recall, however, that a number of similar 'outliers' were found in Norway (see Figures 17.2-17.3 in Chapter 17). In particular, three peripheral communities in this country (Alta, Tromsø, and Bodø) also deviated from the general trend and exhibited a much higher degree of sustainability than would have been expected from spatial considerations alone. It was suggested that the peripheral towns in question are educational, administrative, cultural and economic centres of their respective regions. The presence of colleges, hospitals, and other unique regional functions may have increased the attractiveness of these communities to residents of surrounding areas, mainly at the expense of smaller and less developed urban and rural places in the region.

A similar process may explain the 'excessive' attractiveness of coastal towns in NSW: possible disadvantages of their location in the general setting of urban places are likely to be compensated for by the environmental and recreational advantages of their coastal location. (This conclusion is fully in line with the high statistical significance of two research variables reported in Table 18.2 – proximity to the coast (T=-3.426) and the amount of rainfall (T=2.171).)

The point of inflection at which the MB/NG index reaches the value of 1.0 is extremely important. This threshold indicates that the population growth of a town becomes mainly due to the town's ability to attract migrants and retain current residents. The inland towns of NSW (Set 2) attain this point when the values of IC2 approach values of 0.2-0.3 (Figure 18.2), a level which is almost identical to the threshold of sustainability observed in peripheral areas of Norway (see Figure 17.3 in Chapter 17). Thus, if the distance from a cluster of peripheral towns to the closest population centre of NSW is, for instance, 300 km, an overall population size of some 60,000-90,000 residents appears to be needed to make the population growth of this cluster sustainable (300x0.2x1,000=60,000; 300x0.3x1,000 =90,000).

In the coastal towns of NSW, the same total population of a settlement cluster would generate even higher rates of population growth (Figure 18.2), with values of the MB/NG index well above the threshold of sustainability (1.0). However, in these towns, the values of the MB/NG index are likely to drop sharply when the density of the urban field increases further, as indicated by values of IC2 between 1.0 and 2.0 (Figure 18.2). Using the same threshold of 300 km as an example, we may estimate that the population growth of a 'coastal' cluster may become less attractive if its population size exceeds 300,000-600,000 residents (300x1x1,000=300,000 and 300x2.0x1,000= 600,000). This change was, in fact, hypothesised in Chapter 14 of this book, and is apparently attributed to growing inter-town competition for potential migrants and to growing diseconomies of concentration, particularly in the Sydney area.

IC vs. Homeownership Level

Additional insights concerning the effects of urban clustering on the development of towns can be gained by comparing the values of this index with the extent of private homeownership in the urban localities included in the sets (see Figure 18.3).

The latter indicator (homeownership level) is an extremely important socio-economic datum with long-range implications. Besides an obvious link between the level of private homeownership and wealth, a low level of home ownership (compared to the average regional level) is clear evidence that many residents of a town do not consider it a place of permanent residence. Low values of this index may thus signal a higher probability of an outflow of residents from the locality occurring in the future, particularly during economic downturns.

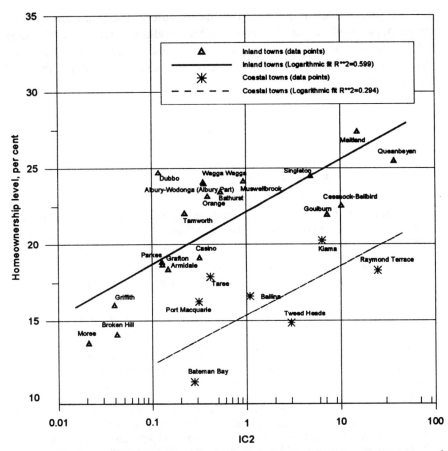

Figure 18.3   **Homeownership levels in differently located towns of NSW (as of 1990-96)**

The proportion of private homeownership tends to increase in both inland and coastal towns as the density of the urban field (indicated by IC2) grows. However, for a given value of the index of clustering, the level of homeownership in coastal towns is substantially lower than in inland localities. This difference is presumably attributed to a high percentage of temporary residents, visitors and tourists in the overall population, and a large share of rental housing compared to inland localities.

As Figure 18.3 shows, in both inland and coastal towns, the level of homeownership tends to increase steadily in line with growing values of the index of clustering. This implies that the population of denser urban clusters is indeed more likely to remain in its current residence and is more ready to invest locally. The reasons for this have been already mentioned in previous chapters. One of these is the presence of a 'safety net' offered by an urban cluster to its residents that manifests itself in more diverse employment and cultural opportunities available within the range practicable for daily commuting. Another possible reason is having a better chance of selling property in a more active housing market should the need for such a sale arise.

Notes

[1] The authors would like to express their gratitude to Margaret Young and Dianne Rudd of the Department of Geography at the University of Adelaide, South Australia for their assistance in assembling and interpreting the data for the present case study.

[2] In estimating remoteness of towns, distances were measured from the closest principal city in either NSW or in neighbouring states (Brisbane in Queensland, and Melbourne in Victoria).

[3] Though annual data would have been preferred for the present analysis, the quinquennial Census of Population and Housing is the only comprehensive source of population movements in Australia (Blake et al, 2000).

[4] Two separate linear-log regression models were computed. In these models, the representation of climatic factors was altered successively, while the representation of all other explanatory variables (population, unemployment, proximity to the coast, etc.) remained unchanged. Although after substitution of rainfall for summer temperatures R^2 dropped only fractionally - 0.704 (temperatures) vs. 0.754 (rainfall), the value of F-statistic decreased considerably – from 11.76 in the 'rainfall' model to 9.12 in the 'temperature' model. This implies a considerably lower degree of generality in the latter case. At first glance, such a significance of the rainfall variable is somewhat surprising since the amount of rainfall seems to diminish continuously as distances from the coast grow. Therefore, it might be expected that the variance of this factor should be accounted for by other explanatory variables included in the model, specifically by the proximity to the coast. The tolerance statistic, reported in Table 18.2, however, indicates that the rainfall variable is responsible for a large share of the variance unexplained by any other factors (some 46.9 per cent). In addition to statistical evidence, a closer examination of the map of rainfall distribution indicates that within a 200-300-km range from the coast, where many of the towns sampled are located, there are substantial variations in annual rainfall. For instance, other things being equal, the amount of rainfall in the north-eastern part of NSW is considerably larger than in its south-eastern part. In addition, west of Canberra, there is a relatively large 'island' of high precipitation, surrounded by much drier areas.

PART V
DEVELOPMENT POLICIES

Each city may be regarded as a magnet, each
person as a needle; and, so viewed, it is at once
seen that nothing short of the discovery of a
method for constructing magnets of yet greater
power than our cities possess can be effective for
redistributing the population in a spontaneous and
healthy manner.

E. Howard, *Garden Cities of To-morrow*

19 Influencing Urban and Regional Growth by Planning Measures

Unlike socio-economic development in general, further urban growth, particularly in densely inhabited core areas, is often undesirable. However, in some cases, particularly in under-populated peripheral regions, population growth is welcome. Such regions, for instance, generally require sustained population growth as a prerequisite for achieving other aspects of development: as the population of a peripheral town increases, it crosses the threshold for higher-level services, and may consequently offer more varied opportunities for employment, social services, and leisure. The development of peripheral areas may also be driven by push factors, rather than by pull factors: Peripheral areas may provide an alternative for the residents of core regions, if their infrastructure is developed and if their level of social amenities is acceptable. When this is not the case, over-population of core areas may result in severe social and environmental problems.

Though the instruments of public policy aimed at enhancing the development potential of individual regions and communities are numerous and diverse, they can be aggregated into five general groups: *a) investment in infrastructure, b) large-scale development projects, c) development funds and incentives, d) a community-oriented approach, and e) an integrated approach.*

According to Parr's (2000) observations, Germany has traditionally held the view that any obstacle to development of a community or region can be overcome by sufficient investment in infrastructure. In France, on the other hand, large showpiece projects, such as automobile assembly plants or a petrochemical complex, have been the preferred policy tools. The UK has until recently relied on grants, loans and even statutory planning restrictions to influence the location of manufacturing activity.

261

In Australia, a flexible approach to regional development has been adopted, according to which the nation's cities are allowed to expand further, while ensuring that the country areas have public services and general living standards broadly comparable to those of the capital cities.

In this chapter, we will deal with each of these five groups of policy instruments briefly, focusing our attention on their drawbacks and advantages.

Investment in Infrastructure

The strong conviction held by some regional planners that investment in infrastructure is highly conducive to sustainable regional development most likely originated from the pioneering studies of von Thünen (1826; 1966 English edition), Marshall (1890; 1892) and Weber (1929), which emphasise the role of transportation cost in the location of agriculture and industries. Subsequently, this concept was developed by Lösch (1938; 1975 reprint), Alonso (1964; 1977), Richardson (1977), and Webber (1973), and applied to the formation of urban settlement by Christaller (1933), Zipf (1949), Clark (1982), and more recently by Krugman (1999), and Fujita and Mori (1996; 1997).

According to these studies, the population growth of towns and regional economic growth (as measured by the availability of employment, incomes, regional product, etc.) depend on accessibility and low transport costs. Therefore, it is often assumed that more investment in infrastructure should result in higher growth, particularly in economically lagging peripheral areas.

However, recent empirical studies appear to show little, if any, evidence that investment in infrastructure indeed has a causal effect on regional development. Thus, recent studies in Israel (see *inter alia* Portnov and Etzion, 2000; Bar El, 2000) failed, in general, to prove that the relationship between infrastructure development and socio-economic growth in peripheral regions of the country had been, in fact, causal.

Similar, rather disappointing, results concerning the effect of infrastructure development on regional economic growth and population change are reported in another recent study, dealing with the effect of *Shinkansen* (high-speed rail transit) on regional development in Japan. Sasaki *et al.* (1997) report that the establishment of high-speed train lines contributed mainly to the development of the central regions of the country, which increased both their regional product and population. At the same time, peripheral regions of Japan either benefited very little from this major infrastructure project or even suffered from a loss of investment and population of about 10-14 per cent, as compared to the *'pre-Shinkansen'* level. The infrastructure project in question thus failed to achieve its goal, but rather contributed to further concentration of population and economic activity in the core areas of Japan and drained development and population resources from the country's less prosperous peripheral regions.

These empirical findings are in line with Parr's (2000) conclusion that 'infrastructure investment, except when it is a recognisable missing ingredient in a region with strong potential, can quickly come to resemble the cargo cult of Papua-New Guinea.'[1]

Large-scale Development Projects

In his influential articles published in 1950 (1964 reprint) and in 1955, the French economist Perroux developed his concept of growth poles and of propelling/propelled industries, and later applied it to regional development (Perroux, 1983 - English edition). According to this concept, growth in a propelling industry or region may generate a 'propulsion' effect on other industries or areas by means of three interdependent processes: a) an effect on prices and flows of goods, b) a transfer of productivity, and c) a transfer of information.

This interesting concept gave rise to a completely new direction of regional studies referred to as the 'growth pole theory.' According to this theory, the establishment of a *pole of growth* in a generally lagging region may stimulate its overall development:

> Experience has shown that an industrial concentration, also referred to as a Large Unit (LU), may act as a magnet for a cluster of additional firms (in retail trade, transport, communication services and the like), if at the outset the space in question was, in economic terms, 'empty'. The additional means required for this process of concentration are either borrowed from other points within the same region, or imported from abroad...These dynamic complementary phenomena are the result of the forces of attraction exerted by the Large Unit, which becomes to some extent a propellant. Once formed, it acts to further expansion, either through demand for raw materials and labour or through supplies of products (*ibid,* p. 142).

In a follow up study, Berry (1973) applied the idea of 'growth poles' to the hierarchy of urban centres arguing that 'impulses of economic change' are transmitted from growth centres along three plains:

- Outward from heartland metropolis to their regional hinterland;
- Hierarchical diffusion from centres of higher-level to centres lower in the hierarchy; and
- Outward from urban centres into their surrounding hinterland (spread effect).

The concept of *circular inter-dependence*, introduced by the Swedish political economist Myrdal (1958), is another contribution to the growth pole theory. According to this concept, better known as the 'principle of cumulative causation,' a single socio-economic event may trigger a wide range of consequences affecting further development of a region or community as a whole:

> The decision to locate an industry in a particular community...gives a spur to its general development. Opportunities of employment and higher incomes are provided for those unemployed before or employed in a less remunerative way. Local businesses can flourish as the demand for their product and services increases. Labour, capital and enterprise are attracted from outside to exploit the expanding opportunities. The establishment of a new business or the enlargement of an old one widens the market for others, as does generally the increase of incomes and demand. Rising profits increase savings, but at the same time investments go up still more, which again pushes up the demand and the level of profits. And the expansion process creates external economies favourable for sustaining its continuation (*ibid*, p. 25).

According to Myrdal, this sequence of cumulative causation works in a similar way if the initial change is negative. For instance, a decision to close down a factory in a particular location may initiate a wide range of negative consequences, resulting in an overall decrease in employment opportunities in related industries and in lower incomes to the local population. According to Myrdal's theory, both positive and negative causation tend to increase rather than decrease interregional inequalities. In this framework, Myrdal distinguishes two types of simultaneous processes:

- The *spread effect* is a centrifugal force which causes the diffusion of growth from growing centres to surrounding areas;
- The *backwash effect* occurs when more developed centres develop further at the expense of less developed surrounding areas. The centres of expansion increase demand and spur investment, which, in turn, boosts incomes and causes a subsequent round of investment.

Hirschman (1958; 1966 reprint) developed a similar explanatory model of regional growth. He defined the flow of capital and labour from underdeveloped and largely unsettled regions to more economically prosperous areas as *polarisation*, while the flow in the opposite direction was referred to as the *trickling-down* effect:

> No matter how strong and exaggerated the spatial preferences of the economic operators, once growth takes a firm hold in one part of the national territory, it obviously sets in motion certain forces that act on the remaining parts. In examining these direct interactions, we shall call 'North' the region which has been experiencing growth and 'South' the one that has remained behind...The growth of the North will have a number of direct economic repercussions on the South, some favourable, others adverse. The favourable effects consist of the *trickling down* of Northern progress...In addition, the North may absorb some of the disguised unemployed of the South and thereby raise the marginal productivity of labour and per capita consumption levels in the South...On the other hand, several unfavourable or *polarisation* effects are also likely to be at work. Comparatively inefficient, yet income-creating, Southern activities in manufacturing and exports may become depressed as a result of Northern competition...A more serious, and frequently observed, polarisation effect consists of the kind of internal migration that may follow upon the economic advances of the North (*ibid*, pp. 187-188).

Core-periphery paradigm is another paradigm of the spatial organisation of development based on assumptions similar to those underlying Perroux's 'growth pole' and Hirschman's 'North-South divide' concepts. According to this dichotomy, whose basics are closely associated with Friedmann (1966), development originates in a relatively small number of centres located at the points of highest potential interaction, defined as the core. Innovative change is concentrated at the core, which dominates over the periphery, which is in turn dependent on it. This dependence manifests itself through the relationships of capital and labour exchanges: Since peripheral regions often lack the resources to sustain their own growth over time, their development potential is largely reliant on processes within the core. This relationship is fundamentally different from the traditional interdependence between a city and its agricultural hinterland. For while in both cases the urban centre provides capital, services and technology, the flow of goods once provided by the hinterland is replaced by a flow of population from the periphery to the core. Core regions thus possess the means of controlling the development of their peripheries and extracting the resources that contribute to their own accelerating growth, which naturally lead to social and political tension (Friedmann, 1966; 1973; Gradus, 1983; Johnston *et al,* 1994; Hansen, 1975; Hansen *et al,* 1990; Stöhr, 1981).

Like Richardson's (1977) location-oriented model and Berry's (1973) model of hierarchical diffusion of regional growth, the core-periphery paradigm emphasises the role of existing urban centres in enhancing the potential for regional growth:

> Impulses for development originate at certain localities and are relayed to other localities in a definite sequence. The pattern of settlements creates a structure of potentials for development that will eventually be registered in indices of regional performance and will condition the evolving character of the society (Friedmann, 1973, p. 23).

The key component of the core-periphery paradigm is the notion of *innovation,* which is viewed as 'the transformation of inventions into historical fact' and considered part of the following conceptual framework:

- The frequency of innovation is directly related to a positive potential for interaction, reflected in the potential for information exchange and communication. Large cities with their developed interaction and communication network are thus major centres of innovation and, respectively, core elements of the regional communication landscape;
- Expansion of the urban system leads to the expansion of inter-city linkages which become the channels for transmitting innovations and thereby areas of accelerated development;
- The frequency of innovation in a given point of space is a function of the power structure of the society. An open system of dispersed power is perceived as more conducive to innovation than a tightly controlled hierarchical system (ibid.).

Between the 1960s and the early 1980s, the above theories, especially that of regional growth poles, were widely embraced by regional planners in an attempt to accelerate development of underdeveloped peripheral regions (see *inter alia* Gradus and Stern, 1980; Kuklinski, 1978; Bivand, 1986). As Hansen (1981) argues, however, optimism relating to the possibility that growth induced in a few centres would generate spread effects into their hinterland was soon replaced by pessimism 'when the expectations of the earlier phase failed to materialise.'

In fact, little evidence has been found to date to support the theory that the creation of regional growth poles could actually boost the development of their hinterland (Hansen, 1975; Kuklinski, 1978; Isserman and Marrrifield, 1987; Mera, 1995; Parr, 1999; 2000). As Parr (2000) commented, large-scale showpiece projects often lead to highly localised development, and may subsequently become 'cathedrals in the desert'. Indeed, some recent empirical studies indicated that though growth may actually occur at 'growth poles,' their establishment is unlikely to cause any substantial 'spill-over' effect to surrounding areas. Their development may even lead to the further depletion of human and capital resources of less developed surrounding communities (Roberts, 1995; Hughes and Holland, 1994; Ma, 1999; Portnov *et al*, 2000; see also Chapter 17 of this book, dealing with the Norwegian case study).

Development Funds and Incentives

Emphasising the importance of public investment and 'positive discrimination' policies in influencing the development of the economically lagging 'South,' Hirschman (1958; 1966 reprint, pp. 199-200) wrote:

> To permit production to proceed on the basis of comparative advantage, Southern exports could be – and have at times been – stimulated through preferential exchange rates. Under such conditions, it might be held that imports into the South should be subject to compensating surtaxes, but this complication can be avoided on the ground that the South could satisfy many of its needs more cheaply in world markets if it were not prevented from doing so by the protection of Northern industries.

Though the policy of public assistance to underdeveloped peripheral regions and communities has been practised in many developed and less developed countries for years, regional development assistance has never reached the scale carried out by the European Union. (For more details on such policies see Balchin, 1990; Portnov and Etzion, 2000; Roberts, 1995; Swales, 1997; Hansen, 1981; Diamond and Spence, 1983; Armstrong and Taylor, 1993; Karkazis and Thanassoulis, 1998).

The enlargement of the (then) European Community increased regional disparities and changed their nature. British entry in 1973 posed the problem of re-conversion of declining industrial regions. The accession of Greece, Spain, and Portugal added to the number of underdeveloped rural areas. The poorest regions in Greece and Portugal have a per capita gross regional product of around 40 per cent of the average for the

European Union while the poorest region of the nine members of 1973-81 (Calabria) comes in at 59 per cent of the average (1987 figures). The GDP per person of Denmark was 2.1 times greater than that of Portugal, compared with a maximum ratio of only 1.5:1 among American states (Bachtler and Michie, 1997; EC, 2000).

In response to these inequalities, large-scale programmes of regional assistance were developed. Currently, the EU Regional Policy consists mainly of four types of structural funds, through which the Union channels its financial assistance to address structural economic and social problems of regions, by means of supporting local industries (Table 19.1):

- *The European Regional Development Fund (ERDF)*. ERDF was set up in 1975 to finance structural aid through regional development programmes targeted at the most disadvantaged regions with a view of reducing socio-economic imbalances between regions of the Union. The ERDF grants financial assistance according to four objectives: a) promoting the development and structural adjustment of regions whose development is lagging; b) modernising and diversifying the economic base of the regions, frontier regions or parts of regions seriously affected by a decline of traditional manufacturing industries; c) promoting rural development by facilitating the development and structural adjustment of rural areas, and d) promoting the development and structural adjustment of regions with an extremely low population density;

- *The European Social Fund (ESF)*. Established in 1960, ESF is the main instrument of Community social policy, which provides financial assistance for vocational training, retraining and job-creation schemes. These are targeted particularly at unemployed youth, the long-term unemployed, socially disadvantaged groups and women;

- *The European Agricultural Guidance and Guarantee Fund* (EAGGF). The purpose of this fund is to provide market support and promote structural adjustments in agriculture. This funds finances price support measures and export refunds to guarantee farmers stable prices;

- *The Financial Instrument for Fisheries* (FIFG). Since 1994, FIFG has grouped together the Community instruments for fisheries. It is applied in all coastal regions, its main task being to increase the competitiveness of the fisheries sector and to develop viable business enterprises in the fishing industry, while at the same time striving to maintain the balance between fishing capacities and available resources (EC, 2000).

Table 19.1 Structural contribution by member state in millions of ECU in 1994-99 (at 1994 prices)

Country	Objectives					CI[f]	Total
	1[a]	2[b]	3 and 4[c]	5[d]	6[e]		
Belgium	730	342	465	272	-	287	2 096
Denmark	-	119	301	321	-	102	843
Germany	13 640	1 566	1 942	2370	-	2 206	21 724
Greece	13 980	-	-	-	-	1 151	15 131
Spain	26 300	2 416	1 843	1110	-	2 774	34 443
France	2 190	3 774	3 203	4171	-	1 601	14 938
Ireland	5 620	-	-	-	-	483	6 103
Italy	14 860	1 463	1 715	1715	-	1 893	21 646
Luxembourg	-	15	23	46	-	20	104
Netherlands	150	650	1 079	315	-	421	2 615
Austria	162	99	387	783	-	143	1 574
Portugal	13 980	-	-	-	-	1 058	15 038
Finland	-	179	336	537	450	150	1 652
Sweden	-	157	509	339	247	125	1 377
U.K.	2 360	4 581	3 377	1267	-	1 570	13 155
EU Total	93 972	15 360	15 180	13778	697	14 051	153 038

Source: EC (2000);
[a] development of economically lagging regions; [b] promoting development in regions affected by industrial decline; [c] improving the conditions of the labour market; [d] promoting the rural development; [e] development of under-populated regions; [f] community initiatives

Within the European Union, regional financial assistance takes place in the form of non-reimbursable grants, subject to co-financing from the Member States, and is channelled through three financial instruments - national programmes; community initiatives, and innovative measures *(ibid.)*:

- *National programmes* account for about 90% of the ERDF budget and are funded on the basis of proposals submitted by the member states;
- *Community initiatives programmes* account for around 9 per cent of the ERDF budget and differ from mainstream national programmes in that they are initiated at the Community rather than the national level;
- *Innovative measures* account for around one per cent of the budget. They cover finance studies, pilot projects or networks designed to test

new policy approaches related to innovation, regional or spatial planning, urban development, and interregional co-operation.

Although a mass influx of funds as a tool of policy can unquestionably increase the rate of economic growth and population attractiveness of a particular geographic area or community, the question is whether such financial assistance can create long-lasting structural changes, or whether it leads simply to increased dependence on the public purse?

Table 19.2, reporting the extent of public regional assistance and selected development indicators of counties in Norway, illustrates a case in point.

As this table shows, remote peripheral municipalities of Norway (Nordland, Troms, Nord-Trødelag, and Finmark) suffered from negative net migration and higher than average unemployment,[2] in spite of receiving higher than average per capita transfers of government funds. Thus, for instance, the transfer of government funds to the Finnmark county in 1997 was nearly 21,000 NOK per capita, compared with only 6,000-12,000 NOK per capita in the country's central counties (Østfold, Akershus and Oslo). One can argue, of course, that if this and other remote peripheral regions of Norway had received no preferential financial treatment at all, their situation would have been even worse. The above example nevertheless suggests that there are objective limits to the efficacy of financial assistance designed to stimulate regional development.

Community-oriented Approach

In a recent review of regional development policies, Parr (2000) suggests a number of embellishments to traditional regional development programs which he refers to as 'compensation mechanisms.' Such compensation mechanisms can he realised by a range of devices, including the following:

- Improving accessibility from peripheral areas to central ones, thus widening the scope for commuting and improving the availability of consumer goods and business services throughout the region;
- Guaranteeing a range of public services at some minimum level in the regions receiving support, perhaps with a significant element of subsidy (as a counter to the possible centralisation of privately provided services);

- Removing obstacles to migration, with assistance for relocation and housing at the favoured areas;
- Establishing a more efficient fiscal system that enables earnings to be remitted from the favoured areas;
- Creating a system of differential taxation, required to support those not affected by other mechanisms of government support for the regional population.

Table 19.2   Development assistance and selected indicators of counties in Norway

County	Transfer of funds in 1997[a]	Total net migration[b]			Unemployment in 1997, %
		1995	1996	1997	
Østfold	7,930	783	720	2,329	2.88
Akershus	5,660	2,623	3,544	4,426	1.65
Oslo	12,405	3,543	4,221	3,501	2.84
Hedmark	10,716	-94	-15	540	2.56
Oppland	10,160	-225	-416	-120	2.49
Buskerud	7,284	631	1,118	1,785	2.17
Vestfold	7,280	972	1,238	2,167	2.58
Telemark	8,896	60	127	521	3.03
Aust-Agder	9,947	411	90	258	2.35
Vest-Agder	8,409	316	372	389	2.47
Rogaland	7,121	-93	504	1,064	2.31
Hordaland	8,636	316	-790	-307	2.93
Sogn og Fjordane	12,154	-139	-114	-491	1.60
Møre og Romsdal	10,004	187	-342	-85	2.00
Sør-Trøndelag	9,288	-20	-133	-74	2.77
Nord-Trøndelag	12,613	-621	-575	-735	3.08
Nordland	13,573	-1,129	-1,654	-1,597	3.07
Troms	14,484	-388	-642	-1,608	2.81
Finnmark	20,971	-767	-1,436	-1,263	4.62

Compiled from: Statistical Yearbook of Norway. Oslo, Statistics Norway (1997), and the Municipality Database, maintained by the Norwegian Social Science Data Service (NSD). [a] Overall transfer of funds from the central government in 1997, NOK per capita; [b] includes both in-country migration and external migration (immigration minus emigration).

A similar, community-oriented, approach underpins the regional development policy for Western Australia (DCT, 1999). This policy is centred around six goals and places a particular emphasis on helping individual communities, rather than on pure economic development of geographic areas and financial assistance to industries and other employment-generating sectors:

- *Community development:* self-sustainability and effective self-representation;
- *Responsive government:* empowering communities to achieve and/or maintain high amenity through equitable access to services;
- *Social and cultural cohesion:* building and maintaining vibrant, vital and cohesive communities recognising the need for equity in the delivery of fundamental services;
- *Economic development:* achieving economically-viable communities providing a variety of fulfilling employment opportunities;
- *Physical infrastructure:* attracting investment in the physical infrastructure essential to retain the population and enhance the capacity of communities to provide all services locally;
- *Environment and natural resources management:* protecting and enhancing habitats and sense of place, and managing natural resources in a sustainable way.

To achieve these goals, the following policy instruments were established *(ibid.):*

- *Improving* transport and telecommunication connections between urban-regional-rural-remote communities;
- *Encouraging* and assisting regional, rural and remote enterprises to target specialised, niche markets;
- *Intervening* to counter the high costs of water, power and serviced-land which are characteristic of small-scale, low-density settlement patterns but which are detrimental to the viability of regional, rural and remote enterprises;
- *Improving* competitiveness of regional, rural and remote enterprises by enhancing core skills of leaders, management and labour.

Although this strategy seems to be well elaborated, two important components are clearly missing. These are the sequence of development assistance and its spatial targets: Are the above measures of regional assistance to be applied to communities of all sizes in centrally located areas as well as in remote peripheral ones? Is the policy in question to be implemented simultaneously in all parts of the region? It is, for instance, questionable whether 'equitable access to services' can really be achieved in all small and isolated communities. It is also unclear whether an attempt to create 'self-sustainable conditions' in each community will not result in a sparse and inefficient dispersal of development resources over a large area - a problem of which regional planners have been well aware of for at least half a century.[3]

Integrated Approach

The policy of population dispersal (PPD) in Israel is an example of regional policy emphasising the role of compound measures in targeting the regional development. Ultimately, this policy is aimed at redirecting population growth and economic development from overpopulated core regions of the country to its underdeveloped peripheral areas.[4] The incentives provided by this policy are of four basic types:

- Planning and development (public housing construction, infrastructure provision);
- Financial incentives to private investors (investment grants, tax exemption, and loan guaranties);
- Allocation of public land (long-term land leases, and price reduction for publicly-owned land); and
- Housing and location aid - low-interest housing loans, housing subsidies, etc. (Portnov and Etzion, 2000).

Given the strategic objectives of this policy, population growth and economic development of the country's periphery in the 1950s-1960s was sustained primarily by directing new immigrants to so called 'priority development zones' (PDZs), in which basic employment and housing opportunities were provided by the government. Since the early 1970s, the policy of direct allocation has gradually been replaced by various governmental incentives designed to encourage private investment, thus increasing the attractiveness of PDZs indirectly. Although the boundaries of PDZs have been subject to numerous changes, they always included (wholly or in part) two peripheral areas of the country – the Northern and Southern districts (Figure 19.1).

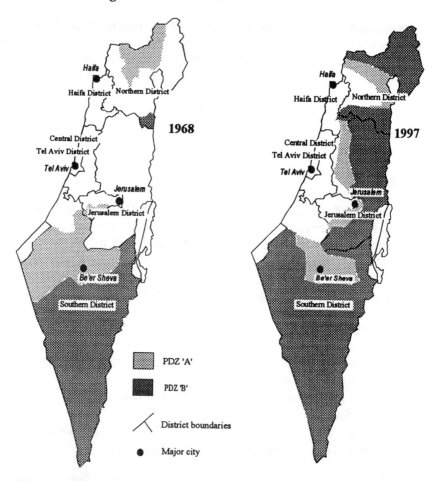

Figure 19.1   Priority Development Zones (PDZs) in Israel in 1968 and 1997 (after Portnov and Etzion, 2000)

Numerous attempts have been undertaken since the early 1950s to evaluate the effects of the policy in question, resulting in largely inconclusive evidence concerning its effects on regional development and population change. (see *inter alia* Drabkin-Darin, 1957; Gradus and Krakover, 1977; Lipshitz, 1996a; Shefer, 1990; Soen, 1977; Portnov and Etzion, 2000). Thus, Portnov and Etzion (2000) acknowledge that despite the fact that between 1948-95, per capita rates of public construction and infrastructure development in most peripheral regions of Israel were considerably higher than those in most core regions, the policy in question failed to reduce the population imbalance between the country's core and periphery.

Conclusion

Traditional regional development policies have one characteristic in common: Nearly all of them emphasise the role of external measures (allocation of funds, infrastructure development, large-scale showpiece projects, etc.) as a tool of encouraging regional growth. However, the efficacy of such external policy measures may be restricted if a region or locality has no inherent growth potential, as determined, among other factors, by its location. In the following chapter, such location characteristics and their possible implications for regional development will be discussed in some detail. Special attention will be given to the development of applied planning strategies aimed at encouraging the potential of urban growth in peripheral development areas in which such an objective is desirable.

Notes

[1] The followers of this cult believe in the imminence of a new age of blessing, to be initiated by the arrival of a special 'cargo' of goods from supernatural sources, which is to solve all the local problems. In expecting such a cargo, symbolic wharves or landing strips and warehouses are built in preparation, and traditional material resources are abandoned - gardening ceases, and food stock is destroyed (EB, 1999 – Cargo cult).

[2] 1997 was selected because it was the most recent year for which data on transfer of funds were available; similar distributions occurred throughout the mid-1990s.

[3] As Hirschman noted (1958; 1966 reprint, pp. 190-191), 'as all governments regardless of their democratic character...need support from all sections of the country, the temptation is strong to scatter the investment effort far and wide. Disconnected roads are built at many points; small Diesel power plants and aqueducts are installed in many towns; even low-cost housing programs which should obviously concentrate on relieving critical shortages and on slum clearance in big cities are often similarly dispersed.'

[4] Similar development policies are found in Europe (Sweden, Norway, United Kingdom, and Greece), Asia (Japan and South Korea), and other countries elsewhere in the world (Balchin, 1990; Diamond and Spence, 1983; Karkazis and Thanassoulis, 1998).

20 Redirecting Priorities and Creating Development Clusters

In a number of countries, (Sweden, Finland, Japan, Korea, Israel, Norway, etc.), redirecting population growth from overpopulated core regions to underdeveloped peripheral areas is an intrinsic goal of regional policy. Following such a policy, regional development in Israel has been guided for many years by the idea of developing a broad network of new towns in the peripheral districts of the country (Gradus and Stern, 1980; Shefer, 1990; Shachar, 1996; Kipnis, 1989; 1996; Portnov and Etzion, 2000). In Norway, remote peripheral communities in the north and along the western coast are continuously supported by the national government through an elaborate system of grants and incentives (Hansen, 1981, Holmøy and Hægeland, 1995, Johansen and Klette, 1997). In Japan, regional policy has been guided for years by the goal of redirecting population growth and economic development from the overpopulated metropolitan areas to less developed local regions by means of large-scale infrastructure projects and restrictive schemes for manufacturing industries in large cities (Abe, 1996; Sasaki et al, 1997; Markusen, 1996). In Australia, the goals of retaining population and sustaining an adequate level of services in the rural areas are intrinsic components of regional development programs of the Commonwealth (Sorensen, 1997; DCT, 1999).

Often, however, such policies appear to have only a limited effect on population and economic processes in priority development areas.

The relationship between the clustering of the urban field and the socio-economic performance of individual urban localities was discussed in some detail in Parts III and IV of this book. There may thus be some value in explaining why the above mentioned policies have often failed to achieve their goals, and in developing alternative approaches. Five aspects of the present analysis seem to be of particular importance in this context.

276

The Relation Between Clustering and Urban Growth

Positive Effects of Clustering

As argued in Chapter 13 and in Chapters 16-18, the formation of dense clusters of urban places is, in general, conducive to more sustainable socio-economic development of urban areas, especially those located in sparsely populated peripheral regions. This link between socio-economic viability of urban places and their location in clusters is attributed primarily to the more varied opportunities for socio-economic interaction which only sufficiently large urban clusters can offer, compared to a scattered pattern of urban settlement. Such a link may justify the concentration of development resources to form a clustered pattern of urban settlement in the geographic areas in which further urban growth is desirable.

Adverse Effects of Clustering

Once an urban cluster grows above a certain population size, further expansion may become increasingly detrimental to the individual towns comprising it. This change is attributed primarily to growing competition among the cluster's members for potential investors and migrants and to increasing diseconomies of agglomeration.[1] (Such competition and diseconomies may increase especially rapidly if a major urban centre is located nearby and interferes with the development of adjacent towns).

The population size of a settlement cluster which when exceeded may have adverse effects on the development of individual towns and may be referred to as the Upper Threshold of Cluster Efficiency (UTCE). At the other end of the scale, the minimum cluster size required for positive effects of clustering to set in, may be defined as the Minimal Threshold of Cluster Efficiency (MTCE). When the former (UTCE) threshold is attained, it may become desirable to switch the focus of development resources from the cluster of urban places that has reached the threshold in question to other urban concentrations in priority development areas.

The Importance of Function Differentiation

Urban clustering is not a simple product of close aerial proximity of towns. Although the location of cluster members within the range practicable for daily commuting is essential for maintaining a daily socio-economic interaction, this precondition alone is clearly insufficient for the ultimate integration of the cluster's members in a single socio-economic unit.

Another essential requirement is the differentiation of functions among the cluster's members, which may create a sufficient diversity of employment and services for the residents of a group of relatively small urban places that form the cluster.

The Relation Between Clustering and Remoteness

In order to be conducive to the sustainable growth of individual towns, the population size of an urban cluster should increase in direct proportion to the distance from the cluster to the closest major population centre of the country (Figure 20.1). The rationale for this is relatively simple: in centrally located geographic areas, residents of small urban communities may enjoy access to a broad range of services and employment opportunities provided by principle cities. The residents of more remote peripheral areas have far fewer such opportunities within their daily commuting range. Therefore, a larger share of services and employment must be provided locally to compensate for remoteness, and larger clusters should be formed to counteract the drawbacks caused by remoteness of the urban cluster from the principle cities.

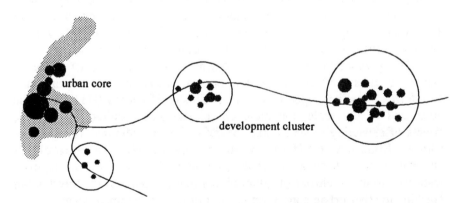

Figure 20.1   Size of an urban cluster as a function of distance from principle cities

The diagram shows that the size of an urban cluster should increase as remoteness of geographic areas grows. This may compensate small urban communities in the cluster for a lack of physical proximity to major population centres of a country, at least to a certain extent, and thus make the growth of peripheral urban clusters more sustainable.

Engines of Development

Neither physical location nor population size and opportunities for functional exchanges alone may guarantee successful development of urban clusters. A clearly identified and well-established motivating force is required to drive the cluster's growth, especially if it is located in a remote peripheral region. There are numerous functions and services that contribute to urban growth, but relatively few provide a sufficiently strong impetus to generate the wide range of regional multipliers essential for sustainable growth. Among such functions are universities and large hospitals, whose role in the formation of principle cities was emphasized in previous sections of he book. Unless a cluster of small peripheral urban communities possesses a considerable comparative advantage such as a coastal location or other unique natural resources, its development must be sustained, at least initially, by the establishment of the above educational and medical facilities that will serve as functional *primum mobiles* of the cluster's growth.

Development Strategies

The present analysis lays the foundation for two complementing development strategies, on which we shall focus our discussion in the following subsections – the formation of development clusters and the strategy of 'redirecting priorities.'

The Formation of Development Clusters

It is suggested that urban development policy in sparsely populated peripheral areas should be directed towards achieving a certain density of the urban field, as determined by the value of the proposed index of clustering (see Section 14 of this book for a more detailed discussion). Possible approaches for implementing this policy are (Figure 20.2):

• *Development clusters with a clearly expressed urban core.* This urbanisation pattern is relevant to peripheral areas which already have existing regional centres comprising relatively large urban localities. The process of urban development in this case may lead to the consecutive formation of a group of satellite settlements situated within the distance practicable for daily commuting to this centre and to each other, and which may form with the regional centre a single economic unit;

- *Development clusters of small urban settlements that have no dominant urban core*. This pattern of urbanisation may be applied to hinterland areas whose current settlement patterns are less intensive, and where existing towns are widely scattered. Under such circumstances, urban development of the region may lead to the establishment of new settlements so as to form development clusters with existing small urban localities. The settlements in such clusters may therefore share some essential functions (employment, educational, cultural, recreational services, etc.), which each of the small localities cannot sustain individually.

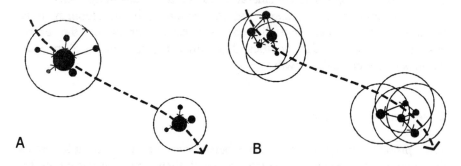

Figure 20.2   Types of urban clusters

A – cluster with clearly expressed urban core; B – cluster of small towns with no clearly expressed urban core.

Setting appropriate targets for the physical size of an urban cluster is extremely important. These targets should vary between the minimal threshold of cluster efficiency   (MTCE) at which positive effects of clustering start to be felt, and the upper threshold of cluster efficiency (UTCE), from which any further increase in the density of the urban field may have adverse effects on the development of individual towns.

In addition, the cluster size should vary as a function of distance from the cluster in question to the closest principle city, so that a peripheral development cluster will have larger population size than one less remote (see Figure 20.1). For instance, if the distance from a town to the closest major city in Israel equals 50 km, it should be part of a cluster comprising about 12 urban localities with an overall population of some 175,000 residents within commuting range, in order to make the population growth of this urban community sustainable. Concurrently, a similar cluster of towns, which is more remote (100 km from the centre), may become sustainable once its total population exceeds 350,000 residents. In larger countries, with less dense patterns of urban development, the population size of sustainable development clusters might be considerably smaller. Thus, for instance, as the present analysis indicates (Chapters 17-18), the population size of such development clusters in peripheral areas of Norway and Australia may vary (with allowance for the distance from the closest urban centre of the country) from 40,000 to 120,000 residents.

Redirecting Priorities

To form the development clusters, a strategy of 'redirecting priorities' may be used (Portnov and Pearlmutter, 1997). This strategy assumes that development resources should be concentrated primarily on a limited number of urban clusters in selected peripheral areas until they reach the above threshold and become sufficiently attractive to migrants and private developers. The localities selected during the first phase of the development process can be located in close proximity to existing urban centres, which have already achieved the above population threshold (Figure 20.3).[2] Support of the selected localities should, of course, provide a balanced investment in housing development and in employment generating economic sectors. The establishment in the cluster of functional 'magnets' such as a large hospital or university may also enhance greatly the cluster's growth potential. In addition to direct government intervention, various forms of indirect involvement such as incentives for private investors and tax exemptions can also be applied.

As soon as the population threshold conducive to sustainable growth is achieved (MTCE), development support may be redirected on a step-by-step basis to other clusters of towns. This process of sequential and hierarchical concentration of resources can thereby be moved deeper and deeper into outlying areas (see Figure 20.3).

One comment is important: Once the overall population size of a development cluster approaches its threshold of sustainable growth, it may itself become one of the major population centres of a country. If so, the cluster in question may turn into the reference point for estimating the target populations of other development clusters located in more remote peripheral areas, using the proposed Index of Clustering as a quantitative tool (Chapter 14).

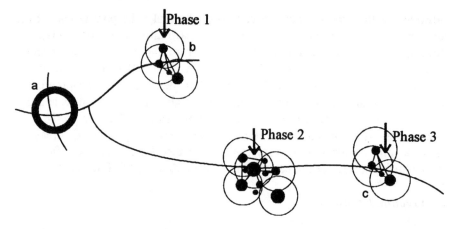

Figure 20.3   **The strategy of redirecting priorities to the formation of development clusters suggested for peripheral development areas**

a – major population centre of the country; b – development cluster; c – concentration of development resources.

The proposed strategy suggests that reaching a certain density of the urban field is an essential precondition for sustaining urban growth in a peripheral region. However, a further increase in the extent of clustering may affect adversely the chances of individual towns to achieve sustainable growth due to inter-town competition for potential investors and migrants and to growing diseconomies of over-concentration. At this stage, the redirection of development priorities may become essential not only for sustaining the long-term growth of the initially selected development cluster (Phase 1), but also for enhancing the development potential of more remote urban concentrations to which the development support is to be transferred at later phases (Phase 2, 3, etc.). The proposed Index of Clustering (IC – see Chapter 14) can be used as a quantitative tool to estimate the 'target thresholds for concentration or redirection of development support.

The proposed strategy of 'redirecting priorities' has certain parallels with Perroux's 'growth pole' theory subsequently developed by Friedmann (1973), Hansen (1975), and Bivand (1981), and implemented in various empirical planning studies (see *inter alia* Kuklinski, 1978; Parr, 1999; Hughes and Holland, 1994; Roberts, 1995). Nevertheless, the differences between these two development strategies are substantial.

First, the strategy of 'redirecting priorities' does not place a particular emphasis on the fact that the selected development communities will 'radiate development impulses' into their hinterland. Rather, it assumes that these communities will *sustain their own growth* due to their relative attractiveness to private investors and migrants. Second, in contrast to the 'growth pole' strategy, the strategy of redirecting priorities defines a certain population threshold, upon reaching which, development assistance can be transferred to other locations. The redirection of development priorities at a certain stage is essential since, as mentioned, a further increase in the size of an urban cluster may affect adversely the chances individual towns have of achieving sustainable growth, due to inter-town competition for potential investors and migrants and to growing diseconomies of over-concentration.

The strategy in question does, however, have certain parallels with Lewis's (1955; 1963 reprint, p.339) concept of industrialisation, though the relationship between urban growth and manufacturing is definitely less straightforward in the modern economy than Lewis envisioned in the early 1950s:

> From the economic standpoint it is better in the early stages of industrialisation to concentrate on building up a small number of well-integrated industrial centres. When these are well established, and industrialisation has got over its growing pains, other centres can be started in much the same way.

The concrete findings of this study - the size of an urban cluster and the intensity of the factors influencing sustainable population growth of urban localities - are definitely specific for the countries covered by the respective case studies. However, the strong non-linear relationship found between the clustering of the urban field and the sustainability of population growth and economic development is probably characteristic of development processes elsewhere. This insight may be of value to planners and decision-makers in any country that experiences acute problems of inter-regional inequalities in population growth and socio-economic development.

Notes

[1] A detailed account of diseconomies of agglomeration can be found in Krugman (1995; 1999), who calls such diseconomies 'the centrifugal forces' of dispersion.

[2] As both Hirscheman (1958; 1966 reprint) and Parr (2000) argue, a selection of certain urban concentrations for exclusive development support may have political implications in democratic societies and thus might be difficult to implement. Governments tend to seek support from all regions in a country and thus may face strong opposition from communities not yet supported. Though a detailed discussion of this problem falls far

beyond the scope of this study, which is concerned mainly with issues of physical planning, one of Parr's (2000) recommendations may be followed by decision-makers: the concentration of development support may be accompanied by the provision of better infrastructure to facilitate commuting and other forms of socio-economic interaction between communities not yet selected for support and those in development clusters.

Bibliography

Abe, H. (1996), 'New Directions for Regional Development Planning in Japan', in
J. Aden and P. Boland (eds), *Regional Development Strategies: A European
Perspective*, Jessica Kingsley Publishers, London and Bristol, pp. 273-95.

Alonso, W. (1960; 1991 reprint), 'A Theory of the Urban Land Market', in P.C.
Cheshire and A.W. Evans (eds), *Urban and Regional Economics*, Cambridge
University Press, Cambridge, pp. 83-91.

Alonso, W. (1964), *Location and Land Use: Towards a General Theory of Land
Rent*, Harvard University Press, Cambridge, MA.

Alonso, W. (1971; 1977 reprint), 'The Economics of Urban Size', in J. Friedman
and W. Alonso (eds), *Regional Policy: Theory and Applications*, The MIT
Press, Cambridge, MA, pp. 334-450.

Alonso, W. (1977), 'Location Theory', in J. Friedman and W. Alonso (eds),
Regional Policy: Theory and Applications, The MIT Press, Cambridge, MA,
pp. 35-63.

Alperovich, G. (1993), 'An Explanatory Model of City-size Distribution:
Evidence from Cross-country Data', *Urban Studies*, vol. 9, pp. 1591-601.

Altman, E.A. and Rosenbaum, B.R. (1975), 'Principles of Planning and Zionist
Ideology: The Israeli Development Town', in J. Friedmann and W. Alonso
(eds), *Regional Policy*, The MIT Press, Cambridge, MA, pp. 680-94.

Armstrong, H. and Taylor, J. (1993), *Regional Economics and Policy*, Harvester,
New York.

Aston, M. (1999), *Interpreting the Landscape: Landscape Archaeology and Local
History*, Routledge, London.

Atkinson, A. (1991), 'Environment and Development: Concepts and Practices in
Transition,' *Public Administration and Development*, vol. 11(4), pp. 401-13.

Atkinson, A. (1992), 'The Urban Bioregion as "Sustainable Development"
Paradigm,' *Third World Planning Review*, vol. 14(4), pp. 327-54.

Australian Bureau of Statistics (1999), *Australia Now – A Statistical Profile*
(Internet Edition).

AEW (2000), *History of Australian Commonwealth*, Australian Embassy in
Washington, D.C. (Internet Edition).

Babarović, I. (1979), 'Rural Marginality and Regional Development Policies in
Brazil', in A. Kuklinski (ed), *Regional Policies in Nigeria, India, and Brazil*,
Mouton Publishers, The Hague, pp. 186-319.

Bacher, J. and Michie, R. (1997), 'The Interim Evaluation of EU Regional Development Programmes: Experience from Objective 2 Regions', *Regional Studies*, vol. 31(9), pp. 849-58.

Balchin, P.N. (1990), *Regional Policy in Britain: The North-South Divide*, Paul Chapman Publishing, London.

Barbier, E.B. (1989), 'The Contribution of Environmental and Resource Economics to Economics of Sustainable Development,' *Development and Change*, vol. 20, pp. 429-59.

Bar-El, R. (2000), 'Regional Infrastructure Investments and Regional Economic Structures', Paper presented at 3rd Israeli-British & Irish Joint Regional Science Workshop on *Public Investments and Regional Economic Development*, Hebrew University of Jerusalem, 14-16 February, 2000.

Barret, G. (1998), 'The Transport Dimension', in M. Jenks *et al* (eds), *The Compact City: A Sustainable Urban Form?* E & FN Spon, London, pp. 170-80.

Beely, B. (1988), 'Migration and Planning: The Turkish Case', in D. Drakakis-Smith (ed), *Urbanization in the Developing World*, Routledge, New York, pp. 159-74.

Berry, B.J.L. (1973), *Growth Centres in the American Urban System*, Ballinger Publishing Company, Cambridge, MA, vol. 1.

Bitan, A. and Rubin, S. (1991), *Climatic Atlas of Israel for Physical and Environmental Planning and Design*, Ramot Publishing Co, Tel-Aviv.

Bivand, R.S. (1981), 'Regional Policy and Asymmetry in Geographical Interaction Relationships, in A. Kuklinski (ed), *Polarized Development and Regional Policies*, Mouton, The Hague, pp. 219-29.

Bivand, R.S. (1986), 'The Evaluation of Norwegian Regional Policy: Parameter Variation in Regional Shift Models', *Environment and Planning C: Government and Policy*, vol. 4(1), pp. 71-90.

Blake, M., Bell, M. and Rees, P. (2000), 'Creating a Temporally Consistent Spatial Framework for the Analysis on Interregional Migration in Australia', *Int. J. of Population Geography*, vol.6, pp 155-74.

Borjas, G.J. (1989), 'Economic Theory and International Migration', *International Migration Review*, vol. 23(3), pp. 457-85.

Bossel, H. (1999), *Indicators for Sustainable Development: Theory, Method, Applications*, International Institute for Sustainable Development, Winnipeg, Canada.

Bourne, L.S. (1975), *Urban Systems: Strategies for Regulation*, Claredon Press, Oxford.

Brown, L.R. and Jacobson, J. (1987), 'Assessing the Future of Urbanization', *State of the World 1987*, W.W. Norton & Company, New York and London, pp. 38-56.

Burnley, I.H., Murphy, P.A. and Jenner, A. (1997), 'Selecting Suburbia: Residential Relocation to Outer Sydney', *Urban Studies*, vol. 34(7), pp. 1109-27.

Carroll, G.R. (1982), 'National City-size Distributions: What do We Know after 67 Years of Research?' *Progress in Human Geography*, vol. 6, pp. 1-43.

Choshen, M. and Kimhi, I. (1996), 'Migration of Jews to and from Jerusalem: Traits of the Migrants and the Causes of Migration, in Y. Gradus and G. Lipshitz (eds), *Mosaic of Israeli Geography*, Ben-Gurion University of the Negev Press, Be'er Sheva, pp. 85-95.

Christaller, W. (1933; 1966 English edition), *Central Places in Southern Germany*, Prentice Hall Inc., Englewood Cliffs, NJ.

CIA, (2000), *The 1999 World Fact Book*, U.S. Central Intelligence Agency (Internet Edition).

Clark, C. (1982), *Regional and Urban Location*, St. Martin's Press, New York.

Clawson, M. and Hall, P. (1973), *Planning and Urban Growth: An Anglo-American Comparison*, The Johns Hopkins University Press, Baltimore.

COI (1974), *The New Towns of Britain*, Central Office of Information/Her Majesty's Stationery Office, London.

Copus, A.K. (1999). 'Peripherality and Peripherally Indicators', *North*, vol. 10, pp. 11-5.

Dampier, W. (1982), 'Ten Years after Stockholm: A Decade of Environmental Debate', *Ambio*, vol. 11(4), pp. 215-31.

DCT (1999) *Setting the Direction for Regional Western Australia*, Policy Framework Discussion Paper, Department of Commerce and Trade, Perth, WA.

De Jong, C.F. and Fawcett, J.T. (1981), 'Motivation for Migration: An Assessment and a Value-expectancy Research Model', in C.F. DeJong and R.W. Gardner (eds), *Migration Decision-Making. Multidisciplinary Approaches to Micro-level Studies in Developed and Developing Countries*, Pergamon Press, New York, pp. 13-53.

Deichmann, U. (2000), *African Population Database Documentation*, National Centre for Geographic Information and Analysis, University of California (Internet Edition).

Diamond, D.R. and Spence, N.A. (1983), *Regional Policy Evaluation: A Methodological Review and the Scottish Example*, Gover, Aldershot.

Dodds, S.H. (1999), 'Pathways and Paradigms for Sustaining Human Communities', *Open House International*, vol. 24(1), pp. 6-16.

Doxiadis, C.A. (1964), *The Ancient Greek City and the City of the Present*, Doxiadis-Associates-Consultants, Athens.

Doxiadis, C.A. (1977), *Ecology and Ekistics*, Westview Press, Boulder, CO.

Drabkin-Darin, H. (1957), *Housing in Israel: Economic and Sociological Aspects*, Gadish Books, Tel Aviv.

EB (1999), *Encyclopaedia Britannica Online*.

EC (2000), *Regional policy of the European Union*, European Commission (Internet Site).

Ehrlich, P.R., Ehrlich, A.H. and Holdren, J.P. (1972), *Eco-science: Population, Resources, Environment*, W.H. Freeman and Company, San-Francisco, CA.

Fedick, S.L. (1997), 'Settlement', in P.Oliver (ed), *Encyclopaedia of Vernacular Architecture of the World*, Cambridge University Press, Oxford, pp. 170-2.

Felsenstein, D. (1997), *Estimating Some of the Impacts on Local and Regional Economic Development Associated with Ben-Gurion University of the Negev*, Negev Centre of Regional Development, Be'er Sheva.

Felsenstein, D. (1998), 'Indices for Distance Measurement in Halacha', in E. Razin and R. Rubin (eds), *Studies in the Geography of Israel*, Hebrew University, Jerusalem, pp. 214-28.

Fialkoff, C. (1992), 'Israel's Housing Policy during a Period of Massive Immigration', in Y. Golani, S. Eldor and M. Garon (eds), *Planning and Housing in Israel in the Wake of Rapid Changes*, Ministries of the Interior and of Construction and Housing, Jerusalem, pp. 169-77.

Fik, T.J. (1991), 'Price Pattern in Competitively Clustered Markets', *Environment and Planning A*, vol. 23(11), pp. 1545-60.

Findley, S. (1977), *Planning for Internal Migration: A Review of Issues and Policies in Developing Countries*, United States Government Printing Office, Washington, D.C.

Fischer, C.S. (1976), *The Urban Experience*, Harcourt Brace Jovanovich, Inc., New York.

Foss, N.J. (1996), 'High-order Industrial Capabilities and Competitive Advantage', *Journal of Industry Studies*, vol. 3(1), pp. 1-20.

Fotheringham, S. (1991), 'Migration and Spatial Structure: The Development of the Competing Destinations Model', in J. Stillwell and P. Congdon (eds), *Migration Models: Macro and Micro Approaches*, Belhaven Press, London and New York, pp. 57-72.

Frenkel, A., Shefer, D. and Roper, S. (2000), 'Does Location Matter for High-Tech Firms? Evidence from Israel and Ireland', Paper presented at 3rd Israeli-British & Irish Joint Regional Science Workshop on *Public Investment and Regional Economic Development*, Hebrew University of Jerusalem, 14-16 February, 2000.

Friedmann, J. (1966), *Regional Development Policy: A Case Study of Venezuela*, MIT Press, Cambridge, MA.

Friedmann, J. (1973), *Urbanisation, Planning and National Development*, SAGE Publications, Beverly Hills and London.

Fujita, M. and Mori, T. (1996), 'The Role of Ports in the Making of Major Cities: Self-agglomeration and Hub-effect', *Journal of Development Economics*, vol. 49(1), pp. 93-120.

Fujita, M. and Mori, T. (1997), 'Structural Stability and Evolution of Urban Systems'. *Regional Science and Urban Economics*, vol. 27, pp. 399-442.

Fulford, C. (1999), 'The Compact City and the Market: The Case of Residential Development', in M. Jenks *et al* (eds), *The Compact City: A Sustainable Urban Form?* E & FN Spon, London, pp. 122-33.

George, P. (1970), 'Types of Migration of the Population According to the Professional and Social Composition of Migrants', in A. Clifford and J. Jansen (eds), *Reading in the Sociology of Migration*, Pergamon Press, Oxford, pp. 39-47.

Golany, G. (1978), 'Planning Urban Sites in Arid Zones: The Basic Considerations', in G. Golany (ed), *Urban Planning for Arid Zones*, John Wiley & Sons, New York, pp. 3-21.

Golany, G. (1982), 'Selecting Sites for New Settlements in Arid Lands: Negev Case Study', *Energy and Building*, vol. 4, pp. 23-41.

Goodland, R. and Ledec, G. (1986), *Neoclassical Economics and Principles of Sustainable Development*, World Bank, Washington, D.C.

Gordon, I. (1991), 'Multi-stream Migration Modelling', in J. Stillwell and P. Congdon (eds), *Migration Models: Macro and Micro Approaches*, Belhaven Press, London and New York, pp. 73-91.

Gradus, Y. (1983), 'The Role of Politics in Regional Inequality: The Israeli Case,' *Annals of the Association of American Geographers*, vol. 73, pp. 388-403.

Gradus, Y. (1984), 'The Emergence of Regionalisation in a Centralized System: The Case of Israel', *Environment and Planning D: Society and Space*, vol. 2, pp. 87-100.

Gradus, Y. and Krakover, S. (1977), 'The Effect of Government Policy on the Spatial Structure of Manufacturing in Israel', *Journal of Developing Areas*, vol. 11, pp. 393-409.

Gradus, Y. and Stern, E. (1980), 'Changing Strategies of Development: Toward a Regiopolis in the Negev Desert', *Journal of American Planning Association* vol. 46(4), pp. 410-23.

Green, A.E., Hogarth, T. and Shackleton, R.E. (1999), 'Longer Distance Commuting as a Substitute for Migration in Britain: A Review of Trends, Issues and Implications', *International Journal of Population Geography*, vol. 5, pp. 49-67.

Green, H.C. (1982), 'Town Design in the Arid Pilbara of Western Australia, in G. Golany (ed), *Desert Planning: International Lessons*, The Architectural Press, London, pp. 15-30.

Greenwood, M. and Stock, R. (1990), 'Patterns of Change in the International Location of Population, Jobs and Housing: 1950 to 1980', *Journal of Urban Economics*, vol. 28(2), pp. 243-76.

Greenwood, M.J. and McDowell, J.M. (1991), 'Differential Economic Opportunities, Transferability of Skills, and Immigration to the United States', *Review of Economics and Statistics*, vol. 73(4), pp. 612-23.

HABITAT (1997), *Monitoring Urban Settlements with Urban Indicators*, United Nations Centre for Human Settlements, Nairobi.

Hansen, J.C. (1981), 'Settlement Pattern and Population Distribution as Fundamental Issues in Norway's Regional Policy', in J.W. Webb, A. Naukkarinen and L.A. Kosinski (eds) *Policies of Population Redistribution*, Geographic Society of Northern Finland, Oulu, pp. 107-27.

Hansen, N.M. (1975), 'Criteria for a Growth Centre Policy', in J. Friedmann and W. Alonso (eds), *Regional Policy*, The MIT Press, Cambridge, MA, pp. 566-87.

Hansen, N.M., Higgins, B. and Savoie, D. (1990), *Regional Policy in a Changing World*, Plenum, New York.

Hare, A.P. (1962), *Handbook of Small Group Research*, The Free Press, London (2nd Edition).

Hare, A.P. (2000), *Social Interaction* (book manuscript in preparation).

Haughton, G. and Hunter C. (1994), *Sustainable Cities*, Jessica Kingsley Publishers, London.

Hirschman, A.O. (1958; 1966 reprint), *The Strategy of Economic Development*, Yale University Press, New Haven, CN.

Holmøy, E. and Hægeland, T. (1995), 'Effective Rates of Assistance for Norwegian Industries', *Discussion paper No.147*, Statistics Norway, Oslo.

Howard, E. (1898; 1985 reprint), *Garden Cities of To-morrow*, Attic Books, London.

Hueting, R. (1980), *New Scarcity and Economic Growth: More Welfare through Less Production?* Amsterdam.

Hudson, F.S. (1976), *A Geography of Settlements*, MacDonald and Evans, Estover, Plymouth.

Hughes, D.W. and Holland, D.W. (1994), 'Core-periphery Economic Linkage: A Measure of Spread and Possible Backwash Effects for the Washington Economy', *Land Economics*, 70(3), pp. 364-77.

ICBS, (1951-1998), *Statistical Abstract of Israel* (Annual), Israeli Central Bureau of Statistics, Jerusalem.

ICBS, (1965-1997) *Local Authorities in Israel:* Physical Data (Annual), Israeli Central Bureau of Statistics, Jerusalem (in Hebrew).

Issar, A. (1999), 'The Past as a Key for the Future in Resettling the Desert', in B.A. Portnov and A.P. Hare, *Desert Regions: Population, Migration, and Environment*, Springer Verlag, Heidelberg, pp. 241-48.

Isserman, A.M. and Merrifield, J.D. (1987), 'Quasi-experimental Control Group Methods for Regional Analysis: An Application to an Energy Boomtown and Growth Pole Theory', *Economic Geography*, vol. 63(1), pp. 3-19.

IUCN, (1980) *World Conservation Strategy: Living Resource Conservation for Sustainable Development*, International Union for Conservation of Nature and Natural Resources, UN Environment Program and World Wildlife Fund, Giland, Switzerland.

Johansen, F. and Klette, T.J. (1997), 'Wage and Employment Effects of Payroll Taxes and Investment Subsidies'. *Discussion paper No.194*, Statistics Norway, Oslo.

Johnston, R.J., Gregory, D. and Smith, D.M. (eds) (1994), *The Dictionary of Human Geography*, 3rd Edition, Blackwell, New York.

Kanafani, A. (1978), 'Transportation and Regional Structure in Underdeveloped Regions', in R. Funck (ed), *The Analysis of Regional Structure: Essays in Honour of August Lösch*, Pion Press, London, pp. 28-34.

Karkazis, J.and Thanassoulis, E. (1998), 'Assessing the Effectiveness of Regional Development Policies in Northern Greece Using Data Envelopment Analysis,' *Socio-economic Planning Sciences*, vol. 32(2), pp. 123-37.

Kates, R.W., Johnson, D.L., and Johnson-Haring, K. (1977), 'Population, Society and Desertification', in *Desertification: Its Causes and Consequences*. Pergamon Press, Oxford, pp. 261-318.

Kipnis, B.A. (1989), *Plant Scale and Manufacturing Policies for Peripheral Regions: An Intercultural Analysis of Israel, Brazil and Belgium*, Aldershot, Avebury.

Kipnis, B.A. (1996), 'From Dispersal to Concentration: Alternative Strategies in Israel', in Y. Gradus and G. Lipshitz (eds), *Mosaic of Israeli Geography*, Ben-Gurion University of the Negev Press, Be'er Sheva, pp. 29-36.

Kirschenbaum, A. and Comay, Y. (1974), 'Dynamics of Population Attraction to New Towns - The Case of Israel, in *Dialogue in Development - Natural and Human Resources*, Proceedings of the 3rd World Congress of Engineers and Architects, Jerusalem, Israel, pp. 18-30.

Klemmer, P. (1978), 'Methods for the Determination of Centrality', in R. Funck (ed) *The Analysis of Regional Structure: Essays in Honour of August Lösch*, Pion Press, London, pp. 54-61.

Kneese, A. V. (1978), 'The Economic and Economically Related Aspects of New Towns in Arid Areas', in G. Golany (ed), *Urban Planning for Arid Zones*, John Wiley & Sons, New York, pp. 123-38.

Krakover, S. (1987), 'Clusters of Cities versus City Region in Regional Planning,' *Environment and Planning A*, vol. 19, pp. 1375-86.

Krakover, S. (1998a), 'Population Dispersal in Israel as Reflected in City-size Distributions', in E. Razin and R. Rubin (eds), *Studies on the Geography of Israel*, Hebrew University, Jerusalem, pp. 255-70 (in Hebrew).

Krakover, S. (1998b), 'Testing the Turning-point Hypothesis in City-size Distribution: The Israeli Situation Re-examined,' *Urban Studies*, vol. 35(12), pp. 2183-96.

Krakover, S. and Morrill, R.L. (1992), 'Long-wave Spatial and Economic Relationships in Urban Development', in *Application of the Expansion Method*, Routledge, London and New York, pp. 161-84.

Krugman, P. (1995), *Development, Geography, and Economic Theory*, The MIT press, Cambridge, MA.

Krugman, P (1999), 'The Role of Geography in Development', *International Regional Science Review*, vol. 22(2), pp. 142-61.

Kuklinski, A., (ed) (1978), *Regional Policies in Nigeria, India and Brazil*, Mouton Publishers, the Hague.

Kupiszewski, M., Durham, H. and Rees, P. (1998), 'Internal Migration and Urban Change in Poland', *European Journal of Population*, vol. 14, pp. 265-90.

Lele, S.M. (1991), 'Sustainable Development: A Critical Review,' *World Development*, vol. 19(6), pp. 607-21.

Levinson, E., Gradus, Y. and Kalati, I. (1994), 'A Profile of the Negev', *The Newsletter of the Negev Centre for Regional Development*, vol. 1(1), pp. 8-10.

Levy, J. M. (1985), *Urban and Metropolitan Economics*, McGraw-Hill, New York.

Lewis, W.A. (1955; 1963 reprint), *The Theory of Economic Growth*, George Allen & Unwin Ltd, London.

Lipshitz, G. (1992), 'Divergence versus Convergence in Regional Development', *Journal of Planning Literature*, vol. 7(2), pp. 123-38.

Lipshitz, G. (1996a), 'Spatial Concentration, and Deconcentration of Population: Israel as a Case Study', *Geoforum*, vol. 27(1), pp. 87-96.

Lipshitz, G. (1996b), 'Core vs. Periphery in Israel over Time: Inequality, Internal Migration, and Immigration', in Y. Gradus and G. Lipshitz (eds), *Mosaic of Israeli Geography*, Ben-Gurion University of the Negev Press, Be'er Sheva, pp. 13-28.

Lipshitz, G. (1997), 'Immigrants from the Former Soviet Union in the Israeli Housing Market: Spatial Aspects of Supply and Demand', *Urban Studies*, vol. 34(3), pp. 471-88.

Lipshitz, G. (1998), *Country on the Move: Migration to and within Israel, 1948-1995*, Kluwer Academic Publishers, Dordrecht.

Lonsdale, R.E. (1998), 'A Century of Shifting Perceptions and Development Issues of Marginality', in H. Jussila *et al* (eds), *Perceptions of Marginality: Theoretical Issues and Regional Perceptions of Marginality in Geographic Space*, Ashgate, Aldershot, pp. 35-44.

Lösch, A. (1938; 1975 reprint), 'The Nature of Economic Regions', in J. Friedman and W. Alonso (eds), *Regional Policy: Theory and Applications*, The MIT Press, Cambridge, MA, pp. 97-105.

Ma, Z. (1999), 'Temporary Migration and Regional Development in China', *Environment and Planning A*, 31(5), pp. 783-802.

McCann, P. and Sheppard, S. (2000), 'Human Capital, Higher Education and Graduate Migration', Paper presented at 3rd Israeli-British & Irish Joint Regional Science Workshop on *Public Investments and Regional Economic Development*, Hebrew University of Jerusalem, 14-16 February, 2000.

MacKellar, F.L. and Vining, D.R. (1995), 'Population Concentration in Less Developed Countries: New Evidence', *Papers in Regional Science*, vol. 74(3), pp. 259-93.

MacNeill, J., Winsemius, P. and Yakushiji, T. (1992), *Beyond Interdependence: The Meshing of the World's Economy and the Earth's Ecology*, The Oxford University Press, Oxford.

Maier, G. and Weiss, P. (1991), 'The Discrete Choice Approach to Migration Modeling', in J. Stillwell and P. Congdon (eds), *Migration Models: Macro and Micro Approaches*, Belhaven Press, London and New York, pp. 17-33.

Malthus, T.R. (1798; 1973 reprint), *An Essay on the Principles of Population*, J.M.Dent & Sons Ltd., London.

Markusen, A. (1996), 'Interaction between Regional and Industrial Policies: Evidence from Four Countries', *International Regional Science Review*, vol. 19(1), pp. 49-77.

Marshall, A. (1890), *Principles of Economics*. McMillan, London (1930, 8th edition).

Marshall, A. (1892), *Elements of Economics.* McMillan, London (1909, 4th edition).

Meadows, D.H., *et al* (1972), *The Limits to Growth: A Report for the Club of Rome's Project on the Predicament of Mankind,* Earth Island, London.

Mera, K. (1995), 'Polarization and Politico-economic Change', *Papers in Regional Science,* vol. 74(1), pp. 175-85.

Michel, F., Perrot, A. and Thisse, J.F. (1996), 'Interregional Equilibrium with Heterogeneous Labour', *Journal of Population Economics,* vol. 9(1), pp. 95-113.

Middleton, N. and Thomas, D., Eds. (1997), *World Atlas of Desertification.* Arnold, London.

Mills, E.S. (1980), 'Population Redistribution and the Use of Land and Energy Resources', in B.J.L. Berry and L.P. Silverman (eds), *Population Redistribution and Public Policy,* National Academy of Sciences, Washington, D.C., pp. 50-69.

Moore, E.G. and Rosenberg, M.W. (1995), 'Modelling Migration Flows of Immigrant Group in Canada', *Environment and Planning A,* vol. 27, pp. 699-714.

Moore, T.G. (1994), 'Core-periphery Models, Regional Planning Theory, and Appalachian Development', *Professional Geographer,* vol. 46(3), pp. 316-31.

Moreno, J.L (1953; 1978 reprint), *Who Shall Survive? Foundations of Sociometry, Group Psychotherapy and Sociodrama,* Beacon House Inc., Beacon.

Myrdal, G. (1958), *Economic Theory and Under-developed Regions,* Gerald Duckworth & Co Ltd., London.

Negev, A. (1993), 'Scented Empire', *Eretz Magazine,* vol.30, pp. 35-52.

Newman, D., Gradus, Y. and Levinson, E. (1995), 'The Impact of Mass Immigration on Urban Settlements in the Negev 1989-1991', *Working Paper No 3,* Negev Centre for Regional Development, Be'er Sheva.

Newman, P. (1993), 'The Compact City: An Australian Perspective', *Built Environment,* vol. 18(4), pp. 285-300.

Nie, N.H., Hull, C.H., Jenkins, J.G., Steinbrenner, K. and Bent, D.H. (1975), *SPSS,* 2nd Edition, McGrow-Hill Book Company, New York.

NSD, (1999), *The Municipality Database,* Norwegian Social Science Data Services, Bergen.

Nordhaus, W.D. and Tobin, J. (1977), 'Growth and Natural Resources', in Dorfman (ed), *Economic of the Environment,* W.W. Norton, New York.

Oliver, P. (ed) (1997), *Encyclopaedia of Vernacular Architecture of the World.* Cambridge University Press, Oxford.

Pareto, V. (1935), *A Treatise on General Sociology,* Dover Publications, New York.

Parr, J.B. (1999), 'Growth-pole Strategies in Regional Economic Planning: A Retrospective View: Part 2. Implementation and Outcome', *Urban Studies,* 36(8), pp. 1247-68.

Parr, J.B. (2000), 'Regional Economic Policy: Lessons from the Developed World for Developing Nations', Paper presented at 3rd Israeli/British/Irish Regional Science Workshop, Jerusalem, February, 14-15th, 2000.

Pavlides, E. (1997), 'Slope', in P. Oliver (ed), *Encyclopaedia of Vernacular Architecture of the World*, Cambridge University Press, pp.150-51.

Pearsall, S.H. (1984), 'In Absentia Benefits of Nature Preserves: A Review,' *Environmental Conservation*, vol. 11, pp. 3-10.

Perman, R. and Stern, D.I. (1999), 'The Environmental Kuznets Curve: Implications of Non-stationarity,' *Working paper #9901*, The Australian National University, Canberra.

Perroux, F. (1950), 'Economic Space: Theory and Applications', *Quarterly Journal of Economics*, vol. 64; - Reprinted in J. Friedman and W. Alonso (eds), *Regional Development and Planning: A Reader*, The MIT University Press, Cambridge, MA, pp. 21-36, 1964.

Perroux, F. (1983), *A New Concept of Development: Basic Tenets*, Croom Helm, London and Canberra.

Plato. *The Laws of Plato* (1979 English Translation by T.L. Pangle), Basic Books Inc., N.Y.

Poot, J. (1996), 'Information, Communication and Networks in International Migration System', *The Annals of Regional Science*, vol. 30, pp. 55-73.

Portnov, B.A. (1992), *Rational Use of Urban Land in Reconstruction Areas*, Stroyizdat, Krasnoyarsk (in Russian).

Portnov, B.A. (1994), *Rational Use of Residential Land in Cities of Siberia: Methods of Urban Regulation*, Doctoral Dissertation, Moscow Architectural Institute, Moscow (in Russian).

Portnov, B.A. (1998a), 'The Effect of Housing Construction on Population Migrations in Israel', *Journal of Ethnic and Migration Studies*, vol. 24(3), pp. 541-58.

Portnov, B.A. (1998b), 'The Effect of Housing on Migration in Israel', *The Journal of Population Economics*, vol. 11(3), pp. 379-94.

Portnov, B.A. (1999a), 'Modelling the Migration Attractiveness of a Region', in B.A. Portnov and A.P. Hare (eds), *Desert Regions: Population, Migration and Environment*, Springer Verlag, Heidelberg, pp. 111-32.

Portnov, B.A. (1999b), 'The Effect of Regional Inequalities on Migration: A Comparative Analysis of Israel and Japan', *International Migration*, vol. 37(3), pp. 587-615.

Portnov, B.A. and Erell, E. (1998a), 'Clustering of the Urban Field as a Precondition for Sustainable Population Growth in Peripheral Areas: The Case of Israel', *Review of Urban and Regional Development Studies*, vol. 10(2), pp. 123-41.

Portnov, B.A. and Erell, E. (1998b), 'Long-term Development Peculiarities of Peripheral Desert Settlements: The Case of Israel', *International Journal of Urban and Regional Research*, vol. 22(2), pp. 216-32.

Portnov, B.A., Erell, E., Bivand, R. and Nilsen, A. (2000), 'Investigating the Effect of Clustering of the Urban Field on Sustainable Population Growth of

Centrally Located and Peripheral Towns', *International Journal of Population Geography*, vol. 6, pp. 133-54.

Portnov, B.A., and Etzion Y. (2000), 'Investigating the Effects of Public Policy on the Interregional Patterns of Population Change: The Case of Israel', *Socio-economic Planning Sciences*, 34(4), pp. 1-31 (in press).

Portnov, B.A. and Pearlmutter, D. (1997), 'Sustainability of Population Growth: a Case Study of Urban Settlements in Israel', *Review of Urban & Regional Development Studies*, vol. 9(2), pp. 129-45.

Portnov, B.A. and Pearlmutter, D. (1999a), 'Sustainable Population Growth of Urban Settlements', in B.A. Portnov and A.P. Hare (eds), *Desert Regions: Population, Migration, and Environment*, Springer Verlag, Heidelberg, pp. 37-60.

Portnov, B.A. and Pearlmutter, D. (1999b), 'Private Construction as a General Indicator of Urban Development: The Case of Israel', *International Planning Studies*, vol. 4(1), pp. 133-61.

Portnov, B.A. and Pearlmutter, D. (1999c), 'Sustainable Urban Growth in Peripheral Areas, *Progress in Planning* (Monograph series), vol. 52(4), Pergamon, London, pp. 239-308.

Ravenstein, E.G. (1885), 'The Laws of Migrations', *Journal of the Royal Statistical Society*, XLVIII(II), pp. 167-235.

Razin, E. (1998), 'The Impact of Decentralisation on Fiscal Disparities among Local Authorities in Israel', *Space & Polity*, vol. 2(1), pp. 51-71.

Razin, E., Rosentraub, M. (2000), 'Are Fragmentation and Sprawl Interlinked? North American Evidence', *Urban Affairs Review* (forthcoming).

Rees, P., Ostby, L., Durham, H. and Kupiszewski, M. (1998), 'Internal Migration and Regional Population Dynamic in Europe: Norway Case Study', *Working Paper Series*, 98(4)., The University of Leeds, School of Geography.

Rephann, T. and Isserman, A. (1994), 'New Highways as Economic Development Tools: An Evaluation Using Quasi-experimental Matching Methods', *Regional Science and Urban Economics*. 24(6), pp. 723-51.

Ribarsky, W., King, D., Gavrilovska, A. and van de Pol, R. (1998), *Time-Critical Visual Exploration of Scalably Large Data*, Springer Verlag, Heidelberg.

Richardson, H.W. (1977), *Regional Growth Theory*, Macmillan, London.

Roberts, J.T. (1995), 'Trickling down and Scrambling up: The Informal Sector, Food Provisioning and Local benefits of the Carajas Mining 'Growth Pole" in the Brazilian Amazon', *World Development*, 23(3), pp. 385-400.

Rogerson, C.M. (1998), 'High-technology and Infrastructure Development: International and South African Experiences', *Development South Africa*, vol. 15(5), pp. 875-905.

Sage, C. (1994), 'Population, Consumption and Sustainable Development', in M. Redclift and C. Sage (eds), *Strategies for Sustainable Development': Local Agendas for the Southern Hemisphere*, John Wiley & Sons, Chichester, pp. 35-60.

Saini, B. S. (1980), *Building in Hot Dry Climates*, John Wiley & Sons, Chichester.

Sale, K. (1985), *Dwellers in the Land: The Bioregional Vision*, Sierra Club Books, San Francisco, CA.

Sasaki, K., Ohashi, T. and Ando, A. (1997), 'High-speed Rail Transit Impact on Regional System: Does Shinkansen Contribute to Dispersion'? *The Annals of Regional Science*, vol. 31(1), pp. 77-98.

Saxenian, A. (1996), 'Regional Network and Industrial Adaptation in Silicon Valley and Route 128', *Cityscape*, vol. 2(2), pp. 41-60.

Schmidt, M.H. (1998), 'An Integrated Systematic Approach to Marginal Regions: From Definition to Development Policies', in H. Jussila *et al* (eds), *Perceptions of Marginality: Theoretical Issues and Regional Perceptions of Marginality in Geographic Space*, Ashgate, Aldershot, pp. 45-66.

Shachar, A. (1996), 'National Planning at a Crossroads: The Evolution of a New Planning Doctrine for Israel', in Y. Gradus and G. Lipshitz (eds), *Mosaic of Israeli Geography*, Ben-Gurion University of the Negev Press, Be'er Sheva, pp. 3-12.

Shachar, A. and Felsenstein, D. (1992), 'Urban Economic Development and High Technology Industry', *Urban Studies*, vol. 29(6), pp. 839-55.

Shefer, D. (1990), 'Innovation, Technical Change and Metropolitan Development: An Israeli Example', in P. Nijkamp (ed), *Sustainability of Urban System: A Cross-national Analysis of Urban Innovation*, Avebury, Aldershot, pp. 167-82.

Shefer, D. and Bar-El, E. (1993), 'High-technology Industries as a Vehicle for Growth in Israel's peripheral Regions', *Environment and Planning C: Government and Policy*, vol. 3, pp. 245-61.

Shefer, D. and Frenkel, A. (1998), 'Local Milieu and Innovations: Some Emperical Results', *Annals of Regional Science*, vol. 32, pp. 185-200.

Sheffer, G. (1978), 'Elite Cartel, Vertical Domination, and Grassroots Discontent in Israel', in S. Tarrow, P.J. Katzenstein and L. Graziano (eds), *Territorial Politics in Industrial Nations*, Praeger Publisher, New York, pp. 64-96.

Shelburne, R.C. and Bednarzik, R.W. (1993), 'Geographic Concentration of Trade-Sensitive Employment,' *Monthly Labour Review*, vol. 116(6), pp. 3-13.

Shilton, L. and Craig, S. (1999), 'Spatial patterns of Headquarters', *Journal of Real Estate Research*, vol. 17(3), pp. 341-64.

Show, D. (1987), "Siberia: Geographic Background', in A. Wood (ed), *Siberia: Prospects for Regional Development*, Groom Helm, London, pp. 9-34.

Smith, W.F. (1975), *Urban Development: The Process and the Problems*, University of California Press, Berkeley.

SN (1994), *Standard Classification of Municipalities*, Statistics Norway, Oslo.

SN (1997), 'Greater Oslo is Winner in Migration', *Weekly Bulletin on Population Statistics*, vol. 34, Statistics Norway, Oslo.

SN (1997-1999), *Statistical Yearbook of Norway* (Annual), Statistics Norway, Oslo.

Soen, D. (1977), 'Israel's Population Dispersal Plans and their Implementation, 1948-1974: Failure or Success?' *GeoJournal*, vol. 1(5), pp. 21-6.

Sonis, M. (1988), 'Interregional Migration in Individual Countries: Israel', in W. Weidlich and G. Haag (eds), *Interregional Migration: Dynamic Theory and Comparative Analysis*, Springer, New York.

Sorensen, T., ed. (1997), *Regional Policy and Practice*, vol. 6(1), ANZRSA Press, Auckland, NZ.

Stambøl, L.S. (1991), 'Migration Projection in Norway: A Regional Demographic-economic Model', in J. Stillwell and P. Congdon (eds), *Migration Models: Macro and Micro Approaches*, Belhaven Press, London and New York, pp. 287-308.

Stambøl, L.S. and Sørensen, K.Ø. (1989), 'Migration Analysis and Regional Population Projections', *Discussion paper No.46*, Statistics Norway, Oslo.

Stillwell, J. and Congdon, P., eds (1991), *Migration Models: Macro and Micro Approaches*, Belhaven Press, London and New York.

Stouffer, S.A. (1940; 1962 reprint), *Social Research to Test Ideas*, The Free Press of Glencoe.

Stöhr, W.R. (1981), 'Development from Below: The Bottom-up and Periphery-inward Development Paradigm', in W.R. Stöhr and D.R. Fraser-Taylor (eds), *Development from Above or Below?* John Wiley & Sons, Ltd., London, pp. 39-70.

Stren, R., White, R., and Whitney, J. (1992), *Urbanisation and the Environment in International Prospective*, Westview Press, Boulder, CO.

Swales, J.K. (1997), 'The Ex-post Evaluation of Regional Selective Assistance', *Regional Studies*, vol. 31(9), pp. 859-65.

Swann, G.M., Prevezer, M. and Stout, D., eds (1998), *The Dynamic of Industrial Clustering: International Comparisons in Computing and Biotechnology*, Oxford and New York, Oxford University Press.

Tsur, B. (1995), 'Aliya Down 3.5% in '95', *The Jerusalem Post*, 31.12.95.

Turner, R K. (1993), 'Sustainability: Principles and Practice,' in R.K. Turner (ed), *Sustainable Environmental Economics and Management: Principles and Practice*, John Wiley & Sons, Chichester, pp. 3-36.

U.S. DOT/FHWA (1990), *Journey-to-Work Trends in the United States and its Major Metropolitan Areas: 1960–1990*, U.S. Department of Transportation, Washington, D.C.

von Thünen, J.H. (1826), *The Isolated State* (1966 English edition), Oxford, Pergamon Press.

Walcott, S.M. (1999), 'High Tech in the Deep South: Biomedical Firm Clusters in Metropolitan Atlanta', *Growth and Change*, vol. 30(1), pp. 48-74.

WCED, (1987), *Our Common Future*, World Commission on Environment and Development, Oxford Univ. Press, New York.

Webber, M.J. (1973), *Impact of Uncertainty on Location*, 2nd Edition, The MIT Press, Cambridge, Massachusetts.

Weber, A. (1909; 1929 reprint), *Theory of the Location of Industries*, The University of Chicago Press, Chicago and London.

Weber, M. (1921; 1958 English edition), *The City*, The Free Press, New York.

Weiss, H. (1986), 'The Origin of Tell Leilan and the Conquest of Space in Third Millennium Mesopotamia', in H. Weiss (ed), *The Origin of Cities in Dry-farming Syria and Mesopotamia in the Third Millennium B.C.*, Four Quarters Publishing Co., Guilford, CN, pp. 71-108.

White, G.F. (1966), 'The World's Arid Zones', in E.S. Hills (ed), *Arid Lands: A Geographical Appraisal*, Methuen & Co Ltd, London, pp. 15-30.

Widdows, R., ed (1996), *Encyclopedic World Atlas*, Oxford University Press, New York (3rd Edition).

Wile, J.H. (1978), 'The Impact of Demand and Cost Changes on the Spatial Dispersion of a Market-oriented Industry', in R. Funck (ed), *The Analysis of Regional Structure: Essays in Honour of August Lösch*, Pion Press, London, pp. 19-27.

Williams, K., Jenks, M., and Burton, E. (1999), 'How Much is too Much: Urban Intensification, Social Capacity and Sustainable Development', *Open House International*, vol. 2(1), pp. 17-25.

Woldenberg, M.J. (1979), 'A Periodic Table of Spatial Hierarchies', in S. Gale and G. Olson (eds), *Philosophy in Geography*, D. Reidel Publishing Company, Dordrecht, pp. 429-57.

Wong, C. (1995), 'Developing Quantitative Indicators for Urban and Regional Policy Analysis', in R. Hambleton and T. Huw (eds), *Urban Policy Evaluation: Challenge and Change*, Paul Chapman Publishing Ltd., Cardiff, pp. 111-22.

WRI, (1997), *World Resources: A Guide to the Global Environment*, World Research Institute, Washington, D.C.

Zheng, X.P. (1997), 'China's Regional Inequalities and Related Long-term Policies', *Review of Urban and Regional Development Studies*, vol. 9, pp. 115-28.

Zipf, G.K. (1949; 1972 reprint), *Human Behaviour and the Principle of the Least Effort: An Introduction to Human Ecology*, Hafner Publishing Company, New York.

Appendices

Appendix 1 MB/NG index (adjusted hyperbolic tangent function)

MB	NG					
	-1800	-1700	-1600	-1500	-1400	-1300
-1800	-2.00	-2.00	-2.00	-1.99	-1.99	-1.99
-1700	-2.00	-2.00	-1.99	-1.99	-1.99	-1.99
-1600	-2.00	-1.99	-1.99	-1.99	-1.99	-1.99
-1500	-1.99	-1.99	-1.99	-1.99	-1.99	-1.99
-1400	-1.99	-1.99	-1.99	-1.99	-1.99	-1.98
-1300	-1.99	-1.99	-1.99	-1.99	-1.98	-1.98
-1200	-1.99	-1.99	-1.99	-1.98	-1.98	-1.97
-1100	-1.99	-1.99	-1.98	-1.98	-1.97	-1.97
-1000	-1.99	-1.98	-1.98	-1.97	-1.97	-1.96
-900	-1.98	-1.98	-1.97	-1.97	-1.96	-1.95
-800	-1.98	-1.97	-1.97	-1.96	-1.95	-1.94
-700	-1.97	-1.97	-1.96	-1.95	-1.94	-1.93
-600	-1.97	-1.96	-1.95	-1.94	-1.93	-1.91
-500	-1.96	-1.95	-1.94	-1.93	-1.91	-1.89
-400	-1.95	-1.94	-1.93	-1.91	-1.89	-1.87
-300	-1.94	-1.93	-1.91	-1.89	-1.87	-1.84
-200	-1.93	-1.91	-1.89	-1.87	-1.84	-1.81
-100	-1.91	-1.89	-1.87	-1.84	-1.81	-1.77
0	-1.89	-1.87	-1.84	-1.81	-1.77	-1.72
100	-0.94	-0.92	-0.91	-0.89	-0.86	-0.83
200	-0.92	-0.91	-0.89	-0.86	-0.83	-0.80
300	-0.91	-0.89	-0.86	-0.83	-0.80	-0.76
400	-0.89	-0.86	-0.83	-0.80	-0.76	-0.72
500	-0.86	-0.83	-0.80	-0.76	-0.72	-0.66
600	-0.83	-0.80	-0.76	-0.72	-0.66	-0.60
700	-0.80	-0.76	-0.72	-0.66	-0.60	-0.54
800	-0.76	-0.72	-0.66	-0.60	-0.54	-0.46
900	-0.72	-0.66	-0.60	-0.54	-0.46	-0.38
1000	-0.66	-0.60	-0.54	-0.46	-0.38	-0.29
1100	-0.60	-0.54	-0.46	-0.38	-0.29	-0.20
1200	-0.54	-0.46	-0.38	-0.29	-0.20	-0.10
1300	-0.46	-0.38	-0.29	-0.20	-0.10	0.00
1400	-0.38	-0.29	-0.20	-0.10	0.00	0.10
1500	-0.29	-0.20	-0.10	0.00	0.10	0.20
1600	-0.20	-0.10	0.00	0.10	0.20	0.29
1700	-0.10	0.00	0.10	0.20	0.29	0.38
1800	0.00	0.10	0.20	0.29	0.38	0.46

Appendix 1 (continuation)

MB	NG					
	-1200	-1100	-1000	-900	-800	-700
-1800	-1.99	-1.99	-1.99	-1.98	-1.98	-1.97
-1700	-1.99	-1.99	-1.98	-1.98	-1.97	-1.97
-1600	-1.99	-1.98	-1.98	-1.97	-1.97	-1.96
-1500	-1.98	-1.98	-1.97	-1.97	-1.96	-1.95
-1400	-1.98	-1.97	-1.97	-1.96	-1.95	-1.94
-1300	-1.97	-1.97	-1.96	-1.95	-1.94	-1.93
-1200	-1.97	-1.96	-1.95	-1.94	-1.93	-1.91
-1100	-1.96	-1.95	-1.94	-1.93	-1.91	-1.89
-1000	-1.95	-1.94	-1.93	-1.91	-1.89	-1.87
-900	-1.94	-1.93	-1.91	-1.89	-1.87	-1.84
-800	-1.93	-1.91	-1.89	-1.87	-1.84	-1.81
-700	-1.91	-1.89	-1.87	-1.84	-1.81	-1.77
-600	-1.89	-1.87	-1.84	-1.81	-1.77	-1.72
-500	-1.87	-1.84	-1.81	-1.77	-1.72	-1.67
-400	-1.84	-1.81	-1.77	-1.72	-1.67	-1.60
-300	-1.81	-1.77	-1.72	-1.67	-1.60	-1.52
-200	-1.77	-1.72	-1.67	-1.60	-1.52	-1.43
-100	-1.72	-1.67	-1.60	-1.52	-1.43	-1.33
0	-1.67	-1.60	-1.52	-1.43	-1.33	-1.21
100	-0.80	-0.76	-0.72	-0.66	-0.60	-0.54
200	-0.76	-0.72	-0.66	-0.60	-0.54	-0.46
300	-0.72	-0.66	-0.60	-0.54	-0.46	-0.38
400	-0.66	-0.60	-0.54	-0.46	-0.38	-0.29
500	-0.60	-0.54	-0.46	-0.38	-0.29	-0.20
600	-0.54	-0.46	-0.38	-0.29	-0.20	-0.10
700	-0.46	-0.38	-0.29	-0.20	-0.10	0.00
800	-0.38	-0.29	-0.20	-0.10	0.00	0.10
900	-0.29	-0.20	-0.10	0.00	0.10	0.20
1000	-0.20	-0.10	0.00	0.10	0.20	0.29
1100	-0.10	0.00	0.10	0.20	0.29	0.38
1200	0.00	0.10	0.20	0.29	0.38	0.46
1300	0.10	0.20	0.29	0.38	0.46	0.54
1400	0.20	0.29	0.38	0.46	0.54	0.60
1500	0.29	0.38	0.46	0.54	0.60	0.66
1600	0.38	0.46	0.54	0.60	0.66	0.72
1700	0.46	0.54	0.60	0.66	0.72	0.76
1800	0.54	0.60	0.66	0.72	0.76	0.80

Appendix 1 (continuation)

MB	NG					
	-600	-500	-400	-300	-200	-100
-1800	-1.97	-1.96	-1.95	-1.94	-1.93	-1.91
-1700	-1.96	-1.95	-1.94	-1.93	-1.91	-1.89
-1600	-1.95	-1.94	-1.93	-1.91	-1.89	-1.87
-1500	-1.94	-1.93	-1.91	-1.89	-1.87	-1.84
-1400	-1.93	-1.91	-1.89	-1.87	-1.84	-1.81
-1300	-1.91	-1.89	-1.87	-1.84	-1.81	-1.77
-1200	-1.89	-1.87	-1.84	-1.81	-1.77	-1.72
-1100	-1.87	-1.84	-1.81	-1.77	-1.72	-1.67
-1000	-1.84	-1.81	-1.77	-1.72	-1.67	-1.60
-900	-1.81	-1.77	-1.72	-1.67	-1.60	-1.52
-800	-1.77	-1.72	-1.67	-1.60	-1.52	-1.43
-700	-1.72	-1.67	-1.60	-1.52	-1.43	-1.33
-600	-1.67	-1.60	-1.52	-1.43	-1.33	-1.21
-500	-1.60	-1.52	-1.43	-1.33	-1.21	-1.07
-400	-1.52	-1.43	-1.33	-1.21	-1.07	-0.92
-300	-1.43	-1.33	-1.21	-1.07	-0.92	-0.76
-200	-1.33	-1.21	-1.07	-0.92	-0.76	-0.58
-100	-1.21	-1.07	-0.92	-0.76	-0.58	-0.39
0	-1.07	-0.92	-0.76	-0.58	-0.39	-0.20
100	-0.46	-0.38	-0.29	-0.20	-0.10	0.00
200	-0.38	-0.29	-0.20	-0.10	0.00	0.10
300	-0.29	-0.20	-0.10	0.00	0.10	0.20
400	-0.20	-0.10	0.00	0.10	0.20	0.29
500	-0.10	0.00	0.10	0.20	0.29	0.38
600	0.00	0.10	0.20	0.29	0.38	0.46
700	0.10	0.20	0.29	0.38	0.46	0.54
800	0.20	0.29	0.38	0.46	0.54	0.60
900	0.29	0.38	0.46	0.54	0.60	0.66
1000	0.38	0.46	0.54	0.60	0.66	0.72
1100	0.46	0.54	0.60	0.66	0.72	0.76
1200	0.54	0.60	0.66	0.72	0.76	0.80
1300	0.60	0.66	0.72	0.76	0.80	0.83
1400	0.66	0.72	0.76	0.80	0.83	0.86
1500	0.72	0.76	0.80	0.83	0.86	0.89
1600	0.76	0.80	0.83	0.86	0.89	0.91
1700	0.80	0.83	0.86	0.89	0.91	0.92
1800	0.83	0.86	0.89	0.91	0.92	0.94

Appendix 1 (continuation)

MB	NG					
	0	100	200	300	400	500
-1800	-1.89	-0.94	-0.92	-0.91	-0.89	-0.86
-1700	-1.87	-0.92	-0.91	-0.89	-0.86	-0.83
-1600	-1.84	-0.91	-0.89	-0.86	-0.83	-0.80
-1500	-1.81	-0.89	-0.86	-0.83	-0.80	-0.76
-1400	-1.77	-0.86	-0.83	-0.80	-0.76	-0.72
-1300	-1.72	-0.83	-0.80	-0.76	-0.72	-0.66
-1200	-1.67	-0.80	-0.76	-0.72	-0.66	-0.60
-1100	-1.60	-0.76	-0.72	-0.66	-0.60	-0.54
-1000	-1.52	-0.72	-0.66	-0.60	-0.54	-0.46
-900	-1.43	-0.66	-0.60	-0.54	-0.46	-0.38
-800	-1.33	-0.60	-0.54	-0.46	-0.38	-0.29
-700	-1.21	-0.54	-0.46	-0.38	-0.29	-0.20
-600	-1.07	-0.46	-0.38	-0.29	-0.20	-0.10
-500	-0.92	-0.38	-0.29	-0.20	-0.10	0.00
-400	-0.76	-0.29	-0.20	-0.10	0.00	0.10
-300	-0.58	-0.20	-0.10	0.00	0.10	0.20
-200	-0.39	-0.10	0.00	0.10	0.20	0.29
-100	-0.20	0.00	0.10	0.20	0.29	0.38
0	0.00	0.10	0.20	0.29	0.38	0.46
100	0.10	0.00	0.29	0.38	0.46	0.54
200	0.20	0.58	0.00	0.46	0.54	0.60
300	0.29	0.76	0.92	0.00	0.60	0.66
400	0.38	0.92	1.07	1.21	0.00	0.72
500	0.46	1.07	1.21	1.33	1.43	0.00
600	0.54	1.21	1.33	1.43	1.52	1.60
700	0.60	1.33	1.43	1.52	1.60	1.67
800	0.66	1.43	1.52	1.60	1.67	1.72
900	0.72	1.52	1.60	1.67	1.72	1.77
1000	0.76	1.60	1.67	1.72	1.77	1.81
1100	0.80	1.67	1.72	1.77	1.81	1.84
1200	0.83	1.72	1.77	1.81	1.84	1.87
1300	0.86	1.77	1.81	1.84	1.87	1.89
1400	0.89	1.81	1.84	1.87	1.89	1.91
1500	0.91	1.84	1.87	1.89	1.91	1.93
1600	0.92	1.87	1.89	1.91	1.93	1.94
1700	0.94	1.89	1.91	1.93	1.94	1.95
1800	0.95	1.91	1.93	1.94	1.95	1.96

Appendix 1 (continuation)

MB	NG					
	600	700	800	900	1000	1100
-1800	-0.83	-0.80	-0.76	-0.72	-0.66	-0.60
-1700	-0.80	-0.76	-0.72	-0.66	-0.60	-0.54
-1600	-0.76	-0.72	-0.66	-0.60	-0.54	-0.46
-1500	-0.72	-0.66	-0.60	-0.54	-0.46	-0.38
-1400	-0.66	-0.60	-0.54	-0.46	-0.38	-0.29
-1300	-0.60	-0.54	-0.46	-0.38	-0.29	-0.20
-1200	-0.54	-0.46	-0.38	-0.29	-0.20	-0.10
-1100	-0.46	-0.38	-0.29	-0.20	-0.10	0.00
-1000	-0.38	-0.29	-0.20	-0.10	0.00	0.10
-900	-0.29	-0.20	-0.10	0.00	0.10	0.20
-800	-0.20	-0.10	0.00	0.10	0.20	0.29
-700	-0.10	0.00	0.10	0.20	0.29	0.38
-600	0.00	0.10	0.20	0.29	0.38	0.46
-500	0.10	0.20	0.29	0.38	0.46	0.54
-400	0.20	0.29	0.38	0.46	0.54	0.60
-300	0.29	0.38	0.46	0.54	0.60	0.66
-200	0.38	0.46	0.54	0.60	0.66	0.72
-100	0.46	0.54	0.60	0.66	0.72	0.76
0	0.54	0.60	0.66	0.72	0.76	0.80
100	0.60	0.66	0.72	0.76	0.80	0.83
200	0.66	0.72	0.76	0.80	0.83	0.86
300	0.72	0.76	0.80	0.83	0.86	0.89
400	0.76	0.80	0.83	0.86	0.89	0.91
500	0.80	0.83	0.86	0.89	0.91	0.92
600	0.00	0.86	0.89	0.91	0.92	0.94
700	1.72	0.00	0.91	0.92	0.94	0.95
800	1.77	1.81	0.00	0.94	0.95	0.96
900	1.81	1.84	1.87	0.00	0.96	0.96
1000	1.84	1.87	1.89	1.91	0.00	0.97
1100	1.87	1.89	1.91	1.93	1.94	0.00
1200	1.89	1.91	1.93	1.94	1.95	1.96
1300	1.91	1.93	1.94	1.95	1.96	1.97
1400	1.93	1.94	1.95	1.96	1.97	1.97
1500	1.94	1.95	1.96	1.97	1.97	1.98
1600	1.95	1.96	1.97	1.97	1.98	1.98
1700	1.96	1.97	1.97	1.98	1.98	1.99
1800	1.97	1.97	1.98	1.98	1.99	1.99

Appendix 1 (continuation)

MB	NG					
	1200	1300	1400	1500	1600	1700
-1800	-0.54	-0.46	-0.38	-0.29	-0.20	-0.10
-1700	-0.46	-0.38	-0.29	-0.20	-0.10	0.00
-1600	-0.38	-0.29	-0.20	-0.10	0.00	0.10
-1500	-0.29	-0.20	-0.10	0.00	0.10	0.20
-1400	-0.20	-0.10	0.00	0.10	0.20	0.29
-1300	-0.10	0.00	0.10	0.20	0.29	0.38
-1200	0.00	0.10	0.20	0.29	0.38	0.46
-1100	0.10	0.20	0.29	0.38	0.46	0.54
-1000	0.20	0.29	0.38	0.46	0.54	0.60
-900	0.29	0.38	0.46	0.54	0.60	0.66
-800	0.38	0.46	0.54	0.60	0.66	0.72
-700	0.46	0.54	0.60	0.66	0.72	0.76
-600	0.54	0.60	0.66	0.72	0.76	0.80
-500	0.60	0.66	0.72	0.76	0.80	0.83
-400	0.66	0.72	0.76	0.80	0.83	0.86
-300	0.72	0.76	0.80	0.83	0.86	0.89
-200	0.76	0.80	0.83	0.86	0.89	0.91
-100	0.80	0.83	0.86	0.89	0.91	0.92
0	0.83	0.86	0.89	0.91	0.92	0.94
100	0.86	0.89	0.91	0.92	0.94	0.95
200	0.89	0.91	0.92	0.94	0.95	0.96
300	0.91	0.92	0.94	0.95	0.96	0.96
400	0.92	0.94	0.95	0.96	0.96	0.97
500	0.94	0.95	0.96	0.96	0.97	0.98
600	0.95	0.96	0.96	0.97	0.98	0.98
700	0.96	0.96	0.97	0.98	0.98	0.98
800	0.96	0.97	0.98	0.98	0.98	0.99
900	0.97	0.98	0.98	0.98	0.99	0.99
1000	0.98	0.98	0.98	0.99	0.99	0.99
1100	0.98	0.98	0.99	0.99	0.99	0.99
1200	0.00	0.99	0.99	0.99	0.99	0.99
1300	1.97	0.00	0.99	0.99	0.99	1.00
1400	1.98	1.98	0.00	0.99	1.00	1.00
1500	1.98	1.99	1.99	0.00	1.00	1.00
1600	1.99	1.99	1.99	1.99	0.00	1.00
1700	1.99	1.99	1.99	1.99	1.99	0.00
1800	1.99	1.99	1.99	1.99	2.00	2.00

Appendix 1 (continuation)

MB	NG
	1800
-1800	0.00
-1700	0.10
-1600	0.20
-1500	0.29
-1400	0.38
-1300	0.46
-1200	0.54
-1100	0.60
-1000	0.66
-900	0.72
-800	0.76
-700	0.80
-600	0.83
-500	0.86
-400	0.89
-300	0.91
-200	0.92
-100	0.94
0	0.95
100	0.96
200	0.96
300	0.97
400	0.98
500	0.98
600	0.98
700	0.99
800	0.99
900	0.99
1000	0.99
1100	0.99
1200	1.00
1300	1.00
1400	1.00
1500	1.00
1600	1.00
1700	1.00
1800	1.00

Appendix 2

Population and location indicators of towns included in the research sets in Israel

Set	Population ('000) in 1970	Population ('000) in 1996	Index of Remoteness, km (IR)	Index of Isolation (IS1)	Index of Isolation (IS2)	Index of Clustering (IS1/IR)	Index of Clustering (IS2/IR)	MB/NG index
Set 1 (central towns)								
Yavne	10.1	27.5	20	14	1321	0.70	66.08	0.67
Qiryat-Ono	14.9	23.4	7	22	1804	3.14	257.71	0.20
Or-Yehuda	12.3	24.1	7	25	1926	3.57	275.17	0.14
Nes-Ziyyona	12.1	22.3	15	18	1629	1.20	108.61	0.90
Rosh-H'Ayin	11.6	27.5	28	18	1267	0.64	45.26	0.04
Average for the set:	12.2	25.0	15.4	19.4	1589	1.85	150.57	0.39
Set 2 (Galilee towns)								
Nazerat-Illit	15.0	40.0	35	11	255	0.31	7.29	1.18
Afula	16.9	35.1	35	9	227	0.26	6.51	0.86
Migdal-H'Emeq	8.8	21.9	27	13	320	0.48	11.87	1.30
Qiryat-Sh'mona	15.1	19.4	70	0	19	0.00	0.28	-0.61
Bet-Shean	11.9	14.9	60	0	14.90	0.00	0.25	-0.49
Average for the set:	13.5	26.3	45.4	6.6	167.5	0.21	5.64	0.45
Set 3 (Negev towns)								
Dimona	22.5	31.2	115	0	31.20	0.00	0.27	-0.32
Ofaqim	9.2	21.6	85	2	189.80	0.02	2.23	0.01

Set	Population ('000) in 1970	Population ('000) in 1996	Index of Remoteness, km (IR)	Index of Isolation (IS1)	Index of Isolation (IS2)	Index of Clustering (IS1/IR)	Index of Clustering (IS2/IR)	MB/NG index
Arad	4.4	20.3	138	0	20.30	0.00	0.15	0.00
Sederot	7.5	18.2	62	2	118.00	0.03	1.90	0.12
Netivot	5.4	15.6	72	2	55.40	0.03	0.77	0.22
Average for the set:	9.8	21.4	94.4	1.2	82.9	0.02	1.06	0.01

Appendix 3

Population and location indicators of selected municipalities in Norway

Municipality	Index of Remoteness (IR), km	Index of Isolation (IS1)	Index of Isolation (IS2) - 1970	Index of Isolation (IS2) - 1997	Index of Clustering (IS1/IR)	Index of Clustering (IS2/IR) - 1970	Index of Clustering (IS2/IR) - 1997	Index of Clustering (mean)	Population, '000 Municipality (1998)	Population, '000 Major town (1997)	MBNG index*
					Set 1 (core)						
Askim	50	11	920.8	1039.1	0.220	18.416	20.782	19.599	13.3	11.6	0.815
Drammen	40	11	845.4	968.4	0.275	21.135	24.210	22.673	54.2	60.4	0.357
Frogn	34	12	924.1	1035.9	0.353	27.179	30.468	28.824	12.7	10.2	1.111
Moss	61	14	980.9	1147.8	0.230	16.080	18.816	17.448	26.2	30.4	-0.214
Ringerike	37	5	735.4	844.5	0.135	19.876	22.824	21.350	27.8	10.6	0.561
Ski	25	11	873.0	984.3	0.440	34.920	39.372	37.146	25.1	11.7	0.839
					Set 2 (periphery I)						
Halden	116	4	228.3	246.4	0.034	1.968	2.124	2.046	26.5	20.7	-0.352
Larvik	132	5	163.1	180.4	0.038	1.236	1.367	1.301	40.1	21.1	-0.178
Porsgrunn	142	5	184.3	203.8	0.035	1.298	1.435	1.367	32.5	35.9	-0.464
Sandefjord	119	6	280.6	301.7	0.050	2.358	2.535	2.447	38.7	34.0	1.148
Sarpsborg	91	6	149.4	164.0	0.066	1.642	1.802	1.722	47.0	39.7	-0.964
Skien	134	6	184.3	203.8	0.045	1.375	1.521	1.448	49.4	34.3	0.250
Tønsberg	99	7	185.4	204.3	0.071	1.873	2.064	1.968	34.3	41.3	-0.375

Municipality	Index of Remoteness (IR), km	Index of Isolation (IS1)	Index of Isolation (IS2) - 1970	Index of Isolation (IS2) - 1997	Index of Clustering (IS1/IR)	Index of Clustering (IS2/IR) - 1970	Index of Clustering (IS2/IR) - 1997	Index of Clustering (mean)	Population, '000 Municipality (1998)	Population, '000 Major town (1997)	MBNG index*
Set 3 (periphery II)											
Elverum	142	2	53.6	64.0	0.014	0.377	0.451	0.414	17.9	11.4	1.250
Gjøvik	124	3	61.0	75.4	0.024	0.492	0.608	0.550	27.0	16.7	0.179
Hamar	127	3	61.0	75.4	0.024	0.480	0.594	0.537	26.4	28.6	-0.054
Harstad	1360	1	30.1	32.6	0.001	0.022	0.024	0.023	23.0	18.6	-0.411
Kristiansund	495	1	32.4	34.6	0.002	0.065	0.070	0.068	16.9	16.8	-1.411
Lillehammer	168	2	53.6	64.0	0.012	0.319	0.381	0.350	24.5	18.7	0.893
Molde	430	2	57.9	59.2	0.005	0.135	0.138	0.136	23.6	17.8	0.214
Narvik	1406	1	30.1	32.6	0.001	0.021	0.023	0.022	18.5	14.0	-1.125
Steinkjer	510	0	8.6	10.4	0.000	0.017	0.020	0.019	20.4	10.4	-0.732
Ålesund	381	1	39.9	42.4	0.003	0.105	0.111	0.108	38.1	24.6	0.048
Set 4 (educational and economic centres of peripheral regions)											
Alta	1920	0	5.6	10.8	0.000	0.003	0.006	0.004	16.5	10.8	0.625
Bodø	1220	0	24.4	33.5	0.000	0.020	0.027	0.024	40.6	33.5	0.339
Tromsø	1650	0	28.9	47.8	0.000	0.018	0.029	0.023	57.9	47.8	0.500

* Averages for 1970-1997

Appendix 4
Population and location indicators of selected Statistical Local Areas (SLAs) in New South Wales (NSW), Australia

Central town of SLA	Closest city	Town set	Population in 1996	IR [km]	IS1	IS2	IC1	IC2	MB/NG in 1986-91 (tanh)
Core towns (Set 1)									
Queanbeyan	Canberra	1	25689	10	3	366.5	0.3000	36.6500	0.963
Lithgow	Sydney	1	11441	100	5	3383.3	0.0500	33.8330	0.165
Maitland	Newcastle	1	50108	40	7	603.5	0.1750	15.0875	0.982
Cessnock-Bellbird	Newcastle	1	17540	60	7	613.5	0.1167	10.2250	0.951
Goulburn	Canberra	1	21293	80	3	576.6	0.0375	7.2075	-0.214
Singleton	Newcastle	1	12519	80	6	385.8	0.0750	4.8225	0.843
Peripheral towns (Set 2)									
Muswellbrook	Newcastle	2	10541	110	4	103.2	0.0364	0.9382	0.426
Bathurst	Sydney	2	26029	160	3	85.8	0.0188	0.5363	0.986
Orange	Sydney	2	30705	200	3	78.1	0.0150	0.3905	0.785
Albury-Wodonga*	Melbourne	2	41491	280	2	99.8	0.0071	0.3564	0.895
Wagga Wagga	Canberra	2	42848	240	1	84.3	0.0042	0.3513	0.998
Casino	Brisbane	2	9990	170	2	54.2	0.0118	0.3188	0.209
Tamworth	Newcastle	2	31865	240	1	53.2	0.0042	0.2217	0.931
Armidale	Newcastle	2	21330	360	3	53.2	0.0083	0.1478	0.948
Grafton	Brisbane	2	16562	300	1	38.7	0.0033	0.1290	0.407
Parkes	Sydney	2	10094	320	1	40.7	0.0031	0.1272	-0.122

Central town of SLA	Closest city	Town set	Population in 1996	IR [km]	IS1	IS2	IC1	IC2	MB/NG in 1986-91 (tanh)
Dubbo	Sydney	2	30102	340	1	40.1	0.0029	0.1179	0.990
Broken Hill	Adelaida	2	20963	500	0.01	21.0	0.0000	0.0420	-0.616
Griffith	Canberra	2	14209	360	0.01	14.2	0.0000	0.0394	-0.301
Inverell	Brisbane	2	9378	400	0.01	9.4	0.0000	0.0235	-0.067
Moree	Brisbane	2	9270	440	0.01	9.2	0.0000	0.0209	-0.087
Coastal towns (Set 3)									
Raymond Terrace	Newcastle	3	12332	25	7	613.5	0.2800	24.5400	1.000
Kiama	Wollongong	3	11711	40	2	255.2	0.0500	6.3800	1.941
Tweed Heads	Brisbane	3	37775	120	7	356.3	0.0583	2.9692	1.000
Lismore	Brisbane	3	28380	220	7	356.3	0.0318	1.6195	1.998
Ballina	Brisbane	3	16056	180	5	196.0	0.0278	1.0889	2.000
Taree	Newcastle	3	16702	160	2	66.3	0.0125	0.4144	1.999
Port Macquarie	Newcastle	3	33709	212	2	66.3	0.0094	0.3127	2.000
Bateman Bay	Canberra	3	9568	120	1	33.4	0.0083	0.2783	2.000
Coffs Harbour	Brisbane	3	22177	240	1	38.7	0.0042	0.1613	2.000

*Albury part.

Index